The STRUGGLE for
YOUR MIND

The STRUGGLE for YOUR MIND

Conscious Evolution and the Battle to Control How We Think

KINGSLEY L. DENNIS

Inner Traditions

Rochester, Vermont • Toronto, Canada

Inner Traditions
One Park Street
Rochester, Vermont 05767
www.InnerTraditions.com

SUSTAINABLE FORESTRY INITIATIVE Certified Sourcing
www.sfiprogram.org
SFI-00854

Text stock is SFI certified

Library of Congress Cataloging-in-Publication Data
Dennis, Kingsley.
  The struggle for your mind : conscious evolution and the battle to control how
we think / Kingsley L. Dennis.
     p. cm.
  Includes bibliographical references and index.
  ISBN 978-1-59477-457-7 (pbk.) — ISBN 978-1-59477-704-2 (e-book)
  1. Spiritual life—Miscellanea. 2. Consciousness—Miscellanea. 3. Civilization—
21st century. I. Title.
  BF1999.D373 2012
  153—dc23

                                                                    2011046484

Printed and bound in the United Stated by Lake Book Manufacturing
The text stock is SFI certified. The Sustainable Forestry Initiative® program
promotes sustainable forest management.

10   9   8   7   6   5   4   3   2   1

Text design and layout by Jack Nichols
This book was typeset in Garamond Premier Pro with ITC Bookman and
Baskerville used as display typefaces.

To send correspondence to the author of this book, mail a first-class letter to the
author c/o Inner Traditions • Bear & Company, One Park Street, Rochester, VT
05767, and we will forward the communication, or contact the author directly at
his website **www.kingsleydennis.com**.

for
Lidia Varela Santiago
for being part of the journey

CONTENTS

Introduction
A FUTURE WE NEED TO WIN
(Or Why We Need a Revolution
in Human Thought)

SATAN'S MEETING

Satan called a worldwide convention of demons.
In his opening address he said,
"We can't keep people from going to pray."

"We can't keep them from reading their holy books and
knowing the truth."
"We can't even keep them from forming an intimate
relationship with their Spirit."
"Once they gain that connection with their inner spirit,
our power over them is broken."

"So let them go to their prayers; let them have their
covered-dish dinners, BUT steal their time, so they
don't have time to develop an inner relationship with
themselves.

"This is what I want you to do," said the devil:

1

"Distract them from gaining hold of their inner spirit and maintaining that vital connection throughout their day!"

"How shall we do this?" his demons shouted.

"Keep them busy in the nonessentials of life and invent innumerable schemes to occupy their minds," he answered.

"Tempt them to spend, spend, spend, and borrow, borrow, borrow."

"Persuade the wives to go to work for long hours and the husbands to work six to seven days each week, ten to twelve hours a day, so they can afford their empty lifestyles."

"Keep them from spending time with their children."

"As their families fragment, soon their homes will offer no escape from the pressures of work!"

"Overstimulate their minds so that they cannot hear that still, small voice."

"Entice them to play the radio or cassette player whenever they drive. To keep the TV, VCR, CDs, and their PCs going constantly in their homes and see to it that every store and restaurant in the world plays nonreligious music constantly."
"This will jam their minds and break that union with Spirit."

"Fill the coffee tables with magazines and newspapers."
"Pound their minds with the news twenty-four hours a day."
"Invade their driving moments with billboards."

"Flood their mailboxes with junk mail, mail-order catalogs, sweepstakes, and every kind of newsletter and promotion offering free products, services, and false hopes."

"Keep skinny, beautiful models on the magazines and TV so their husbands will believe that outward beauty is what's important, and they'll become dissatisfied with their wives."

"Keep the wives too tired to love their husbands at night."

"Give them headaches too!"

"If the women don't give their husbands the love they need, the men will begin to look elsewhere."
"That will fragment their families quickly!"

"Give them distractions to distract them from teaching their children the real meaning of life."

"Even in their recreation, let them be excessive."
"Have them return from their recreation exhausted."

"Keep them too busy to go out in nature and reflect on creation. Send them to amusement parks, sporting events, plays, concerts, and movies instead."
"Keep them busy, busy, busy!"

"And when they meet for spiritual fellowship, involve them in gossip and small talk so that they leave with troubled consciences."

"Crowd their lives with so many good causes they have no time to seek power from the Spirit."
"Soon they will be working in their own strength, sacrificing their health and family for the good of the cause."

"It will work!"
"It will work!"

It was quite a plan!

The demons went eagerly to their assignments causing people everywhere to get busier and more rushed, going here and there. Having little time for their inner spirit or their families. Having no time to tell others about the power of being human and to change lives.

I guess the question is, Has the devil been successful in his schemes?

The above tale is a useful allegory that helps to paint a picture of the thesis of this book: namely, that for long periods of human history active forces have been penetrating our world, seeking to keep humanity "asleep" and distracted from inner life. These forces are aware of the true power of human consciousness, and the social power structures used to influence and manipulate the masses would collapse if true human potential were exercised. Therefore, in the pursuit of control and power certain forces active upon the Earth aim to artificially suppress the natural evolution of human consciousness.

As the title of this book suggests, humanity is caught in a struggle and our consciousness is the battleground. It may come as unnerving news to some that humanity is constantly being bombarded by forces and events beyond our control. This does not make us impotent, however; all natural organisms are under the influence of external forces. Yet there are other forces at work on humanity. These forces are deliberate, social, more often than not man-made, and manipulate with intent. They aim to persuade if possible and coerce if necessary. These forces seek to target the remaining spaces where humanity has a modicum of "free choice" and "free will." To some degree these forces are part of the requirements of civilization, helping to shepherd and organize a burgeoning population. Yet over and above this organization are exploitative forces that work *against the laws of conscious evolution*. These forces and the need to overcome them are the subject of this book.

The perpetual battlefield is what we know as our everyday lives: our education, our work, our leisure, our emotional and spiritual well-being, and our conscious thinking. Yet the armaments of this struggle are not guns, tanks, airplanes, bombs, or battle cruisers. It is much more subtle than this. It is less hardware and more software. It is, in effect, a silent war. And I hope to show that it is a war that is central to the tragic physical scourges occurring on our beautiful planet. It is a war that targets not only the present but also the very long-term future(s) of our civilization. And it has been going on for as long as human societies have existed on planet Earth. What is this war? It is a *battle for our minds*—how *we think*. In short, it is the *war of consciousness*.

Cultural evolution—the growth and expansion of civilizations—has always been closely tied with the ingenuity of human vision. The power, and hopefully wisdom, of human vision has been a principal factor in the rapid progress of humankind over a short span of historical time. Biological evolution is, let's face it, a slow mover. Through genetic inheritance and species reproduction, physical organisms evolve over geological time. Yet cultural evolution is quicker; it works through a series of memes and external artifacts (art, literature, monuments, etc.) that affect the human neural system. In other words, we pass on information culturally and each successive generation builds on these models in the hope of evolving better models. However, quicker still is *neurogenetic evolution*—that is, a combination of an elevation of brain capacities with an upgraded nervous system. Neurogenetic mutation is itself a driver of conscious evolution. In this model external impacts are required to stimulate the mutation, and take the form of increased empathy between people brought on by global flows of information and communication (such as in the "global brain" metaphor), an increase in solar radiation/energies, and changes in the Earth's magnetism. Such impacts resonate with the human nervous system and through biological fields of energy (biofields) may well assist in mutating organic DNA. DNA is thus an evolutionary acceleration tool. Further, any attempt at information embargo (or quarantine of neurogenetic impacts) can be seen as a form of neurocensorship. This is an important concept within the framework of this book.

How this can be so? Well, relatively new developments in biophysics have indicated that all biological organisms are made up of a liquid-crystalline medium. Further, that DNA is a liquid-crystal lattice-type structure, which some refer to as a liquid crystal gel, whereby body cells are involved in a *holographic* instantaneous communication via the emitting of biophotons (a source based on light). As I discuss in chapter 7, this implies that all living biological organisms continuously emit radiations of light that form a field of coherence and communication. The liquid-crystalline structure within living systems is also responsible for the direct current (DC) electrodynamic field that permeates the entire body of all animals. It has also been noted that the DC field has a mode of semiconduction that is much faster than the nervous system.[1] The electrical field of the human body is important in terms of its resonance with external impacts. The human nervous system, and likewise DNA, is extraordinarily sensitive and receptive to external signals, impacts, and energies. In short, DNA receives, processes, and responds to environmental conditions at an astounding rate of change. Without the participation of DNA mutational adaptation and change, we would not have evolution on this planet as we know it. Further, it is likely that the next stage of humanity's evolutionary development will involve a change in the vibrational nature of our DNA. After all, DNA directly affects how the human nervous system functions, and the history of life and of humanity is often defined in terms of the evolution of the nervous system. It is important then to know that human DNA does not exist within some sealed vacuum and can be influenced by external impacts and energies.[2]

Many esoteric and spiritual traditions have posited that DNA can be accessed and programmed over time, through deliberate conscious intention and by the vibrational frequencies of language, words, and thought (such as in well-documented shamanistic practices).[3] Investigators such as John C. Lilly and Timothy Leary have discussed meta-programming the human "biocomputer" by accessing the DNA through various transpersonal methods.[4] Now, however, we are gaining scientific advances into some of the potential properties of DNA. Biophysics informs us, with scientific legitimacy, how the external environment can influence human DNA.[5] This gives new perspective to the adage "You are what you eat," but in this case we are not so much talking about food but about *external impacts* and how we consciously ingest these impacts. In other words, how we think—our conscious intentions—can and does have an influence on our nervous system. Therefore, our state of mind, whether positive or negative, has a significant influence on the physical state of our biological nervous system. It also plays an important role in our psychic development—whether or not we are open to new ideas, creative thinking, visionary concepts, and concerns for self-actualization. We would do well to remind ourselves that the human being is an unfinished project. We have the capability for so much more: for instigating our own paths toward self-actualization. Yet if everyone were inspired to pursue such goals to the detriment of conditioned cultural roles (such as consumerism, debt slavery, passivity, and so forth) there would be a crisis of cultural power and governance. So has something been holding us back?

It is interesting to note that the Maya have a spiritual history that makes mention of a flaw in human DNA. According to Hunbatz Men, a Mayan daykeeper and teacher of Mayan science:

> Our DNA during the Mayan cycles of the last twenty-six thousand years has been encoded with a flaw that can, ultimately, become a source of de-evolution. This flaw causes us to believe that we are separate from the Divine Source. For us to evolve identity, this flaw was required. But now it is time for us to move into communion with the Divine.[6]

Whether or not this flaw is an actual truth, it still retains significance because the human identity of "separation" has been exploited for centuries as a way of maintaining social control over populations. Whether it is reinforced through layers of social processes and institutions, through the media and entertainment industry, or through religious and spiritual doctrines, it has served as an obstacle against neurogenetic evolution. We are now, as a species, at a point in our evolutionary journey where it is imperative that we advance and develop our state of consciousness and understanding. Our present evolutionary state is limited in terms of perception and thus we lean toward a material comprehension of our "realities." For example, the luminous matter we observe in the universe with the aid of our technological instruments is only about 0.5 percent of all calculated mass, and what we actually see directly with our eyes is even less.

What we actually take to be our reality is in fact only a thin slice of electromagnetic light. Our physical bodies (our biological and sensory apparatus) allow us to construct our world and live within a meaningful materiality because we share certain similar vibratory levels. However, it now seems that our energetic/vibratory level has been maintained rather than surpassed. Why is this? It may well be that a "blockage" has occurred during the further evolution of human consciousness. If this is the case, as I contend it is, then it is high time for this blockage to be removed. Yet the situation we face is that there are a myriad of terrestrial and social forces at work that appear to be in collusion to sustain and even amplify these particular blockages.

Certain allegorical esoteric teachings also suggest that there has been a deliberate blockage placed on the human energy system. One of these is Gurdjieff's concept of the *kundabuffer,* which was allegedly placed in humankind to stop us from achieving objective consciousness and thus to shield us from knowing of the "terror of the situation." The kundabuffer was a blockage installed in order to cause human beings to "see reality upside down," as well as to engender in them sensations of pleasure and enjoyment. Yet it also became responsible for egotism, vanity, selfishness, and other similar conceited traits. Such traits then keep humankind distracted and caught up in their own trivial concerns, wasting vital energy that could be used in more advantageous pursuits. Likewise, the teachings of Don Juan, as outlined by the writings of Carlos Castaneda, describe how humanity's "glowing coat of awareness" is diminished from birth by predatory forces that leave humanity with barely enough energy for a basic sedentary existence.

Other similarities abound in "channeled" information that suggests that human DNA was stripped down to only a two-stranded version. These and other sources hint at the possibility of an obstruction on the evolution of higher consciousness within humanity. The result of this is an inability to transcend destructive and divisive tendencies now widespread within the human condition. In what appears to be almost parallel to the Fall, as described in biblical texts, humanity has sunken from the Golden Age into a lowly existence plagued by unconscious behavior and forgetfulness. We can see this mirrored in Plato's assertion that "Humans are on Earth like beings stricken with amnesia." Through such a lens it appears that the collective psyche of humanity is dominated by the more primitive material concerns of service to self and the notion of a separate identity free from external responsibilities and constraints. Under such conditions it is extremely difficult for humanity to develop "objective consciousness." And this way of behavior also makes humans susceptible to being brought under the manipulative exploitation of those who feed off power: namely, dictators, zealous leaders, corporations, and state institutions. Within this "fallen state" (an upside-down reality) the sedative offered in recompense is the easy addiction to sexual stimuli and sedentary pleasures. Humans, we are told, are susceptible to self-gratifying desires and pleasurable pursuits, and often in detriment to their own capacities for self-actualization. Destruction and wars, murders and mutilations are the actions of unconscious groups and individuals. Our actions globally are the manifestation in the physical realm of a species that has a diminished access to its collective spiritual essence.

Whether or not we choose to believe or adhere to these suggestions within esoteric teachings, most of us could perhaps agree that *there seems to be something in the way.* With all the goodwill and intentions within our hearts, why is it we cannot collectively rise above this malaise? And why does it seem that the majority is being ruled by a minority of mad people? Are we all the inmates on some lunatic-asylum planet? Don't the universal laws of creation and sustenance support life-engendering traits rather than suffering? With these questions alone it would seem that there is something amiss within the general psyche of humanity. It could well be that for far too long the majority of humans have been under the yoke of the powerful few—from priestly elites of Egypt and Babylonia; from the Romans and the cyclic domination of empires and from the various religious institutions that have herded the many. In the end, we may know nothing other than servitude. Centuries of social slavery could, after all, have hard wired us to become passive and meek to authority. We have only to refer to the infamous Stanley Milgram experiments to realize that we would do almost anything if a person in a white coat told us to.[7] In other words, we have been quite thoroughly socially conditioned to accept and submit to various displays of power. The question today is how these forces of control seek to pacify and distract the human conscious spirit. It is the hypothesis of this book that ongoing elements within human societies have been interfering with the natural growth and expression of human consciousness, which, at our present stage, may affect the potential for the next phase of neurogenetic evolution.

However, I also believe that humanity is now crossing a threshold—a transition period, if you like. And this period is characterized by a greater influx of energies made available to assist in this now-overdue shift on the evolutionary journey. Neurogenetic "mutations" are already appearing—the rise of gifted individuals, seers, sensitives and psychics, and visionaries—and more importantly an accelerating rise in the collective awareness of individuals. Humanity is beginning to awaken to both the current limits of perception and to the inherent capacity for greater things. Governments are being hounded by well-organized and, on the whole, intelligent protests. Thousands of well-structured nongovernmental organizations (NGOs) are currently operating to counteract the greed of corporate and national policies, an abundance of information is now available through global communication channels (noticeably the Internet), and bottom-up decentralized practices of knowledge sharing are now becoming the norm among people. The awareness of humanity is expanding. Yet obstacles still remain: the Awakening still has not reached a tipping-point.

Since the advent of industrialization more and more people have become urbanized. And with this urbanization has come a mechanized organization of life. Through the necessity of complexity, internal structures become simplified into categories. As renowned historian Arnold Toynbee pointed out in his *A Study of History* there is a tendency "visible in both biological and social development, toward a diminution in size and increasing simplification, going along with a higher degree of internal organization and refinement."[8] Through the industrialization process nations develop into a technical and mechanized structure. While this is an explanation of brevity, its general message remains valid. As populations increase so does the need for adequate and efficient mechanisms of control. And not only control, but distraction too. So the worker became granted the role of the consumer. No longer was the working-class hero falling foul of alienating tendencies (as Karl Marx once highlighted). The worker was soon able to purchase the very goods he was helping to build. And why? Because the economy needed to grow, and the upper class was not wide-ranging enough to buy up all the demand. So demand was widened in a ploy to stimulate greater supply. Economies and trade expanded rapidly once all members of the society were able to purchase the goods. The worker became the consumer, and social mechanization tightened its grip. In the twentieth century we might have been led to believe that these old paradigms would be transcended by more enlightening processes. Yet as historian Lewis Mumford pointed out over seventy years ago:

> True: the industrial world produced during the nineteenth century is either technologically obsolete or socially dead. But unfortunately, its maggoty corpse has produced organisms, which in turn may debilitate or possibly kill the new order that should take its place: perhaps leave it a hopeless cripple.[9]

The "new order" that emerged from the nineteenth-century industrial world only succeeded in increasing the mechanization of human life in developed countries. People in these societies are living within mental and perceptual constraints because of being immersed within a highly artificial, mechanical, and controlled way of life. Those people living in less-developed countries are hampered less by mechanization and more by brute force, illegitimate regimes, and basic needs of food and shelter. For the purposes of this book, however, I focus primarily on the mechanized cultures of developed and developing technological societies (technocultures). In these regions people may have a greater potential to access resources for material and spiritual change. And this potential for change—primarily an aspect of human vision—threatens the incumbent power structures. For this reason, I contend that there has been a concerted effort to distract people's thinking away from the "terror of the situation" (to use Gurdjieff's phrase). Yet it is not only the power of human consciousness that is being stalled—it is also human energies.

So why do we need a human revolution? Well, we've already had an industrial revolution whereby nations learned to harness the power of physical energy reserves (coal, oil, and so on) for growth. Now we need to harness the power of psychic energy reserves (consciousness) in order to spur our next stage of human evolution.

People rarely question (or at least not often enough) that they might be under the yoke of constrictive and rigid structures. This is primarily because of the illusion of freedom. For example, if a prisoner never sees the bars of his cell, why would he think he is in a prison? Yet our sense of reality is deliberately engineered in order to assume the structure of satisfaction so that we don't go seeking other forms of reality outside these structures. Or if we are not placated through satisfaction, then we are subdued by limited resources, such as being tied into the credit/debit economy or survival mode. Another tactic now increasingly being used is that of constructed fear. Events of fear are being arranged in order to attack the collective psyche of people and to realign focus on physical concerns. Our fear is manipulated, heightened, and eventually harvested. This tactic also promotes fear waves of bioenergy to halt, or obstruct, the energetic evolutionary impulse of humankind. These subjects form the content of this book.

We are being sold short not only on who we are but also on what we can become. As a consequence, we are selling our future(s) short; and not only for ourselves but also for the new generations to come. These are indeed critical times: crucial change is upon us and is moving over the face of the Earth. Humanity will be forced into change, and how we deal with it will be a measure of our maturity as a species. Energy will be made available to us at the same time that many existing structures will be collapsing around us. And during this tussle and shuffle there will be an all-out struggle for our minds. What will we choose to think? How will we choose to engage our consciousness? When will we stop being herded like dumb cattle through artificial and unnatural perceptive and cognitive systems? If we don't start to ask these questions, then those who exercise power over us will never have to provide the answers. I thus argue throughout the book that humans are enmeshed within an all-embracing and all-inclusive social matrix. This refers to the array of bodies (social institutions, social norms, laws, education, religion, and so forth) that are woven together to form the workings of a control society. And in control societies there are both covert and overt strategies for the cultural conditioning of behavior and thought, as I discuss in the early chapters of the book.

By way of an analogy, imagine we are living as if within a very small room of a house. Our lives are shaped by the awareness of this one room. The reach of our perceptions is limited to the four walls. Yet now and again someone has a "vision": they get up and leave the room. They explore the rest of the house and often come back to inform us. Sometimes we listen to them, worship them, and put flowers at their feet in submission. Other times we collectively stone them for blaspheming against our natural belief systems. As Gopi Krishna put it:

> According to a long list of mystics and sages over millennia, and also according to a whole array of psychic and unexplained phenomena, then the physical world we live in, the objects, events, laws,

and universal rules that we believe in—are not, in reality, what they appear to be. . . . It is like we live in a magical castle with thousands of rooms . . . and we spend our lives wandering from room to room, discovering new things and creating hypotheses from the new findings. . . . But we never discover the foundations upon which the house is built—we enter this castle at birth and leave it at death under the influence of a spell cast by our brain.[10]

Our brains are responsible for the reality we perceive because it is our primary filtering apparatus. Yet like all good hardware it is merely processing the inputs it receives. It is a matter of "garbage in, garbage out." In this sense much of what occurs as daily life can be seen as a construct or, if you like, a program. Our social lives exist within a myriad of competing conditioning programs, the majority of which are aimed at bringing a person's focus out onto the external physical and away from internal reflections. We therefore need to be more conscious of how these processes operate. For example, over the decades many in the developed nations have been lured into a fetishlike relationship with commodities; this then lures people into a credit/debt society that ties them into a virtual prison. The exact same pattern is beginning to replicate itself within the newer, developing technocultures such as China and other Asian countries.

And so we come to the grand Modernity Project: a carefully constructed act of globalization that seeks to turn diversity into a standardized mass. Of course, for economic growth to continue expanding new markets have to be found. And the world is just too used to having continued expansion—having limits to growth is just not an option. So national and transnational structures have been established to provide for both demand and supply; and in the meantime, people's minds are being cleverly manipulated. So far we have supported these systems by acquiescing to their presence, yet they are only transitory structures and many of them are now fighting for their survival. The years ahead will prove to be a period of change on all fronts—physical, emotional, mental, and energetic. Most important of all, human consciousness will be the target of a variety of influences, both positive and negative. It is the outcome of this clash that will be key to the future. Are we going to allow for the natural path of neurogenetic evolution to take place? And are we going to be able to ride out these changes and focus our conscious energies onto a constructive and viable future? These are the questions we need to ask ourselves.

I have attempted in this book to explore and present these issues. My understanding is that the real struggle is over how human consciousness is controlled, influenced, and ultimately directed. The answer to this will determine whether we build for ourselves a harmonious future integral to our "spaceship Earth" home, or whether we allow a further blockage of human evolution. Some of the earlier chapters do indeed examine some of these bleaker issues. However, I assure you that the outcome is nothing other than positive for the human species. Partly, I admit, because I cannot conceive of any other acceptable alternative. Chapter 1, "Governing the Social Mind: Propaganda, Power, and the Masses," looks at some of the techniques of engineering the social mind. Both propaganda and social psychology are seen as serving the construction of the masses, which are, as Doris Lessing reminds us, the prisons we choose to live within.

Chapter 2, "The Modernity Project: The Rise of Scientific Technique," examines the modern technoculture in terms of postindustrial society, consumerism, and the nature of a hyperreality. This chapter also discusses how a scientific rationalism has emerged that supports modern structures of power and control. Also examined are strategies of social fragmentation and distraction, such as the influence of our media and entertainment. Chapter 3, "Living under Quarantine: The Manufacture of Social Control," looks specifically at the global techno-digital networks of control and how these serve as a form of "informational embargo." The chapter also addresses the covert "silent methods" used for social manipulation, such as our economic credit/debt systems and our increasing information databases. Chapter 4, "Undue Influence: Playing Games with the Mind," goes into more detail about how current (and undisclosed) technologies are actually harmful to the physical and mental well-being of people. The chapter examines the possibility of directly targeting a person's thought processes in order to manipulate mental processes and consciousness from afar. These themes are, by their nature, rather bleak and unnerving. Chapter 5, "Constructions of Fear: The Armageddon Meme," examines how by establishing a climate of fear then helplessness and dependency can be created, which in turn suppress the strength of human consciousness. In this respect, subjugation through crisis is a common theme. Also discussed is the state of a permanent-war economy and what I refer to as terrifying peace. The chapter also discusses the spread of specific "Armageddon memes" of imminent catastrophe and how they serve to further weaken the individual's state of being.

Chapter 6, "Winning the War of Minds: Changing the Mental Game-Play," finally turns the tide and looks at the positive changes set to occur within the field of human consciousness. This chapter addresses the concept of a conscious universe and thus how human consciousness interacts with the informational fields around us. Also discussed are some of the changes within the vibrational frequencies now arriving within the Earth's biosphere. The coming years, it is said, will see a period of heightened human excitability. Chapter 7, "Our Evolutionary Futures: Agents of Mutation," takes a look at the biology of consciousness and how certain built-in mechanisms for neurogenetic evolution may be manifesting. Specifically, the chapter discusses how the human body produces energy fields and its implications for quantum consciousness. Chapter 8, "Ushering in the New Life: A Reenvisioning of Society and Spirituality," asserts that we can co-create a more harmonious and positive future by adapting to a lifestyle that corresponds with our conscious hearts and minds. That is, it would be to our collective benefit if our materialistic cultures were more accepting to spiritual influences as a means of aligning with the natural and cosmic order. Finally, Chapter 9, "New Perceptions: Creating Energetic Change in Ourselves," examines how with "new horizons" for human consciousness, being ready for change means having the ability to nurture new mental and emotional energies. By learning how to free up energy, a person is then able to save some energy from daily usage and wastage. This stored energy can then be used for a person's own focused intentions, awareness, and increased perceptions.

Now, are you ready to *take back your mind*?

1
GOVERNING THE SOCIAL MIND
Propaganda, Power, and the Masses

What we live through, in any age, is the effect on us of mass emotions and of social conditions from which it is almost impossible to detach ourselves. Often the mass emotions are those which seem the noblest, best and most beautiful. And yet, inside a year, five years, a decade, five decades, people will be asking, "How could they have believed that?"

DORIS LESSING

(FROM *PRISONS WE CHOOSE TO LIVE INSIDE*)

There is a famous thirteenth-century Persian poem that tells the story of an old woman who upon encountering an eagle on her windowsill captures it, for she has never seen an eagle before. The old woman looks at the strange bird and finally says, "What a funny-looking pigeon!" She then proceeds to clip its wings, straighten its beak, and trim its claws in order to change the appearance to suit her own ideas of what a bird should look like. In this Persian poem we have a mirror of human thought: altering the unfamiliar or the "other" to make it acceptable and to make it fit with present perceptions. And here we also have an analogy for the social mind: clipped and trimmed in order to fit a basic model.

Throughout our lives we are subjected to indoctrination by a systemic structure of processes and institutions. Within this conditioning environment beliefs almost "grow" into us. And once they are a part of our socially constructed selves they are sustained, reinforced, and protected, often unconsciously, by psychological processes of perception. With few rare exceptions, all people are brought up within specific culturally defined environments (or templates). A person's dominant social milieu then attempts to offer a variety of accepted sociocultural norms of thought and behavior. These may operate through various forms, such as personal faith, religion, science, language and emotions, denial and doubt, happiness and fear, safety and security (identity and belonging), well-being and materialism. Once ingrained, a person is liable to perpetuate such traits, believing them to have been obtained through "free thought." In the end, we reinforce beliefs that have grown into us, accepting and defending them as our own. So when we say, "I don't believe," what we often in fact mean to say is, "I automatically reject everything my brain is not wired to receive." The end result is that for most of us we only believe those things we want to believe or that fit within our perceptual paradigms and/or experiences. And because we have committed ourselves to such beliefs we then feel it imperative that we support the investment we have made. After all, who likes to be proved wrong? Not only do we often strive to support our own cherished beliefs but we also end up agreeing with anyone or anything that appears to be in agreement with us. For example, have you noticed how we often "vote" for positive online reviews of things we like, such as a book or a film, yet will ignore or be unlikely to find helpful the disagreeable reviews. By nature people seek to affirm their structures of beliefs and identity by promoting activities and experiences that serve to reinforce and validate their own conditioned sets. People rarely seek out experiences that will actively challenge their perceptions and thus create uncertainty and/or doubt. How many far-right conservatives would spend time reading the latest socialist newsletter? The fixed idea is the enemy of freethinking.

Yet in order to get along successfully in life it is important to fit in with the crowd, to avoid being a social misfit or an alienated individual. We have to learn how to get along with everyone else. We are, after all, social animals. To attempt to live according to other than the norm of accepted social behavior and thought has usually led to difficulties and certain degrees of estrangement. It can be said, especially in these current times, that leadership increasingly belongs to the mediocre. And whereas the famous edict of the Temple of Apollo at Delphi stated "Know Thyself," such ideals have eroded, or at least diminished, in successive generations. Such ancient temples have been replaced by the edifices of education, religion, law, and politics. Various individual traits and capacities have become "authorized" by a select few cultural and/or religious iconic institutions. Many people may not be fully aware of these processes operating in their lives, for the impacts are often gradual rather than sudden. And the process begins early on in a person's life.

Such patterning often begins very early in a child's life and is usually from the formative impacts and experiences. The patterning process goes through several stages. The first stage has been named Limited Perceptions and this is where the child comes to believe certain things about the world around her simply because she doesn't see anything else. The child's perceptual range is thus reinforced through the immediate environment. These initial belief sets are then strengthened by stage two. This stage is named Perceptual Set, whereby the child's attention is drawn to sets that reinforce the current programmed patterns.[1] For example, when you buy a new car you suddenly see that model everywhere on the road, whereas before you didn't notice it. Thus initial impressions are reinforced and further cemented. And the human social animal is prone to clinging stubbornly to first impressions, even when they are later contradicted by information (known as the primacy effect). These processes of early indoctrination might be open to later reevaluation if not for continuing sets of social reinforcement. Many aspects of society are set up to provide each person with successive impacts of like-minded conditioning. For example, the area where a child lives will influence which school she goes to and the kind of children she meets and hangs around with. This can exert a strong influence on the type of academic progress she is likely to make. And all through these early years of schooling the child will most probably meet like-minded others who will support her early programming and worldview. On top of this the child will be subject to beliefs that have been imposed by her parents. These beliefs provide a structure to filter and create a worldview and will be used to interpret all subsequent experiences. The formative years of childhood education are often a wasted opportunity. At this crucial time when a child's attitudes and intelligence are being formed, instead of spending long hours under the influence of a group of mature, loving family members from which to copy behaviors and draw their self-image, a child is often under the influence of other immature children and tired, overworked teachers.

Since children learn and develop by observing and mimicking other people, when they spend all day in school with similar, immature children as models of behavior, they construct a likewise undernurtured set of behaviors. As a consequence many children leave school with a head full of sums yet they are insensitive, imbalanced, and generally confused. If children pass through this stage without having acquired a degree of security and self-esteem, then it is likely that they will live through adulthood with the same lack of security and self-esteem. The result is that such an adult has formed no real power within himself, which creates an underdeveloped sense of self. He will have no real inner authority, which may itself be deliberate on the part of institutional education. And without inner authority a person will require an external authority to tell him how to think and feel, what is allowed, and what he must do—which is exactly what the governing authorities in any power structure wish for.

The combined effects of these processes—early childhood indoctrination, parental socialization, and educational impacts—are often successful in conditioning an individual to a specific cognitive and perceptual reality. Once established these belief sets then form a kind of dependency.

> The combined effects of childhood indoctrination and the socialization process, at its most successful and effective level, serves to blinker an individual to reality and create a dependence on a belief system—any belief system.[2]

The unconscious indoctrination of childhood is liable to leave a person open to further layers of conditioning, as well as reinforcing a sense of acceptance and belonging. Collective society further serves to reinforce and modify most physical, mental, and emotional behavior. Thus the person who is deemed most socially valuable is often the person who has demonstrated his ability to adopt (and adapt to) consensual social behavior and patterns. And when such individual beliefs are never, or rarely, called into question by the social milieu it is easier for a person to forget why he holds them. Remember that beliefs are not facts: a belief is a belief because it is neither knowledge nor truth. It is a conviction of faith—a thought backed by emotional attachment. When examined many beliefs are found to have resulted from indoctrination through various processes, such as emotional language and heavily laden associations. Examples here include love of country (patriotism, nationalism), love of god, love of family and tribe, love of principles and a sense of moral self. For many of these beliefs a whole group of people—even a nation—may sacrifice much in defense of shared emotional investment. And if a majority of people share the same beliefs then it is unlikely they will be called into question. To do so could result in a person exhibiting "abnormal" behavior. What actually passes for "normal" behavior is what adjusts to the biological and psychological collective. To stand apart from mass behavior is often considered abnormal. It is thus the case that:

... most of us are indoctrinated throughout our lives, often without knowing it. Beliefs almost "grow" into us. They are then sustained and protected, usually unconsciously, by the physiological and psychological processes of perception.[3]

Many beliefs and associated behavior patterns continue with us into adulthood. Just as the need for a child to be loved and accepted is a powerful incentive, many people later join different causes and/or ideologies to fulfill a need to belong. The need to be accepted and receive attention is often the greater cause, making the ideological cause superficial. Without realizing it a person is often more likely to desire a sense of social belonging that they may have been denied elsewhere.[4] Within this milieu a person is more likely to be influenced to say and do the same as others around them.

The need to be one with a group, to have group approval and therefore social approval, means that individuals will very often change their attitudes *themselves,* to fit with the norm, instead of having to be persuaded .... The passive power exerted by social norms is all the stronger than overt power because it is bowed to unconsciously.[5]

Such is the powerful pull of social conformity. People cannot be fully trusted to say and do what *they think is right* if others around them are all expressing an opposite opinion. This is because the pull toward social conformity, whether conscious or unconscious, is just too strong. The danger here is that in such environments a person is more likely to give away personal responsibility than act on it. A group more generally exhibits a lack of responsibility on the part of its members, since each person thinks that the overall responsibility can be shared and individual blame does not accrue. The result is that each person reinforces the other's inertia. Thus nonaction actually becomes the accepted norm within the group. This inertia is then reinforced and validated, often through personal rationalization, since so much has been invested in the group. To be wrong could inflict much individual angst; it is therefore better to rationalize one's actions as correct. This fear of responsibility is a product of socialization and renders an individual less capable of dealing fluidly with the uncertainties and complexities of a full life. The result is that there is a tendency for people to prefer to submerge themselves within the mass: in other words, to be a silent part of the collective behavior of the crowd. And it is this exact type of behavior that has been repeatedly seized upon by dictators and rogue "leaders" as a way of gaining authority and legitimacy.

Obedience to authority figures* is a trait that has long been conditioned within an individual. From a young age a child is exposed first to parents, then to schoolteachers, then to uniformed civil servants, and finally to bosses. An individual is thus trained how to operate, and respond correctly, within the established hierarchical social system. This creates the belief that a person is never totally free in her behavior; she is almost always under the authority of someone above her who influences events. Paradoxically, many people insist to themselves that they have personal freedom, yet externally they fear exhibiting "too much" freedom. People who conform most are likely to have the least tolerance for uncertainty and ambiguity. Social conformity has thus inculcated a feeling of safety: belonging is a safe haven where a person is protected. Yet such emotions—of comfort and discomfort—are often programs socially conditioned from birth. Much of our human behavior thus stems from the influences that have shaped us. Yet what is often not realized is the degree to which these social forces are deliberately constructed in order to mold and govern a collective mass. Through social, religious, educational, and media institutions specific knowledge systems are established and often serve to supply a consensual and bland array of stimuli. The reality of the situation is that we are subtly coerced to enroll in systems of imitation through which we

*See Stanley Milgram's famous experiments on obedience to authority.

are trained to memorize information that is passed on as knowledge. This information is then reinforced through authoritarian institutions (such as science and "expertism"), thus making it appear as true. Even what is labeled as common knowledge may not be what it claims to be: "The more you look at 'common knowledge,' the more you realize that it is more likely to be common than it is to be knowledge. No real knowledge is common."[6]

On the other hand, alternative systems of thought are often labeled as subversive and subject to human acts of modification and/or dismissal. In this manner specific physical, mental, and emotional patterns are engrained, reinforced, and modulated by human institutions. One of the most subversive and subtle of these institutions is propaganda.

PROPAGANDA AND THE MASSES

The ancient Greeks used persuasion as a form of rhetoric and regarded it highly as a rational means for argument and communication. Such persuasive debates can themselves be seen as an ancient form of propaganda. Yet throughout history the need to persuade and influence has always been manipulated by those people in power as a means to maintain authority and legitimacy. The extreme of this is the now infamous use of Nazi propaganda. Somewhat ironically it was Joseph Goebbels (Hitler's head of the Ministry of Popular Enlightenment and Propaganda) who said, "Propaganda is a much maligned and often misunderstood word. The layman uses it to mean something inferior or even despicable. The word *propaganda* always has a bitter aftertaste."[7] Yet while the Nazis developed their powerful propaganda under the auspices of the Ministry of Popular Enlightenment, other nations had their own ministries for the manipulation of the public mind. In Britain it was the Ministry of Information; in the United States, the Office of War Information; and in the USSR it was the Committee of the Communist Party. Another way to think of it, as George Orwell referred to it in his novel *1984,* is as the

Ministry of Truth. The legitimacy of government power, it would appear, revolves around creating and maintaining the "mass mind" of the people.

Propaganda in various forms has always been employed as part of the dissemination of information and/or beliefs. Whereas in past centuries this was predominantly related to religious doctrine it later became particularly rampant during times of ideological struggle, such as in the French and American revolutions. In the twentieth century, however, propaganda was transformed into a deliberately organized weapon of warfare. What national governments learned from the two World Wars was that public opinion (the mass mind) was a vital factor in securing ongoing power struggles. So not only did governments need to ensure that sufficient numbers of people were willing to die for the national cause, but also that in relative peacetime the very same people were willing to become the most compliant consumers. The overall manipulation of the mass public mind thus became no longer a matter of speech making; it had to become a pervasive presence within the lives of each individual. In this sense:

> Culture was reduced to the lowest common denominator for mass consumption, with the masses generally seen as politically apathetic yet prone to ideological fanaticism, vulnerable to manipulation through the media and the increasing sophistication of propagandists.[8]

Within the context of "mass society" propaganda morphed into a mechanism for not only engineering public opinion but also as a means for consolidating social control. The increased "mechanization" that came in with the Modernity Project (chapter 2) conditioned people into an almost unconscious need for propaganda. That is, people expected to be fed regular installments of information and to feel secure and protected by such knowledge. Propaganda (in this context the regular and consistent influx of government-sponsored information) serves not only to imprint but also, more effectively, to reinforce and expand on existing sets of conditioning. The manufacturing of consent* is now endemic to modern technological societies. It also involves some rather dubious invasive strategies to interfere with the brain processing of large numbers of people, as later chapters will discuss. Yet do we really believe that our minds are so open to such manipulated coercion?

Edward Bernays has often been called the father of public relations, as his teachings and research spurred the postwar years of propaganda. Bernays, a nephew of Sigmund Freud, utilized psychological and psychoanalytical ideas to construct an informational system (propaganda) capable of manipulating public opinion. Bernays, apparently, considered that such a manipulative apparatus was necessary because society was composed of too many irrational elements (the people) that could be dangerous to the efficient mechanisms of power ("democracy"). During both World Wars propaganda had been used to astounding success, by all governments involved, in gaining public support for wartime efforts (and atrocities!). This led, as if naturally, to the same principles and processes being employed during peacetime for the organization and persuasion of the social masses. Below are a series of extracts taken from Bernays's now classic book *Propaganda,* which serves to illustrate the thinking behind the development, improvement, and implementation of mass mind techniques.

> The conscious and intelligent manipulation of the organized habits and opinions of the masses is an important element in democratic society. Those who manipulate this unseen mechanism of society constitute an invisible government which is the true ruling power of our country. We are governed, our minds are molded, our tastes formed, our ideas suggested, largely by men we have never heard of. This is a logical result of the way in which our democratic society is organized. . . .

---

*A term employed by the linguist and cultural critic Noam Chomsky.

. . . It remains a fact that in almost every act of our daily lives, whether in the sphere of politics or business, in our social conduct or our ethical thinking, we are dominated by the relatively small number of persons . . . who understand the mental processes and social patterns of the masses. It is they who pull the wires, which control the public mind, who harness old social forces and contrive new ways to bind and guide the world. . . .

. . . As civilization has become more complex, and as the need for invisible government has been increasingly demonstrated, the technical means have been invented and developed by which opinion may be regimented. . . .

. . . This new technique may fairly be called the new propaganda. It takes account not merely of the individual, nor even of the mass mind alone, but also and especially of the anatomy of society, with its interlocking group formations and loyalties. It sees the individual not only as a cell in the social organism but as a cell organized into the social unit. Touch a nerve at a sensitive spot and you get an automatic response from certain specific members of the organism. . . .

. . . The invisible government tends to be concentrated in the hands of the few because of the expense of manipulating the social machinery which controls the opinions and habits of the masses. . . .

. . . We can effect some change in public opinion with a fair degree of accuracy by operating a certain mechanism, just as the motorist can regulate the speed of his car by manipulating the flow of gasoline. . . .

. . . The group mind does not think in the strict sense of the word. In place of thoughts it has impulses, habits and emotions. . . .[9]

The social mechanism of regimenting the mass mind was, in Bernays's thinking, the logical extension of any democratic society. In fact it represented the very intellectual heart of efficient democratic rule. Bearing in mind that the above quotations were published in 1928 we can expect the mechanism of mass manipulation to have progressed to a very advanced degree. Jacques Ellul, a social philosopher, recognized that propaganda was an "indispensable condition for the development of technical progress and the establishment of a technological civilization."[10] By this Ellul meant that propaganda was needed in order to integrate the individual into a technological world. In line with Bernays's thinking, as a society becomes inherently more complex it utilizes more advanced technological tools in the drive to retain and organize order. The need to influence the opinions and actions of individuals and groups through specific psychological manipulations is the result of a highly technological and populated civilization. This is the same principle whether it applies to Egyptian, Roman, or modern Western empires. There is too little room to have too many radical and independent thinkers. Standardization is the key to an orderly society of high population. Yet this very method of consensual consciousness and controlled patterns of thinking is anathema to the natural expression of individual evolutionary impulses. Thus a trade-off has been implemented—only we, the people, were never consulted on the issue.

It can be said that the intention of current and future societies is to construct a socio-cultural-political edifice that exists within a technological infrastructure and that operates both overt (visible) and covert (nonvisible) forms of mass social control. This will, by necessity, involve the monitoring and suppression of unacceptable forms of individual and collective consciousness. Such unacceptable forms are likely to be characterized by flashes of inner realization and the innate human desire for evolution. Further, this evolution will be in line not with external forms of artificial structures but instead with the human blueprint for conscious and spiritual development. However, postindustrial societies have further hampered the expression of individual development and creativity as an extension to the earlier feudal class systems.

The urban migration of people from the land provided a necessary workforce for industrial output and also provided the foundations on which to build a more appropriate and efficient "state mechanism" for social control. Urban densities and the mass migration to city life enabled propaganda to become more efficient, pervasive, and effective. The introduction of social-influencing mechanisms was not solely to engender a change in people's allegiances or beliefs; it also entailed a concerted effort to destabilize a person's critical faculty. In order for this to be effective it was necessary to implement various kinds of propaganda techniques. The best-known form of propaganda is the vertical type, which comes directly from a top-down authority figure. Examples are dictators, leaders, prime ministers, and presidents. Yet a lot of what passes for propaganda, or mass persuasion, is not considered as such by people or even so-called experts, as it consists of more of a horizontal form. These forms exist throughout developed societies and are often seen as pillars of the community; their power lies in the fact that they exist already firmly *inside the system*. Such examples are education, work training, social services, and financial systems. In society these propaganda apparatuses are known as institutions. Whereas vertical propaganda needs a fixed apparatus such as media and communication, and is thus more visible, the horizontal forms work much more subtly through people and human organizations and are thus much less visible as forms of manipulation. More about these forms of social control will be discussed in chapter 2.

On a more visible front, modern programs of social influence could not exist without the mass media. Today it exists as a combination of expertise and knowledge from technology, sociology, social behaviorism, psychology, communications, and other scientific techniques. Almost every nation needs a controlled media if it is to regulate and influence its citizenry. By way of the media a controlling authority is able to exert psychological influence on people's perception of reality. This capacity works hand in hand with the more physical components, such as enforcing the legal system and national security laws (surveillance and monitoring). State control, acting as a "psychological machine," instigates specific psychological manipulations in order to achieve desired goals within its national borders (and often beyond). Examples of these psychological manipulations include the deliberate use of specific cultural symbols and embedded signifiers that catalyse conditioned reflexes in the populace. Whether we realize it or not we are indoctrinated to react predictably to specific signs, symbols, words, and images. These triggers have included *Red* and *Communist* during the United States' 1950s McCarthyism; or *Muslim terrorist* during the currently constructed "War on Terror." Targeted reactions can thus be achieved, making the populace open to further manipulation in this state. This is a process of psychic re-formation that works repeatedly to soften up the people through continued and extensive exposure to particular stimuli. *These are the symbols we live by—artificial and man-made—in order to construct a compliant society.*

Today's media, which includes the dominant presence of advertising, extensively uses the notions of attractors and attractor patterns to target audience consciousness. This type of symbol manipulation is often referred to in the business as neuromarketing. Media corporations are using the huge growth in global communications to further shape their science of targeting human consciousness. In the case of neuromarketing many advertisers first audience test their commercials using brain-scanning techniques in order to know which part of a person's brain is being activated by the specific strong attractors. For example, specific attractors can bypass the logical part of the brain and impact the emotional part. So in the film industry, the advertisers place an award symbol (such as an Oscar or Golden Globe) that has proved to be an effective strong attractor that influences the emotional part of the brain. The philosophy here is to adjust the level of consciousness of an advertisement in relation to the measurable level of consciousness of the consumer.* Advertisers are aware that a person's consciousness passes on messages indirectly to the body in the form of galvanic skin response, pupil response, electrical nerve response, and so forth, and so every element of the screen promotion must elucidate the correct conscious reception. In order to achieve this correct set of attractor patterns all elements are deliberately worked on: the music, the visuals, the script, the voice. Interesting, symbolic strong attractors that have the most impact to persuade the audience include visuals such as smiley faces and cute animals (especially dogs wagging tails and kittens purring). In terms of voice they include words such as *honesty, integrity, freedom, hope and change, friendship,* and so on. For this reason politicians use a great deal of these attractor patterns in their speeches and promotional material.†

Further "softeners" placed deliberately within the everyday social include the availability of overwhelming indulgences. These range from a world of desirable objects; material pleasures; and sensual, erotic stimuli. Yet such softeners act as "distracters" that displace an individual from their conscious self and inner focus. In this way the target population is being driven away from innate and fundamental needs for inner development toward the outer projection upon material (status) gains. This drive for active distraction shifts a person toward what feels good rather than what is right. The individual is then given over to a new myth, one created artificially by the society of which they are a part. However, such triggering mechanisms cannot create something out of nothing. A conditioned reflex can only be set up if preconditioned reflexes have already been established. This is the function of childhood conditioning and educational institutions (as well as the influence of preconditioned parental guidance). Psychological levers are thus established

---

*This idea, as well as that of neuromarketing, was given to me in personal correspondence by Darryl Howard, who sent me his research "Advertising in the New Paradigm" (Darryl Howard & Associates).

†Anyone wishing to know more on this subject should investigate neurolinguistic programming (NLP).

to mobilize the populace into action and reaction when necessary by the evocation of these various state-specific myths.

In this way each particular society has means at its disposal to create and maintain a well-defined population set that could be utilized for needs such as overt nationalism and war. Individuals within a culture are embedded, to various degrees, with its conditionings, symbols, and shared characteristics. Thus when these cultural forms change (or are changed) the individual is affected. This is why it is important to have the personal power to step back from the entrapment of cultural conditionings. Such symbols are extremely well studied by the state power apparatus; they have long tweaked and fine-tuned such trigger mechanisms. After all, the whole is supposed to function like a programmed machine (or even a machine in breakdown, if that is the intent). However, because of the rise in population mobility (in part due to rapid transit and more fluid borders), such distinct population sets are now less certain and defined. Because of this, more stringent measures of monitoring, control, and suppression are required (as discussed in later chapters). Society is not a static entity; it is a living organism that is constantly changing, adapting, and shifting. Thus propaganda methods will not succeed if they address the old and past symbols and not the modern. For the industrial nations of the developed world, life and culture have now shifted into their modern phase (or what some would even call the postmodern phase). In order to manage the transition the authority apparatuses had to establish the Modernity Project. At the same time, a modern technosociety serves to validate the sense of an evolving culture and to evoke the promise of a better future. Yet this modernity, by its own need to act as an efficient machine, must further control the citizenry. Thus propaganda is needed in order to set up the people for their own mental, emotional, and at times physical manipulation. Such carefully managed manipulations are not readily visible, or even acknowledged by people, since they are often staged around basic needs.

● ● ●

The state apparatus and its propaganda perform a service by responding to particular needs that the citizenry have become dependent on (rather than independent of). These include both material and psychological needs such as security, shelter, food, work, and belonging. Social propaganda institutions also emphasize and strengthen the shared myths of modern developed societies: that the meaning of life is happiness and wealth can provide it; history began within the advent of civilizations ca. 12000 BCE (around the Levant and Mesopotamia); that history develops in continuing progress, and the progress of technology is continuous; and that everything is matter and physical. When such myths are then scientifically validated they become, in modern parlance, self-evident. Once self-evident they are rarely questioned, and when they are, the questioner is usually labeled as belonging to fringe elements, such as the burgeoning alternative-history theorists. Hitler said, "The bigger the lie, the more chance it has of being believed." Those people who believe themselves immune to propaganda (the "I can distinguish truth from lies" variety) are more liable to fall victim to it. They are not aware of the subtlety and pervasiveness of the processes that are endemic in society. As already stated, propaganda techniques are not always visible. Often such processes function to change the psychological climate of a nation in order for changes to be willingly asked for by the people, such as through the dissemination of fear (see chapter 5). This establishes consequences, which often cannot be brought about by more direct methods. Willing minds are the target, and methods are various and often nefarious.

Methods in use include how nation-states use the "reality of truth" by releasing *seemingly accurate statistics* of plausible situations. Again, this is the "expert in the white lab coat" tactic. For such propaganda/information to be effective it cannot be too far from the truth; in other words, it must have the appearance of reality. Trade, employment, and financial figures are an example of this. And which members of the general public have the knowledge and/or resources to check and confirm such figures? And who really cares? People who do know are usually those who have a vested interest in maintaining the illusion, such as traders and financiers. And when a nation releases its unemployment figures, are they really counting the many who are jobless but not signing up for unemployment benefits or the dispossessed or immigrants? As a norm, statistics of a negative connotation are usually drawn from the smallest possible pile. And once a false (or "doctored") claim is disseminated and accepted by the public, it becomes established and hard to deconstruct or invalidate (unless persuasive anti-propaganda is just as effective). Political propaganda is not the same as sociocultural propaganda; the latter seeks to organize peoples' behavior into known patterns that are beneficial to the ruling powers of the nation. This reflects a complete style of life rather than momentary opinions (as in political propaganda). And a complete style of life is also exactly what is exported to other countries as a product.

Particular dominant nation-states have always acted to export their way of life to other less-dominant nations in order to compel others to strive for a particular model of life (colonialism). Now, colonialism (direct intervention) has been replaced by globalization (indirect intervention) by way of attracting the people of other nations toward a specific Western model of life, thereby gaining both political and financial power over foreign territories. Yet not only are physical territories gained; the social psyche of the populace is also targeted as a means of gaining influence and power. Part of this is to create a new consumer base for the influx of material goods; the other part is to condition the consciousness of the people toward the rise of a standardizing culture. Diversity, yes, but only when it exists under the overall umbrella of *managed unity*.

Modern societies are being set up to accommodate both individualism and the mass collective. Yet the forms that the accepted "individualism" take often hide the workings of a mass psyche—the "allowed liberty" that is provided to the modern person in pursuit of material gains, as long as there is a contribution to the overall plan of the ruling authority. Liberty, then, is an expression of mobility within a prescribed system: it does not denote *liberty external to the system*. Examples are the rock clichés that the mainstream media (MS media) love to promote and use to adorn their front pages—such as the raging antics of musicians Morrison, Hendrix, Cobain, and so forth, which later morphed into copycat corporate-rock PR. In essence, such "rebels" are allowed, and even encouraged, because their antics sell records. Rebelliousness in these forms is thus another contribution to a consumerist society, albeit in a less obvious way. And today there are many ways in which individualism is allowed to manifest. The problem for any ruling power is how to contain the spread of information dangerous to the system. Has this not always been the case? Today the issue is much broader because what people think and share is of much greater power than it has ever been.

What has changed the game plan over the past two decades is the rise of a distributed and decentralized mode of communication between individuals worldwide: the Internet. Its presence has spurned the growth of individuals seeking information between themselves, which is often external to the consensus of various nation-states. This has had the effect of defragmenting people away from conditioned patterns of propaganda and belief systems. This bottom-up intervention has seriously compromised the patterning techniques of ruling authorities. Efforts are now under way to censor information sites that are critical of the state (China, Iran, Turkey, Australia, and others), and to corporatize the Internet into paid subscription access (United States). The U.S. Senate was debating a new bill in June 2010 that sought to give the president the power to shut down the complete Internet for civilian access and to hand it over to CYBERCOM (the U.S. military cyber command) in the event of "cyber attacks." Although the bill did not pass at the time its implications were well recognized by various governments. As an example, during the "Arab Spring" uprisings many Arab governments tried to shut down national access to the Internet. Egypt, especially, was successful in shutting down all internet providers in the country. Other more covert methods employed to counter-affect public consciousness include the use of civil and military technologies to deliberately and wirelessly interfere with the human mind (some of these techniques will be discussed in chapter 4).

The diversity of the information coming from the MS media gives the illusion of independent reporting and news. Yet the MS media of any given nation is owned by a small handful of corporate entities with high-level state relations. An individual is thus attracted to a particular newspaper relative to his views, beliefs, lifestyles, and so forth, all of these "diversified patterned behavior" within the system. The MS media caters to these needs by operating a variety of newspapers that support these mythical standpoints, whether they are politically left, right, left/right of center, liberal, independent, this, that, or any other of the positions available for the "diversity within the unity" of the mass mind. The MS media makes a deliberate point of focusing on the disasters, troubles, and problems that besiege the world rather than the ordinary, everyday, or positive. In this light the world appears incoherent and cruel, emphasizing the individual's need for security, and the *willing security of authority*. The person within the developed modern society must feel safe and far away from the fragmentation of the world. The collective authority of society offers a safe haven, a ritual belonging, which keeps such beasts at bay. The system today is very advanced at being able to supply an individual's needs. One of these hidden needs is the instilled habit of obedience; because of conditioned passivity within a techno-savvy environment a person may unconsciously desire authority and command. In this way a person gives away her inner authority to an external source, which is usually an external power (the state). This act of dependency, whether perceived or not, forms a relationship of need that almost totally bypasses the inner creativity of the individual. In such a system individuals and groups lose their capacity for handling responsibility. With decreased responsibility, self-power is weakened. This environment deadens the communication between a person's outer and inner life—that is, the process for self-actualization becomes hampered, especially since the society that caters to the person's life needs does not supply positive feedback for open consciousness expression.

This state of coerced passivity, which diminishes a person's responsibility and sense of self, opens the way for increased state monitoring and surveillance (chapter 3). In this manner, a majority of the masses will accept (or even desire) such "security" measures. At the least, surveillance will not appear out of the ordinary for most citizens. It is a step-by-step process; rather like the boiling-frog syndrome; our collective "hot water" is being boiled in incremental steps so that we do not notice that we are being boiled alive. And when we do finally feel the burning, it will be too late. Preparation is the key, and governance of the collective mind of society has been a gradual process.

Why do we not feel violated by this conditioned socialization? Why do we not confront it within ourselves? The reason is partly because a human being has learned to justify every little thing. We reason it out and create, whether real or false, some justification for our circumstances. And in the end, we are all too willing to blame ourselves rather than saying, "Hey, I don't deserve this. I am not in the wrong. *I am better than this.*" Usually we feel that we must have done something wrong. This is our great weakness, and in behaving so we diminish the power of our inner authority and block the communication with our self. Guilt debilitates us physically as well as mentally and emotionally. If our processes of self-justification are not powerful enough we may then suffer from feelings of alienation. In these states we are more liable to commit antisocial acts, which then serve to strengthen a nation's legal and policing institutions. In this weakened, or pacified, psychological state the individual is then open to attach to any exterior source, which offers compensation for the person's own perceived failings. Once an external attachment is made, the beginnings of dependency are created. And a person begins to think less and less for herself and more in tune with prescribed patterns.

Prescribed social conditioning, via state institutions, standardizes the current ideas for any epoch. They supply the specific stereotypes; thought patterns; and required moral, social, and political standards. These then become reconfirmed through a variety of processes (government, media, sport, and so forth), which crystallizes them within the population. How many thought processes are truly are own? When you express an opinion, is it really your very own unique opinion, or is it something that you have assimilated and *accepted as your own* from other sources? How many of us believe the universe started with the big bang? That aliens do not exist, and we are not being visited by UFOs? That evolution began from a primordial soup of chemicals? That Atlantis, or other ancient prehistoric civilizations never existed? And so on . . . and so on . . . the list goes on. . . . What really are our beliefs? And why? Do we even know for certain why we are here? You would have thought someone should have cracked this mystery by now, wouldn't you?

Yet these and other crystallized thought patterns end up filling the consciousness of each person. We become clogged to such a degree that our inner consciousness (inner self) finds little room for expression or communication. In effect, we are being "nurtured" to block our own innate and natural talents, capacity, and functioning. In the end, each person is trained to "judge" and "critically evaluate" by such crystallized attitudes and standards. So when a person expresses public opinion as his own, he is no longer expressing a part of himself. These processes *take away our minds*. If we ever want to take back our minds we need to become more aware, more mindful, and more active in the face of social conditioning. Just take a look at our social behavior, at the obvious manifestation of the mass social mind: the veneration of film stars, adoration of artificially constructed heroes, celebrity psychosis, political lunacy, and nationalistic fervor. In these instances we are anything but co-creative and self-actualizing individuals.

Despite this rather bleak assessment there is opportunity for positive change and awakening. It is happening right now, all around us and in multitudinous ways. This is why the power structures in operation are literally working overtime and "upping the ante" in a bid to fight off the awakening of human potential and inner power. I contend that the years ahead will be significant in tipping the scale away from a suppressed state of human consciousness toward an unprecedented burst of conscious evolution. And as the human being continues to evolve, both individually and collectively, we will each come to recognize that any external power structure that attempts to control the *inner* consciousness of the individual is much more harmful and sinister in its ability to disturb human development than any attempts to control physical events.

However, until the individual awakens to her self-evolution we as a group will increasingly be under the power and influence of the modernity project, as I will examine in the next chapter.

2

THE MODERNITY PROJECT
The Rise of Scientific Technique

Scientific technique is much more than just the impact of new technology on the machinations of society. It is the use of science, in its most calculating and inhumane ways, to analyze, control and guide societies in a desired direction.

BERTRAND RUSSELL

True modern propaganda can only function within the context of the modern scientific system.

JACQUES ELLUL

The term *modern* usually conjures up images of progress, development, and betterment. After all, we have been led to believe that being modern implies that one is at the forefront of change. And so it is with many modern societies; they are developing a way forward that is supposedly for the betterment of the citizens. Further, this Modernity Project, which is a form of science, technology, and organization for postindustrial societies, is the inevitable result of positive progress. However, as Russell suggests in the opening quote, science also means that techniques are now available for the better analysis, management, and control of the people. This form of *scientific technique,* as Russell calls it, is in some ways the inevitable outcome of increasingly mechanized and rational societies. With improved methods for the organization and management of social practices, more concentrated forms of power and control are made possible. This is what is now meant by social forms of *technique.*

Technique is not necessarily about machines or technology, although it does include them. It is primarily about the ability of and methods to increasingly organize and create efficient order. It is about strategies of power and the rationality of control. It could be said that technique is actually the means to enact processes of increased mechanization. This is especially so now, in the twenty-first century, when so much technology has become embedded into our very social fabric. Rather than being convenient to us, our *techno-mechanized system* is turning us into the convenience. The last bastion of defense and protest is human consciousness: not only how we think but also how we create and manifest our own inner power and authority. It appears that this has now become the ultimate target for social technique: the containment and control of human consciousness.

The Modernity Project seeks to establish scientific technique as a means to absorb and integrate the human being into everything. In the end, a person is not external to anything; there is no "outside" as each individual is absorbed into the very fabric of the system. The danger here is that this momentum leads not toward unified diversity but toward a very real looming standardization. Such techniques as employed in society include the whole array of social-conditioning processes—from institutions such as school, church, work, media—to tools such as propaganda and modern communications. It is an all-embracing and all-inclusive *social matrix.* By using the term *social matrix* I am referring to the array of bodies (institutions, laws, police, education, religion, and so forth) that are woven together to form the workings of a control society. And in control societies there are both covert and overt strategies for the cultural conditioning of behavior and thought. Institutions and organizations within a social matrix act to concentrate specific forms of power through an array of social networks and hubs. As philosopher Bertrand Russell noted in his investigations into scientific technique:

> The completeness of the resulting control over opinion depends in various ways upon scientific technique. Where all children go to school, and all schools are controlled by the government, the authorities can close the minds of the young to everything contrary to official orthodoxy. . . . It may be hoped that in time anybody will be able to persuade anybody of anything if he can catch the patient young and is provided by the State with money and equipment.[1]

Social technique becomes an intermediary not only between a person and her environment but also between a person, her own knowledge base, and her inner self. Such techniques when applied through social institutions strengthen the primacy of matter and serve to bury the manifestation and potential of the human spirit. It is akin to throwing an electronic Faraday cage (a shield against electric and EM fields) around the individual, isolating her from the flux and flow of natural energies. The human being is increasingly assimilated into a world devoid of magic, mystery, and wonder. These realms or spaces of enchantment become superstition and "primitive," effectively blocking inherent channels of communication and connection. The human being becomes disqualified from a more expansive world of perception and is instead pulled down—or distracted by design—into a constricted, material, magic-less world of prohibitions and hard knocks. There is increasingly less room available for the creativity and expression of the human spirit. The once individual responsibility of self-control has now been turned into a state function: that of a top-down authoritative procedure of control of self. The end goal of this design is for sustained internal coherence of the society. This ensures control and continuity. Again, quoting Russell:

It is to be expected that advances in physiology and psychology will give governments much more control over individual mentality than they now have even in totalitarian countries. Fichte laid it down that education should aim at destroying free will, so that, after pupils have left school, they shall be incapable, throughout the rest of their lives, of thinking or acting otherwise than as their schoolmasters would have wished.[2]

Many of our modern global societies now exhibit a "technical consciousness" that operates through regulation, rationality, and calculated efficiency—the very opposite of the natural, the organic, and the spiritual. The necessary prior conditions include: a relatively quick period of technological development, rapid urban growth, an organized economic structure, a social atmosphere receptive to the rise of technical institutions, and a clear national/state intention for control.

The use of *technique* in today's modern societies is not about advancing and developing each individual's freedom. Rather, it is based on a calculus of efficiency that operates to sacrifice the autonomy of the individual for the automation of the collective. Within this system there is a limitation of choice. Or, in other words, a person is given the perception of choice within an environment of having no real choice. Within this technical-social matrix entertainment and other distraction industries serve their primary roles: they entertain us into contentment and containment. Or, as one critic noted, they "amuse us to death."* Thus the technosocial matrix aims to bring satisfaction to those individuals who comply with the system. It is a barter, or trade-off, whereby contentment is bought by the act of compliance. Yet it is important for the populace that this relationship is not considered, or felt, as subjugation. Rather it is a compromise necessary for good social order.

---

*These are the words of the cultural critic Neil Postman. See his *Amusing Ourselves to Death*.

Further, the rise of scientific technique also carried with it the capacity for extensive suppression and devastating social genocide. Such capacity was demonstrated during Nazi Germany's "Final Solution" program, which became an exercise in technical termination. One example was the orchestrated use of the IBM Hollerith punch-card technology to cross-tabulate and organize the prisoners. According to investigative journalist Edwin Black, the punch-card technology was used to gather identity information about European Jews from collating censuses, registrations, and ancestral tracing programs, which led to the classification of concentration-camp slave labor and associated work projects.[3] Other examples of scientific technique include eugenics, the Human Genome Project, and national criminal DNA databases.* Films that explore such issues include *Code 46* (Michael Winterbottom) and *Gattaca* (Andrew Niccol). Russell was aware of these potential trends when he published the following in 1952:

> Although this science will be diligently studied, it will be rigidly confined to the governing class. The populace will not be allowed to know how its convictions were generated. When the technique has been perfected, every government . . . will be able to control its subjects securely without the need of armies or policemen.[4]

Scientific technique is now securely a modus operandi of the Modernity Project. And in these global times this technique is now able to extend worldwide and to operate through differing cultures, and finally toward a global standardization. This enforced social "development" or "progress" is artificial and subordinates the organic nature of living beings. It is also against the natural world and through conquest and control it regulates and exploits all natural resources. It is the manifestation of emerging global technocultures.

---

*The UK National Criminal Intelligence DNA Database is currently the world's biggest DNA database, with several million profiles and tens of thousands added each month.

TECHNIQUE AND TECHNOCULTURE

The modern project of the construction of a technical-social matrix has two distinct features: 1) it limits and also suppresses the participation of the individual in both social evolution and conscious evolution; 2) its growth is self-augmenting, meaning it can and does operate beyond the need for both human intervention and eventually human capacity. Thus as technical development increases, the role of the human being diminishes. This begs the question: Is this process irreversible? Well, up to a point, it can be reversed. However, in order to reverse or stop this accelerating trend much disruptive change, even chaos, will be experienced. This function-creep of increased rationalization and control of social life has been described by the German sociologist Max Weber as the iron cage. This pervasive technical complex is also responsible for the vast machinery of agricultural farming and global food distribution, energy monopolization and distribution, the medical establishment, global trade, and so forth. These almost universal institutions have served to immerse as many cultures and peoples as possible within a constrained and standardized living matrix of control.

Within nation-state structures there are various manifestations of *technique* that appear within both the physical and social sciences. For example, in biology there are obligatory vaccinations, medical inspections, and health institutions. In physics the emphasis is on the universal myth of matter as primary and separate rather than in the connected nonlocal relationship between the observer and the observed. In the social sciences the emphasis is on researching social management, behavior and norms, and the study of the masses. It is interesting to note in this context that the pioneering field of communication studies was in fact heavily funded by the CIA and other U.S. intelligence services (to the tune of $1 billion in the early 1950s). Modern communication research, as was developed within academia, indirectly served to assist state and military institutions to better understand, manipulate, and exploit both individuals and social groups.[5] Also, in such areas as planning and development and transport networks, the emphasis is not always on efficiency and aesthetics; at times social structures of mobility have been utilized as artifacts for urban control. Such examples include deliberate attempts to deny sections of society access to specific infrastructures of transport, energy, and information.[6] In this regard:

> Technique cannot be otherwise than totalitarian. It can be truly efficient and scientific only if it absorbs an enormous number of phenomena and brings into play the maximum of data. In order to co-ordinate and exploit synthetically, technique must be brought to bear on the great masses in every area. But the existence of technique in every area leads to monopoly. . . . Technique can leave nothing untouched in a civilization. Everything is its concern.[7]

The Modernity Project seeks to establish a global technical civilization (that is, one constructed on techniques of power and control). Thus certain technical necessities are required in order to allow growth while simultaneously endeavoring to curtail specific physical and mental freedom within predefined limits. This has led to a digital age of databases and digital identities. If not curtailed it is likely that this digital Orwellianism will become a global phenomenon and, more importantly, the global standardized norm (see chapter 3).

The technoculture of modernity has no taboos; nothing is sacred and nothing is safe from being exploited and manipulated to serve its ends. Such a matrix cannot accept that there are rules outside of it; in fact it continually propagates new rules in order to expand its reach. The strategy is expansion and containment. It is the nature of a civilization based on *technique* to move toward ever increasing centralization. This inevitably will lead toward a global "unifying" political and economic system and world government. This has the danger of rendering power faceless and untouchable. The individual is left without any person to blame or hold accountable. Telephones are answered by voice programs, queries are dealt with by e-mails, taxes and state exams are computerized, and all information is data based. Individual conscious creative expression is further dumbed and numbed. The problem with this coerced path of social development is that if it goes on for too long then the possibilities for adaptive change will be reduced to such a minimal level that the society is liable to stagnate. In other words, it has ceased to be an evolving organism. And when such evolution is no longer possible, the evolutionary experiment has proved a failure and soon becomes the cause of its own destruction. The choice, as one thinker put it, is between evolution or extinction.[8]

As state control over the individual increases it is likely to lead to further disintegration of the family unit. As is already well documented, industrial change split up strong rural families and communities, herding the workforce into cramped urban housing conditions. The breakup of rural communes, communities, and extended families mirrored a shift from a more decentralized feudal power system into a state-centralized authoritarian model. Family life became subjected to industrial regiments of work schedules. In some instances, as in poorer labor areas, the family unit took on the character of an industrial unit. In recent times the lessening of social taboos around divorce and single-parent families has allowed the relatively easy breakup of families and family relationships. It has even been alleged that feminism and the women's liberation movement were carefully funded strategies by the powerful elite in order to disrupt maternal roles, to break up tight family units, and to push women into tax-paying work. Within this allegation lies the story that the elite bankrolled women's liberation because the bankers wanted to be able to tax the "other half" of the population, and that they got children into school at an earlier age, thus enabling them to be indoctrinated into accepting the state as the primary family, breaking up the traditional family model.* Apparently well-known feminist Gloria Steinem has been on record as saying that the CIA bankrolled *Ms.* magazine as part of the same agenda of breaking

---

*See interviews with film-producer Aaron Russo held shortly before his death.

up traditional family models. Whether these allegations have any truth or not, it is enough to know that such theories exist and are circulating covertly. Regardless of theories, social patterns and trends in Westernized countries show a marked shift of women from the home and into the workforce. This must have had an impact on family bonds. Also, since women have traditionally been the backbone of thriving communities, the regimentation of women's lives into commercial work has allowed the further commercialization of home and child-rearing functions. Once family practices become a part of consumption patterns, then the potential for community relationships become buried under the spread of commercial interests and debts. This is a further erosion of individual, family, and community bonding, which has been a source of strength throughout our human history.

Modern technocultures are moving toward rendering traditional democratic doctrines obsolete. They present the facade of a free and open democracy while operating within a reality of closed choices. We, the people, choose from a limited selection whom we did not select. This is another example of the illusion of free will. And when the technical apparatus has completely absorbed the people, the state structure becomes totalitarian, *even if this is not recognized as being so*. It cannot be otherwise since the mode of operation—a mechanized ordering of individuals—is totalitarian action. This is so even if the particular nation-state appears liberal, democratic, or otherwise. Social critic Herbert Marcuse defined *modern totalitarianism* as "not only a terroristic political coordination of society, but also a non-terroristic economic-technical coordination, which operates through the manipulation of needs by vested interests."[9]

The idea of the nation-state is a relatively recent invention, yet one that is still very real to each individual. Also, the modern totalitarian state is not the same as the old images we have of public brutality and torture. This would represent waste of useful psychic energy and would risk angering the populace. The modern version of the totalitarian state is one of technical efficiency, digital rendering, and data flows. In other words, a Database Nation (database-ization). This type of totalitarian doctrine is not one of barbarism nor dictatorship; rather it constructs a pleasing, entertaining (read: distracting) society that breeds willing conformity through convenience and services. It will provide apparent leverage of critical thought and opposition while simultaneously suppressing and manipulating the collective psyche of the people. By its very nature such a social system halts, or at least hinders, the evolution of consciousness. And in its place is often inserted, as artificial conditioning, a subconscious obedience to authority (refer again to Milgram's experiments). The concept of justice in such societies is replaced by the overt necessity for order and stability. This is then reinforced through fear strategies in order to establish and maintain a required need for security (see chapter 5). Not to have a trusted structure of security would suggest the alternative of chaos and disorder. Within complex social systems the threat of chaos—and thus the loss of social privileges—is usually enough to gain support for constraining security measures.

Many modern societies are thus moving toward a convergence: a centralization of power and control through an advanced complex of institutions that monitor, regulate, and, when necessary, manipulate people, information, minds/thoughts, and behavior. In one sense it is an incredible achievement. On the other hand it is extremely chilling that such an agenda was ever allowed to come into being and grow in the hearts of people.

Of principal concern are the strategies that deal with the control and manipulation of a person's inner life, specifically their mind and consciousness. This is an altogether different element of control within the overall technical matrix and social apparatus. This pervasive creature seeks our approval and support, to the point where we not only give away our minds and inner authority, but also willingly give up our right to conscious evolution. This is none other than a practice of psychic manipulation. Even the spiritual life is targeted by the social matrix of *technique*. Strategies here include the widespread dissemination of *mis*-information, *dis*-information, and distraction doctrines. These include certain (yet not all) New Age and esoteric beliefs that hold out for Ascension, being airlifted to safety via friendly UFOs, or crystal-gazing apathy. Both the material and the spiritual aspects of our lives have been invaded and corrupted in order to control and manipulate both sides, similar to how major financiers often back both sides in a war so it is always a win-win situation. It appears that many of us today are walking a fine line with regard to technique. He who maintains that he can escape it completely "is either a hypocrite or unconscious."[10] The modern globalizing technoculture is shifting toward an all-enclosing system whereby the individual will find it increasingly more difficult (and even near impossible) to both materially and spiritually disengage from the sociotechnical matrix.

Within such modern societies psychic development and conscious evolution are replaced by psychological and emotional gratifications. Without these "services" the population will lose the will to participate, as there would seemingly be no benefits to such action. This is one of the functions of consumerism and the entertainment industry.

FRAGMENTATION AND CONSUMERISM

Increasingly many of us are now living everyday lives in an environment that is ever more symbolic and disembodied. Just take a look at our global digital economies to see the peak of symbolic existence. Now this symbolic environment is becoming stretched to exhaustion: economy, consumerism, media and entertainment, technology, warfare. There is a danger that the symbolic will overtake the actual, pushing real human experience and values into the background. And within the realm of the symbolic lies the core of power that manipulates and controls.

Within a highly symbolic technoculture the lines between fulfil-ment/emptiness, honesty/corruption, and liberty/containment begin to blur into false constructions and subjectivities. All these contribute to an increase in social fracturing with the result that further social constriction will be deemed necessary in order to maintain a sense of order. And if people feel an encroaching sense of emptiness, grief, stress, boredom, and anxiety, then the entertainment industry and other distractions will become more dominant in our lives. Through such means people are enticed and drawn into apathy and are vulnerable to becoming dependent—even infantilized—by an all too easily available switch-on culture. In Japan, for example, in the growing phenomenon of Hikikimori, or self-isolation, more than a million young people are staying in their rooms for unhealthy periods of time, sometimes years. The demands for instant gratification grow and the response time diminishes.

There is real potential here for imbalance and also the opposite: an increased growth in people seeking extremes—extreme excitement and pleasure in order to escape from the fear of boredom and anxiety. Retail therapy (that is, consumerism) has always been a favorite anaesthetic. Yet in the light of current financial woes and the instability in economic markets, consumerism is becoming too expensive for many people without credit. Nonetheless, this does not stop people in the privileged West who have been weaned on the milk of easily available goods. Those who continue to buy and hoard on credit find themselves in deeper debt and deeper stress, affecting individual and family health. Such an increasingly toxic environment only fuels the soaring growth of the corporate health institutions. Tranquilizers, antidepressants, and Viagra are the world's most popular drugs for the human body: a pharma-fueled dance of pumping us up and deflating us. In the eyes of one cultural critic:

So very many ways to gauge the pain: serious obesity among children has increased more than 50 percent in the last fifteen to twenty years; severe eating disorders (bulimia and anorexia) among college women are now relatively common; sexual dysfunction is widespread; the incidence of panic and anxiety attacks is rising to the point of possibly overtaking depression as our most general psychological malady; isolation and a sense of meaninglessness continue to make even absurd cults and TV evangelism seem attractive to many.[11]

Such a critique of modern technocultures paints a picture of rising incoherence, fragmentation, and imbalance. Remember that having *more* will never compensate us for being *less*. The global spread of the social model that offers to fulfill the created demand for quick "desire for satisfaction" is rather a model that peddles distraction. Such social models are also peddling the false belief that everything can be obtained at the push of a button—if only you adhere to the social norms and requirements, just like the rat who was rewarded with food if it pressed the correct button each time. It may be that in a similar way we, the people, are being asked to respond in kind when our buttons are pressed.

Part of our required behavior is to make consumption a way of life. It is as if the buying and use of consumerist goods has become a social ritual whereby we nurture our ego satisfactions and well-being. How we buy (our consumption patterns) has now become embedded in values of social status, social acceptance, and prestige. We are literally branded by what we buy (like hot-iron-branded cattle). Yet many of us proudly display our brands and tags like social markers. In return such displays are often rewarded in the social matrix by conditioned responses of approval, admiration, respect, envy, and so forth. People are being made to feel good for doing trivial things. Similarly we are being handed the illusion that we have a free choice in our consumption patterns: "The apparent widening of individual consumer choices actually shrinks the field of social choices. . . . This politics of commodity . . . offers the feel of freedom while diminishing the range of options and the power to affect the larger world."[12] Again, it is the *politics of distraction*. People are being offered "freedoms" that are carefully selected in order to ensure minimum disruption of the real issues: the perfect magician's sleight-of-hand trick. Voting is a good example of this mechanism. As the infamous slogan says, "If voting changed anything, it would be illegal."

People need to feel that they have a choice, whether it is a real or false choice. We choose between what we are provided rather than going outside of those choices. We lean toward what distracts us or what we feel keeps us satisfied. We are fed a cocktail of pseudochoice, dreams, desires, hopes, and endless escapes. No wonder people often confuse reality and what they see at the movies. They both read from the same script. Perhaps we should consider why there are so many efforts afoot to make us respond in required ways. And why is it that many of us hunger for such fulfillments, such need for meaning? Is there something that we are not being told, such as the power of individual consciousness?

Unity within each individual—strength of connection between the external and inner selves—is a force too concentrated for the social matrix. In order to be manageable and (relatively) compliant people need to be kept distracted and, generally speaking, fragmented. This is increasingly provided by the structure of urban living. Dense, crowded, sprawling city life, with its increased dependence on external institutions for such basics as food, warmth, and work, deepens the sense of a mechanized system and further strips the individual of inner authority. The readiness for obedience to authority is instilled in such an environment. As Richard Heinberg notes:

> As civilization has provided more and more for us, it's made us more and more infantile, so that we are less and less able to think for ourselves, less and less able to provide for ourselves, and this makes us more like a herd—we develop more of a herd mentality—where we take our cues from the people around us, the authority figures around us.[13]

The social matrix of *technique* (the Modernity Project) has sought to establish a modified human environment that has replaced the organic space. Most people now eat, sleep, work, and play according to the clock rather than in line with their own natural rhythms. Traditional rhythms of life and nature (including biological circadian rhythms) have been replaced by mechanical regulations of time. The individuals in such technocultures no longer operate through "living time" but within fragmented divisions of work time, or, rather, clock-time. Although more people may be increasingly working from home there are still routines to be followed: online/physical meetings, dropping off/collecting the children, food shopping, evening leisure time, and so on. Hinterlands of grass and nature have been replaced by stone and concrete. Experience with natural materials and resources (wood and soil) has been taken away from the hands of most people. More than ever we are dependent on services that can work with these materials. How many of us have the aptitude to repair, build, or invent with such resources? Most likely we ring for voice-mail services when something stops working. Soon we will lose the ability to read maps because we are so accustomed to the sweet or husky voice of the built-in satellite-navigation system—tracked yet secure. Such an artificial milieu deprives us of our natural human adaptability, resourcefulness, and inner authority. Yet in order to allow the human body to tolerate such a fragmented unnatural regime certain "release mechanisms" are orchestrated to recalibrate the individual.

These are dutifully supplied by allowances such as legal alcohol, weekend blowouts, competitive sports, regional/national/international rivalries, holidays and fiestas, media satire, legal protests, and so forth. The weekend blowout is an excellent example in which people are encouraged to "release" themselves, have a good time, and indulge in entertainments and then arrive back on the job bright and early Monday morning. A precedent to this pattern was established on the slave plantations in the American South. According to an actual slave narrative, plantation owners often supplied the slave workers with a little pocket money to spend exclusively at the plantation shops.[14] At certain times of the year, such as Christmas, the slaves were allowed several days respite from their arduous work. This time was almost entirely spent in reckless whiskey drinking and wild drunkenness—a necessary release from pent-up emotions. This would inevitably lead to disputes, arguments, brawls, and violent clashes between the slaves. After several days of manic intoxication the plantation owners found that the slaves were quite willing and eager to return to ordered work as a way to get back some semblance of order and ritual in their lives. Most modern societies are structured in just such a manner, through the *work-release* mechanism, which also serves to fuel the economy.

However, certain releases are not allowed, such as those supplied by illegal intoxicants like marijuana, class-A narcotics, and LSD. While statistics show that alcohol-related deaths far exceed those from drug abuse, the real crux is that alcohol provides a stimulus that quickly recedes, leaving the person once again capable of engaging with the social world. Alcohol addiction comes only after extreme and sustained use. Class-A narcotics, however, are likely to create addictive tendencies quite early on in their use, thus rendering an individual less useful to society and as a worker and consumer. Instead of becoming a participant within the economy they become a burden. This is, of course, opposite to the requirements of the social matrix. Narcotics such as marijuana and cannabis, on the other hand, often create states that are pensive, abstract, antilinear (right-brain activity), and trigger thought patterns that are likely to consider notions outside the restrictive milieu of the social matrix. Marijuana and cannabis use are not conducive to a person's returning to willing Monday morning work, as its induced states can be more euphoric than alcohol. Also, its residual traces are more prone to reflection than the dreaded hangover. Thus, such narcotics are often considered as a bane to ordered society despite their historical and widespread use. However, no doubt the most socially controversial narcotics are those that result in consciousness expansion and psychedelic states, such as LSD and DMT-botanic natural sources of psilocybin and ayahuasca. The use of such mind-expanding substances goes far back into recorded history in indigenous cultures. Shamanic accounts of ritualistic ingestion and trance states fill many anthropological accounts and still attract thousands of aspirants annually. There has even been well-researched documentation to suggest that ancient prehistoric cave art owes its expression to such shamanic practices of plant-induced mind-altered states.[15] And when LSD became a Western cultural phenomenon in the 1960s—largely due to the exploits of Dr. Timothy Leary—the power structures came down like a barbed clamp. LSD, it seemed, was a step too far for the social-control institutions to accept, especially when Leary was promoting his slogan "Turn on, tune in, drop out." Within the social matrix such dropping out is not an economically viable option.* Thus certain release mechanisms are allowed within technocultures.

These examples show how social environments are constructed and managed with the intention of providing strict frameworks for the physical and mental behavior of their citizens. Of course, social parameters are necessary if one does not wish for anarchy and complete chaos. The argument here is not that the constructions of society are a bad thing; rather these structures for human organization have been hijacked by vested interests that wish to exploit social environments for their own ends. And in order to achieve this goal there has had to be, by necessity, a concerted effort to distract, manage, and even usurp the consciousness of human beings. After all, social living should provide each person with the tools for co-creation, community life, friendship, and trust. Instead it provides an atmosphere of competition, rivalry, hostility, anonymity, and mistrust. For many people this need for friendship is provided by media personalities and film stars. The media has become the perfect vehicle for constructing the social mirage of the hyperreal.

MEDIA AND HYPERREALITY

It seems—or rather *appears*—that the global world increasingly hinges on signs and symbols that often translate into ineffectual gestures. Technocultures more and more drag people into accelerated connections, relations, and extended tasks. The Argentine writer Jorge Luis

---

*I am not condoning drug use here, but merely pointing out some social implications.

Borges once famously wrote of a great empire that created a map so detailed it was as large as the empire itself. The actual map itself grew and decayed as the empire conquered or lost territory. When the empire finally crumbled, all that remained was the map. This imaginary map finally became the only *remaining reality* of the great empire: a simulacrum, a simulation of the physical reality that now encompasses everyone. In some sense we can say that today's world is moving further toward existing within a simulation of reality. Our world is increasingly given meaning and order through symbols and signs, reducing the human experience to moving between artifacts that construct and maintain a perceived reality. Much of this is orchestrated through global media and the worldwide "cultural creep" of uniform, standardizing Western lifestyle patterns. Some cultural critics, such as the French philosopher Jean Baudrillard, felt that many societies were becoming so reliant upon the simulation that they were losing contact with the physical real world.[16] Through the consumerist mass production of objects and desirables, people's attention and focus is increasingly driven toward superficial attainments and false value systems. The global media, through movies, television, and printed material, shoulders much of the responsibility for blurring the sense of meaning and values and for deliberate distraction techniques, and, of course, for the incredible amount of propaganda and mental/emotional manipulation that lies at the heart of global media. When there is intent to flood people's consciousness with images that are often *more real than the real,* this sense of hyperreality is in danger of eroding the presence of meaning and significance.

This shift toward propagating banal reality lies at the heart of the ever-increasing centralized control of the media. It is somewhat worrying to learn that most Western media organizations are owned by only a handful of giant corporations: News Corp, Viacom, Time-Warner, Disney, Vivendi, and Bertelsmann. For example, Disney (The Walt Disney Company) is the largest entertainment and media multinational in the world. Disney owns the TV networks ABC, Disney

Channel, ESPN, A&E, and the History Channel, as well as publishing, merchandising, and theater subsidiaries. They also own Walt Disney Pictures, Touchstone Pictures, Hollywood Pictures, Miramax Film Corp., Dimension, and Buena Vista International, as well as eleven theme parks around the world. News Corp comes in as the world's second-largest media multinational, with an incredible range of TV and satellite channels, magazine and newspaper holdings, worldwide record companies and publishing companies, including a strong presence in Asian markets. Similarly Time-Warner owns more than fifty magazines, a film studio and various film distributers, more than forty music labels (including Warner Bros., Atlantic, and Elektra), and several TV networks (such as HBO, Cartoon Network, and CNN). Viacom owns TV networks CBS, MTV, VH1, Nickelodeon, Comedy Central, Paramount Pictures, and nearly two thousand cinema screens as part of their media empire. Likewise, Vivendi owns 27 percent of U.S. music sales via labels such as Interscope, Geffen, A&M, Island, Def Jam, MCA, Mercury, Motown, and Universal. They also own Universal Studios, Studio Canal, Polygram Films, Canal+, and numerous Internet and mobile phone companies. Then there is Bertelsmann, which, as a global media corporation, runs Europe's second largest TV, radio, and production company (the RTL Group) with forty-five TV stations and thirty-two radio channels; Europe's largest printing and publishing firm (Gruner & Jahr); the world's largest English-language general trade-book publisher (Random House); the world's largest book and music club group (Direct Group); and an international media and communications service provider (Arvato AG).

The MS media is free to offer up a kaleidoscopic view of world events like a broad canvas of fleeting colors. Each day the mosaic changes and events, tragedies, disasters, coups, and politics flash before the eyes like a glitter ball. As a result the viewer rarely has the chance to focus on one issue, and thus remembers very little. Nor is there the need to remember a specific event, as the next day it is likely to be replaced by another item of news. In this way, the average viewer is granted her "nourishment" and feeling of open news while at the same time being denied any real truth of the situation or any depth of knowledge.

The MS media and entertainment industry also manipulate viewers' emotions through the continual images of sexual arousal and abuse to the point whereby many of us are desensitized and more accepting of sexual misconduct. The media of escapism allows us to live out our fantasies in what is considered a less harmful way. It is supposed to placate us, to make us forget the drudgery of our repetitive lives. It also provides us with an external platform on which to project, supplies a conversation space/talking point among friends and/or work colleagues, or offers a buffer zone to cover up the embarrassment of a noncommunicative family. There are also those few who are motivated to mimic the acts of celluloid, whether through violence or sexual perversion. Sexual energies are channeled into exploited fantasies and indulgences. No doubt the few who do indulge are considered worth the trade-off against the millions who are mollified and happily passive in front of the screen. The creative capacity of human imagination is being substituted for a ready-made set of imaginative programming. We don't need to imagine for ourselves when the whole stage show is presented to us in magnificent Technicolor and computer-generated imagery (CGI). We have our tickets for the flight into unreality. Another more worrying possibility is that television can act as a factor in causing arrested development within younger children. Child researcher Joseph Chilton Pearce has published findings that indicate how television prevents the higher brain in children from developing as television engages solely with the lower (a.k.a., reptilian) brain. If the higher brain is not activated sufficiently through external stimulations—which it rarely is from child institutions—then at age eleven the brain begins to destroy many of its unused neurons. This can lead to a permanent condition of arrested development. This points to a serious lack of proper stimulants for many children in overly institutionalized and controlled social environments. Also, our brains do not fully mature until we are around age twenty-five, which explains the early targeting of children through advertisers and conditioning institutions.

Further, according to recent research, children under the age of four who watch television are 20 percent more likely to develop attention-deficit disorder (ADD) by the age of seven than children who don't.[17] We have to take a quick scan of the types of modern disorders affecting children today to realize that there has been a dramatic increase in negative social influences: ADD (attention-deficit disorder), ADHD (attention-deficit-hyperactivity disorder), ODD (oppositional-defiance disorder), PDD (pervasive developmental disorder), AS (Asperger's syndrome), SID (sensory-integration dysfunction), and ASD (autistic-spectrum disorder). In the U.S. one out of ten young people are mentally ill and more than seven million have ADD; cases of ADHD are up 600 percent since 1990 and autism is now considered an epidemic.[18] Our young children are the fastest-growing segment of the prescription drug market, coerced into the need to consume Ritalin, Prozac, Risperdal, and Concerta. The controversial drug Ritalin can shrink a child's size and weight (according to scientific reports), and can cause permanent changes to the brain. Prozac has been known to cause violent behavior and high incidence of depression and suicide. "These children, who can least handle drugs, are given the most powerful, and medicated at the same rate as adults. The insurance industry gives incentives for medication and disincentives for therapy or more natural substances."[19] We can also add to this mix the barrage of soft drinks (aspartame), junk food, alcohol, toxic pollutants, food additives, chemically treated material, and the general exposure to electrical fields and electromagnetic radiation. In part because of these negative influences there also has been a marked increase in the number of children suffering from food allergies and nutrition disorders. Conditions include, but are not limited to, thyroid disorders, amino-acid deficiencies; inflamed intestines; and immune-system disturbances from ingestion of pesticides, growth hormones, irradiated food.

As if to add fuel to the fire the MS media is now pronouncing that eating healthily can cause mental disease. A recent report in a reputable UK newspaper described how fixation with healthy eating can be a sign of serious psychological disorder.[20] The report goes on to say that this "disease" is called *orthorexia nervosa,* which is basically Latin for "nervous about correct eating"! Of course, because it has a Latin name it must not only be medically correct but also a smart diagnosis. It is as if the mainstream prefers everyone to continue eating junk food that seems to not only affect the sensitivity of the individual but also to increase dis-harmony, as mentioned above. As is now common within our corporate modernity many directors from large food corporations sit on the boards of directors of large media and pharmaceutical corporations—a corporate-industrial complex based on greed and the control of social/market forces. It is no wonder that so many of our children are losing the plot!

On top of this the corporate entertainment industry has proved to be an incredible tranquilizing abstraction and addiction to distraction. It provides an antidote to the very poison of the system to which it itself is an intrinsic part. It also provides a space whereby techno-savvy advertisers can use well-polished techniques—such as an exact combination of startling and symbolic imagery—to train viewers' brains and to impact individual reasoning. These impacts, it has been suggested, reshape brain structure to some degree, numb the nervous system, interfere with the prefrontal lobes, and become, in many cases, a causative factor in ADD. The cycle just continues as the corporate-entertainment-industrial complex forms our institutional megaliths. Yet for the most part people are content and happy in such social systems, as long as they can be provided for. And for those who are finding everyday life difficult, the entertainment industry is even more important for them. So when all hell breaks lose at work, at least you have *The Golden Girls* or *Friends* waiting for you on the home screen! As the social critic Jacques Ellul observed, "This demonstrates the complete adaptation of technical amusements to technical society and to their sociological function."[21]

Of course, this does not apply to all creative entertainment, as there is much independent material that is of quality and value. However, such creative endeavors usually find release only if they can make money for their backers. In terms of MS news it is always important to check the source when reading a news item; that is, is it of an independent source or is it "according to a government source"? The MS media is largely fed via global news services, the two largest being Reuters (now Thomson Reuters) and the Associated Press. This again constitutes a centralization of news information, as well as the various well-established political press offices. When such sources (especially PR offices) disseminate information as truthful news they are doing nothing more than was parodied in Orwell's *1984* as Newspeak. Independent media, such as is rampant on the Internet, has served to neutralize some of the overwhelming persuasive power of the MS-media propaganda. For this reason there are concerted efforts afoot to curtail and censor elements of the Internet. In other words, this means there is considerable corporate and political will to rein in the Internet under the umbrella of corporate and governmental/state control, or at least the surveillance of its use.

However, for many of us media and technological communications are now an extension of our daily lives. By being an extended part of us we are drawn in to their events and are enthralled in their dramas. They appear as an amplification of our own senses, relating, interpreting, and transcribing the world back to us. In essence, our technological extensions become our externalized nervous systems. According to media guru Marshall McLuhan:

> Today, after more than a century of electric technology, we have extended our central nervous system itself in a global embrace. . . . When our central nervous system is technologically extended to involve us in the whole of mankind and to incorporate the whole of mankind in us, we necessarily participate, in depth, in the consequences of our every action.[22]

In McLuhan's words our every action involves us with the world around us through our "extended embrace." The danger here is that humanity collectively becomes enmeshed within a technological embrace that is then manipulated to erode individual/personal freedoms and one's sense of inner authority. Therefore, while this situation has the potential for a radical revolution in collective consciousness and shared empathy (see chapter 6), it also prescribes the pattern for extensive and pervasive social control and ordering (chapter 3).

As global MS media and the extension of hyperreality and simulacre creep into our daily lives we each become numb to the violations, wars, carnage, and outrages that pass off as media spectacles. Also worrying is that our younger generation is becoming ever more desensitized to extreme content as video games increasingly merge with military simulations and violent content. Children's entertainment gradually merges into "militainment" as warfare gaming and first-person shooters become bestsellers and a gaming phenomenon. The simulation of violence and military machismo makes the macabre the unreal, the inconsequential and the fanciful. Immersion is permitted at the press of a button, and instant, on-demand gratifications satiate distraction and attention. This indeed can be a dangerous mix of painless pleasures taught to be available at the effortless touch of a button. It can become all too easy to slip into a distractive regime of escapism and pleasurable indulgence. In February 2010 a twenty-two year old South Korean man was charged with murdering his mother after she nagged him for spending too much time playing online games. After murdering his mother the young killer then went to a nearby Internet café to continue playing his games. Another recent example is that of a young couple, again in South Korea, who in September 2009 returned home from a twelve-hour gaming binge to find their three-month-old daughter dead. The couple were later arrested and charged with starving their daughter to death after it emerged the couple was more interested in raising an online baby (called Anima) in a popular role-playing game called Prius Online. Research published in the UK in February 2010 also showed evidence of a link between excessive Internet use and depression.* Of course, there are always exceptions, and we also need to recognize that some online gaming material can stimulate children's brains through complex puzzle-solving and strategy-based games. However, based on the lowest-common-denominator approach, it appears that the mass market is more successful in selling aggressive, addictive material to the general buying public.

Literally, then, we need to start *taking back our minds,* bringing consciousness to the forefront, giving it priority within our lives, and nurturing our own inner authority. Failing to do so could seriously allow us to glide into the arms of mass global governance that seeks to stagnate the evolutionary mechanism of human consciousness.

Each person is gradually being forced to adapt to the new technologized social matrix and to exist within a "mass society" or to face being excluded from all the services provided by immersion in a collective society. Yet this forced adaptation requires a degree of psychic mutation, one away from neurogenetic evolution and toward conscious stagnation. Many social institutions within technocultures are geared toward a particular mutation of a person's mind, emotions, and consciousness. Today we often refer to it as social conditioning. Yet the varieties of processes and bodies that render this possible are extremely complex and have been well developed over the years. Over the past one and a half centuries humankind has been shifting toward the structure of a mass society. This modern project of *massification* has been rapidly accelerated through the Modernity Project of globalization. Yet at the same time it has been necessary to condition humankind for this new type of mental and psychological reality. My view is that for a positive style of planetization to function we need to assist the emergence of a conscious perceptual shift (a neurogenetic leap). This shift in consciousness would facilitate a co-creative and intercommunicative global humanity (see later chapters). The alternative, as I have outlined so far,

---

*Published by Leeds University (UK). For journal abstract see http://content.karger .com/produktedb/produkte.asp?doi=277001.

is a controlling global system that stifles human consciousness and is in danger of slowing down and hindering the necessary evolution of collective humanity and the expansion of our civilization. Again, noting Ellul:

> The process of massification takes place not because the man of today is by nature a mass man, but for technical reasons. Man becomes a mass man in the new framework imposed upon him because he is unable to remain for very long at variance with his milieu.[23]

Ellul refers here to the socializing pattern of *technique* to render an individual as within a mass, not through individual choice but rather because by nature a person cannot remain long in a state of friction with their environment. The system, as if natural to its character, brings all people into its process of increasing *massification*.

The danger here is that people who live in highly techno-mechanized societies are under the influence of a psychologically subversive environment. This environment has succeeded, to some degree, in making the rational appear irrational, and the irrational as rational. Or, as some mystics like to assert, we live in an upside-down, topsy-turvy world. Another example of this is how humanity's connections and alignment with natural rhythms has been severed through the introduction of an artificial conception of time. The official change over to the Gregorian calendar (a.k.a., the Western calendar) in 1582 subjected nations and their peoples to an artificial time that many indigenous elders have noted does not synchronize with any natural cycle and serves only to disempower human beings by obscuring the relationship between humans and the cosmos. Mayan daykeeper and elder Hunbatz Men says of this: "Today we have an imposed civilization personified by humanity's manipulators. . . . This forces humanity into the abyss of physical and spiritual destruction by a few groups that control the majority of humankind—all of which amounts to a conspiracy against the human race and Mother Nature."[24] Hunbatz Men believes that this alienation of human beings from synchronizing with the natural world also alienates people from the present moment. Thus the Gregorian calendar system has led humanity into a severe case of amnesia.

As it is, to most people the development of more technical, "efficient," and "functional" social structures appear as both inevitable and agreeable aspects of the progress of civilization. Further, they appear as inevitable because such technological advancement and economic complexities are construed as being beyond the reach of the ordinary person. This step-by-step drive toward herding people into an increasingly controlled social environment also, by its intrinsic nature, seeks to eliminate evolutionary agents. Evolutionary agents are people in every society who are the first to mutate/evolve away from the norms of social conditioning and to point the way toward the next stage in human evolution (chapter 7). New modes of realization, awareness, and conscious behavior are now urgently needed if individuals are to break away from these controlling environments. In the next chapter I examine how digital networks of control are shifting us evermore toward physical, mental, and spiritual quarantine.

3
LIVING UNDER QUARANTINE
The Manufacture of Social Control

The Open Conspiracy is the awaking of mankind from a nightmare, an infantile nightmare, of the struggle for existence and the inevitability of war. The light of day thrusts between our eyelids, and the multitudinous sounds of morning clamour in our ears. A time will come when men will sit with history before them or with some old newspaper before them and ask incredulously, "Was there ever such a world?"

H. G. WELLS, *THE OPEN CONSPIRACY*

A comfortable, smooth, reasonable, democratic unfreedom prevails in advanced industrial civilization, a token of technical progress.

HERBERT MARCUSE, *ONE-DIMENSIONAL MAN*

For a long time now there have been various social voices calling out for global unification for a new world order. These calls have been based largely around the emergence of a single world government.

Formed by the increasing centralization of political, social, military, and economic bodies—such as the United Nations, the World Bank, International Monetary Fund (IMF), European Union, NATO, and so forth, it would appear reasonable and rational to assume that somewhere along the line we will arrive at a world government with global military and economic bodies. In fact we are almost there now in some respects. This "global project" has been called by various names, whether it is the *new world order, world commonweal,* or *World Pax.* Yet this modernizing project for a new world order is nothing more than a reshaping—*historical engineering*—of the old orders for recent times. As one acclaimed scholar has pointed out, in both old and new world orders the central goal has been control: "Control of the population is the major task of any state that is dominated by particular sectors of the domestic society and therefore functions primarily in their interest. . . ."[1] Such sectors are the minority elite who pursue controlling strategies to "engineer" world affairs in line with their aims. And these aims are for the most part based on greed and power, and the need to keep the masses contented and docile.

However, some of these global ideals have come under ideological guises or socialist agendas, while others have come in the form of scientific rationalism. H. G. Wells, for example, was an advocate for the *world commonweal/World Pax* vision, which he saw as a convergence of commonly shared human idealism. The awakening of the people, thought Wells, would give them cause to rise in order to drive forward a historical, biological, and sociological agenda toward global unification. Wells's vision was a kind of "workers of the world unite" scenario similar to the original Marxist ideals, which Wells labeled as the Open Conspiracy.

> Now the most comprehensive conception of this new world is of one politically, socially, and economically unified. . . . Many there are at present who apprehend it as a possibility but do not dare, it seems, to desire it, because of the enormous difficulties that intervene, and

because they see as yet no intimations of a way through or round these difficulties. They do not see a way of escape from the patchwork of governments that grips them and divides mankind.[2]

This post-Socialist vision, however, still regarded existing controls and "forms of human association" as part of the new common world directorate. Also Wells believed that the Western countries were better suited to this transition, which would be a natural progress of rising scientific rationalism and technological capacity. Again there is a pattern here in that rational thinking has been adopted as the vehicle in which to present specific agendas most suitable to hierarchical power structures. And it is through the rationalism of the elite scientific establishment that global governance found its most articulate expression. British philosopher Bertrand Russell has been one of the most eloquent writers in presenting a coherent picture of the powerful capacity for scientific rationalism to govern world order.

A scientific world society cannot be stable unless there is a world government. . . . Unless there is a world government which secures universal birth control, there must from time to time be great wars, in which the penalty of defeat is widespread death by starvation. . . . To deal with this problem it will be necessary to find ways of preventing an increase in world population. If this is to be done otherwise than by wars, pestilence, and famines, it will demand a powerful international authority. This authority should deal out the world's food to the various nations in proportion to their population at the time of the establishment of the authority. If any nation subsequently increased its population it should not on that account receive any more food. The motive for not increasing population would therefore be very compelling.[3]

The picture painted here is one of cold rationality that places birth control under the auspices of a world government. Food distribution too comes under the responsibility of the global unified authority. As Henry Kissinger, another elite-establishment political figure, once remarked in 1970, "Control oil and you control nations; control food and you control the people." Recent research places multinational corporations behind the push toward controlling global food supplies.

We can see that the control and management of global food supplies has been a priority for decades. The 1974 UN World Food Conference in Rome outlined the necessity of maintaining sufficient world grain reserves, especially since the price of grain had shot up dramatically by the huge increase in oil prices during the early 1970s oil crisis (at one point world oil prices had risen by 400 percent). At this time the U.S. export strategy in the 1970s was to further control food trade supplies, which led to moves to consolidate power as 95 percent of all grain reserves in the world were under the control of six multinational agribusiness corporations—Cargill Grain Company; Continental Grain Company; Cook Industries Inc.; Louis Dreyfus; Bunge; and Archer Daniels Midland—all but one of which were U.S.-based companies. The U.S. long-term strategy was to dominate the global market in grain and agriculture commodities, as outlined in the early 1970s under Richard Nixon. However, in order for the U.S. to become the world's most competitive agribusiness producer it had to replace the traditional American family-based farm with the now widespread, huge factory-farm production. In other words, traditional agriculture was systematically replaced with agribusiness production through changes in domestic policy. For example, domestic farm programs that had previously protected smaller farm incomes were phased out during Nixon's term in office. This policy was then exported overseas to developing countries in a bid to make U.S. agribusiness more competitive and to get a foothold in foreign markets.[4]

Alongside food and nutrition is health, and health care has also shifted in many nations toward corporate control and institutional power. We have only to consider the recent fiasco concerning the over-hyped swine-flu pandemic to see how large pharmaceutical corporations hold great sway over health care issues and World Health Organization (WHO) declarations. In some regions the legal enforcement to accept swine flu injections is a setting eerily reminiscent of Aldous Huxley's *Brave New World*. As Russell outlines:

> Diet, injections, and injunctions will combine, from a very early age, to produce the sort of character and the sort of beliefs that the authorities consider desirable, and any serious criticism of the powers that be will become psychologically impossible. Even if all are miserable, all will believe themselves happy, because the government will tell them that they are so.[5]

This scenario (albeit speculative) conjures up a psychological (injunctions) as well as chemical (diet, injections) tyranny that seeks to create an assenting and malleable citizenry. Of course, to many people this will sound like science fiction or mere conjecture. I admit that overt evidence may seem to be lacking, and that philosophical discourse does not necessarily indicate intention or fact. However, there is alarming evidence (if one follows the increasing emergence of decent investigative journalism) that social control structures are indeed highly manufactured and in play. There are covert control structures operating both within and between nation-states that would be beyond most people's conceptions. This is not total fantasy. We have only to look into global food supplies, intellectual property rights, financial institutions and central banking, DNA collecting, digital databases, and surveillance mechanisms (to name a few) to realize that many people are living in an increasingly quarantined environment.

The general definition of *quarantine* is an enforced isolation or a restriction of free movement imposed on people or animals to prevent the spread of a contagious disease. I contend that this definition is quite close to the bone, in that humanity is experiencing a heightening of physical and mental restriction. And the contagious disease? Well, this happens to be human consciousness. Only it isn't a threat to each individual person, but rather to the power structures of the encompassing social matrix.

To compare human social life with a type of quarantine is dramatic and suggests a spreading totalitarianism masquerading as liberal democracies. However, I feel that this comparison is apt, as it not only suggests a physically restrictive environment but also one that hampers the expression and growth of consciousness. As the preceding chapters have endeavored to explain, there are a great number of processes at work within modern societies that function to guard, guide, and manipulate how people think. Further, I contend that the primary factor these socializing control structures are guarding against is the acceleration, expansion, and expression of human consciousness and its attendant spiritual awareness. What this infers is that social evolution is no longer (if it ever was) a natural process; rather modern sociotechnical development is now carefully orchestrated around the central issue of power and control. Also this issue of control is concerned with how to manage an ever-growing human population, and to manage it in ways that are beneficial to ruling power hierarchies. This agenda requires technology (the consequences of *technique*) to further regulate and manipulate the free expression of human activity. Some of these socializing processes were outlined in the two previous chapters and include institutions such as education, family, health, work, and entertainment/leisure. In this sense people/citizens are very much *disciplined* into specific behavior and perceptual traits that are suitable to the particular nation-state. In this chapter I will expand on these earlier themes to examine how other subtle forces are at work in our societies to entrap people into weblike systems of control. Further, these processes act as a form of quarantine for the active expression of human consciousness.

Discipline can have varying degrees of manifestation. Whereas in past societies there were public executions and very real physical threats to one's life to instill discipline, nowadays this has shifted to more covert forms of control and influence. The disciplinary patterns in past Western societies concerned the fixed movement between school (or "workhouse") to factory or the army barracks. In today's modern social matrix this has been replaced by more fluid and pervasive control environments that have no finish. Whether it is the family, education, or career, and because social mobility is now much more fluid for the majority of people, the presence of control must be pervasive throughout rather than as an overt edifice. In other words, social control must operate as a pervasive system that permeates all aspects of life if it is to have a chance of long-term and sustained success. This necessitates an agenda of total integration, including not only the physical side of life but, perhaps more importantly, the mental, instinctual, and spiritual sides also. The ultimate dystopian future, for example, could be described this way:

> It will not be a universal concentration camp, for it will be guilty of no atrocity. It will not seem insane, for everything will be ordered, and the stains of human passion will be lost amid the chromium gleam. We shall have nothing more to lose, and nothing to win. Our deepest instincts and our most secret passions will be analyzed, published, and exploited. We shall be rewarded with everything our hearts ever desired. And the supreme luxury of the society of technical necessity will be to grant the bonus of useless revolt and of an acquiescent smile.[6]

We should be careful, therefore, to note that the illusion of liberty can be used as a powerful form of control and domination—such as the democratic right to free and fair elections, as the "free election of masters does not abolish the masters or the slaves."[7]

Yet the fact that this book can be published and distributed, alongside many others that critique established systems (whether political, religious, spiritual, and so forth) shows that a shift in the capacity for shared awareness is growing. Of course, such books, generally speaking, need to make a profit. But their ability to make a profit signals that there is a growing readership for such information and thought. This marks an important trend toward the need for positive change and conscious liberation. Without a change in thought and perception there can be no real change. We change the reality of our lives by first changing our minds. No revolution was ever begun without the burning flames of thought.[8] Art too has served as an avenue of awareness and expression (both overt and covert) as well as a sleepy distraction. In the past art proved to have the potential to be dangerous and subversive. As only one example we have Martin Luther's Protestant Reformation, which began with the printing and dissemination of the *95 Theses* in 1517. However, these amounted to changes, adaptations, and modifications *within* the system (that is, still within the belief system of religious doctrine). Today's reformation requires that people become aware of the system itself and the need to evolve beyond its restrictive forms. This is the most radical and at the same time one of the most necessary roles for artistic expression. Joseph Goebbels (Nazi Germany's propaganda minister) was acutely aware of this potential when he stated, "You are at liberty to seek your salvation as you understand it, provided you do nothing to change the social order." This amounts to nothing more than running around within our own playpen. If scientific rationalism had its extreme way we might find that a revolutionary/reactionary potential would cease to exist. As Russell points out:

> Children will, as in Plato's Republic, be taken from their mothers and reared by professional nurses. Gradually, by selective breeding the congenital differences between rulers and ruled will increase until they become almost different species. A revolt of the plebs would become as unthinkable as an organised insurrection of sheep against the practice of eating mutton.[9]

As suggested by the prior brief discussion on media, great emphasis is put on who has access to what information. Information is crucial to the manageability of a social-control matrix. Many countries are so sensitive about this that they prioritize the control, availability, and flow of information. This applies not only to overtly restrictive regimes such as China (the "Great Firewall"), but also to so-called democratic nations such as the United States, Australia, and European countries. Despite the rapid growth in underground and independent news sites (thanks mainly to the Internet), the majority of us are still living with a managed *information embargo*.

Control over the flow and content of information is essential to any technoculture that is moving toward increasing digitization and database-ization (later this chapter). Such societies are predicated on the flux of data flows that construct and manage social lives, privileges, and identities. To a large degree the manufacture of social control is about the management of information. That's why, in subtle and ingenious ways, modern technocultures have been constructed around the establishment of an implicit *information embargo*. In varying degrees people exist, both physically and psychically, within a form of social quarantine. Furthermore, the methods employed to reach these ends can be very quiet indeed.

SILENT WEAPONS FOR CONTROLLED ENVIRONMENTS

Modern technologized societies now have at their disposal incredible capacities for the instigation of social control and for the manipulation of social consciousness. We should ignore these capacities at our peril. Also, the mechanisms for control are now appearing in developing societies.

> Technology serves to institute new, more effective and more pleasant forms of social control and social cohesion. The totalitarian tendency of these controls seems to assert itself in still another sense—by spreading to the less developed and even to the preindustrial areas of the world.[10]

The critical role of technology for social control of the masses was laid out very clearly by the one-time U.S. National Security Advisor Zbigniew Brzezinski. In his book *Between Two Ages: America's Role in the Technetronic Era* (1970) Brzezinski discussed how the information society would have to provide an amusement focus such as "spectator spectacles" like mass sports and television in order to provide "an opiate for increasingly purposeless masses." He goes on to write that "new forms of social control may be needed to limit the indiscriminate exercise by the individual of their new powers."[11] Brzezinski, as a high-ranking expert on political affairs, was aware of the rise in the consciousness of the people and how this would affect the capacity of power structures to maintain the mask of democracy. Brzezinski wrote that a "global human conscience is for the first time beginning to manifest itself," but that "the new global consciousness, however, is only beginning to become an influential force. It still lacks identity, cohesion, and focus."[12] What was needed, to Brzezinski's thinking, was the deliberate move toward a Technetronic Era (a technoculture) that would facilitate more pervasive and subtle social control over the masses. In what seems an eerily prescient scenario Brzezinski stated that

> the capacity to assert social and political control over the individual will vastly increase. It will soon be possible to assert almost continuous control over every citizen and to maintain up-to-date files, containing even the most personal details about health and personal behavior of every citizen in addition to the more customary data. . . . These files will be subject to instantaneous retrieval by the authorities. Power will gravitate into the hands of those who control information. . . . This will encourage tendencies through the next several decades toward a Technetronic Era, a dictatorship leaving even less room for political procedures as we know them.[13]

Brzezinski's stated vision is close to the type of surveillance and database society that is currently in place in many developed nations.

However, the main aim is to construct a social environment that is not immediately and/or obviously threatening.

Although many dominant forms of social control are now technological in nature and design, their application is not always so. Integration into a comprehensive social matrix has overt and visible forms of force at its disposal, if it needs to use them. Yet the more efficient means are those that act pervasively to compel willing compliance. After all, when we ask for something to be given to us, are we really being forced to receive? Thus the construction of need plays an important role in social control. Another way to put this is that the ruling powers often create/invent and unleash a specific problem in a way to catalyze public reaction. Only then is the solution offered to the general public as a response to our needs. This equation of *problem-reaction-solution* was cleverly portrayed in the film *V for Vendetta* as well as by other acute thinkers.* Other social mechanisms and processes such as finance, consumerism, education, entertainment, and work, also are able to serve as consciousness-distracting sources.

One interesting critique of how the social matrix operates was released, controversially, under the title of *Silent Weapons for Quiet Wars*. There is much controversy surrounding the origins and credibility of this document; however, regardless of its authenticity it still has a point to make. And this point is that on the back of well-researched economic scholarship undertaken at Harvard University in the early 1950s,[14] the notion of economic social engineering became feasible. Shortly after it is alleged, in this document, that

in 1954 it was well recognized by those in positions of authority that it was only a matter of time, only a few decades, before the general public would be able to grasp and upset the cradle of power, for the very elements of the new silent-weapon technology were as accessible for a public utopia as they were for providing a private utopia.[15]

*The phrase *problem-reaction-solution* has been popularized by David Icke.

The notion of social engineering via social processes, aided by increased technological capacity, is said to be at the heart of Western power structures. In other words, tools for social control could be operative within a manipulated economy and social psychology. The report outlines how these processes were forms of "silent weapons" in that instead of firing bullets they fired data bits, and instead of coming from guns they came from computers—a sophisticated modeling of societal management and control. Because of this nature the use of such weaponry would go unnoticed by the majority.

> The public cannot comprehend this weapon, and therefore cannot believe that they are being attached and subdued by a weapon. The public might instinctively feel that something is wrong, but because of the technical nature of the silent weapon, they cannot express their feeling in a rational way, or handle the problem with intelligence. Therefore, they do not know how to cry for help, and do not know how to associate with others to defend themselves against it. ... When a silent weapon is applied gradually to the public, the public adjusts/adapts to its presence and learns to tolerate its encroachment on their lives.[16]

This form of manipulative "quiet warfare" would be based around control of national and global economies, resources, property, commodities, workforce/labor, security forces, law, media, education, tax, data surveillance, and health.

The primary strategy outlined in the report is the use of diversion, which requires keeping the general public ignorant of the real issues of importance by distracting them with trivial things. This is achieved by:

1. Disengaging their minds, sabotaging their mental activities, by providing a low quality program of public education in mathematics, logic, systems design, and economics, and by discouraging technical creativity.

2. Engaging their emotions, increasing their self-indulgence, and their indulgence in emotional and physical activities, by:

    a. unrelenting emotional affronts and attacks (mental and emotional rape) by way of a constant barrage of sex, violence, and wars in the media especially the T.V. and the newspapers.

    b. giving them what they desire in excess "junk food for thought" and depriving them of what they really need.

3. Rewriting history and law and subjecting the public to the deviant creation, thus being able to shift their thinking from personal needs to highly fabricated outside priorities.[17]

Diversion tactics thus make full use of such social institutions as media/entertainment, education, and work in order to supply a range of stimuli that keep peoples' minds focused on external distractions. This diverts real attention away not only from more important issues, such as economic trends and power structures, but also from internal communication with the self and from self-actualizing practices. Human consciousness has been dumbed down by being fed a constant barrage of trivia and nonprogressive or growth-oriented material. The human spirit has been conspicuously starved of real uplifting and self-evolving "nutrients." Because of this we have been collectively experiencing a lower vibration in psychic energy and visionary potential.

One of the major manipulations being played on the people is the management of a false and thoroughly artificial economy. Because we see money as being so fundamental to our lives we often fail to scrutinize how it actually operates. Money does not necessarily denote paper currencies, yet it should possess the following characteristics: it should be a store of value (like gold and silver has historically possessed); it needs to be accepted as a medium of exchange; and it needs to be a unit of account so it can be divisible into smaller/larger units of worth. However, our national and global system of monetary exchange is nothing other than a human creation. Communities first devised the means of exchange, which began as barter economies using animals, food, and so forth, and even today many barter communities exist that prefer to operate within a different value system of exchange (usually one that is more practically useful for the people involved). Yet today's system of monetary exchange is not only more standardized in terms of exchange value, but it is also little more than an accumulation of debt.

John Kenneth Galbraith, the famous Canadian American economist, famously said, "The process by which money is created is so simple that the mind is repelled." And in fact he was right: money creation is a fantastically simple illusion of wealth. The words say it all—*money is created*. It is an artificial construct of consensus value. That is, people worldwide accept the varying rates of currency exchange and, importantly, the value of goods tied to monetary exchange. The value of money may well be a shared illusion that we all buy into, yet it is a very necessary one if we are to engage in our everyday lives. And money creation goes something like this:

An individual goes into a bank with $1,000 and deposits the money in an account. The individual now has a $1,000-asset in storage and the bank has a $1,000 legal responsibility for custodianship. Now, the rules on bank accountability allow each bank to loan out a proportion of the money they have on deposit, which, in theory, is about 90 percent. Since most banks keep only a very small fraction of their actual deposits in reserve in their bank, this procedure is called "fractional reserve banking." Banks are now in a position to start making lucrative financial deals, since they make no money from holding on to people's money (unless charging for bank services or debt interest). These financial deals operate through activities such as merchant banking and investment banking. These sectors deal with high-level business and private equities, and with underwriting and securities. The other, more commonly known type of banking is commercial banking. In our example, a commercial bank can loan out 90 percent of the initial $1,000 deposited, and thus provide $900 for another borrower. This $900 is now in circulation and may get passed on to another person as payment, which then may be deposited back in the commercial bank. If a bank now has this $900 on deposit it can loan out 90 percent of it, an additional $810. If the bank then receives this $810 from another person, it can loan out 90 percent against this, which is $729. This process goes on and on until, for example, the initial $1,000 has now developed into $10,000. However, only $1,000 is actually held in reserve by the bank. The $10,000 it may hold in various accounts is money created out of the original lump sum. It is still very real in terms of purchasing power, yet it represents $9,000 of debt. All of the $9,000 was *loaned into existence* without ever being physically created. The money was "backed" by the initial holding, yet the new "wealth creation" does not exist as physical money. Thus if every person went to the bank to reclaim their part of the $10,000 (called a "bank run") the bank would not be able to pay because they would not actually have the money on account. The bank may then be forced to pay back as much as feasibly possible before entering bankruptcy. In effect, each person has her money as long as everybody doesn't ask for it at the same time, and as long as everybody doesn't start defaulting on their loans. On top of this there is the interest payment that has to be paid back with each loan. This again means that more money needs to be paid back than originally exists.

What this tells us is that money growth is a process of debt accumulation. First, bank credit is money *loaned into existence,* and thus is a debt upon which further debt (interest) must be paid. The second type of money creation comes from the central banks, which have the exclusive authority to lend money (that is, print money), which is then exchanged for government debt. The central bank for each nation has the sole monopoly on creating currency as legal tender. In other words, government spending and money in circulation is backed, yet again, by debt. Further, the majority of central banks in the developed world are "independent," which means they are privately owned and thus beyond political interference. Did I just say that right? Did I say that money creation (printing money), government debt, and private debt are all under the authority of private institutions? Yes, I did. As Mayer Amschel Rothschild (1743–1812), one of the world's most famous bankers, once said: "Give me control over a nation's currency, and I care not who makes its laws." Anyone wishing to know more details has only to investigate the history of the central banking system.

To continue, the creation of money is therefore a debt-creation process. All monies are backed by debt. At the everyday bank level all new money is *loaned into existence*. At the government and state level, all money is simply printed out of thin air and then exchanged for government debt. Both types of debts are also accompanied by interest payments on the debt. We can thus say that money is backed by debt and this debt must pay interest. So here comes another question: If interest is accumulated on top of the debts, then where is the money to cover these extra interest payments? Answer: it doesn't exist *unless extra money is loaned into existence to cover the interest payments on outstanding debt.** And every year the amount of debt, because of interest growth, is expanding by *x* percentage. As each debt expands on previous percentage growth it becomes an exponential system. What this means is that the amount of debt circulating will always be more than the amount of available money. It also implies that the global banking system not only is *perpetually expanding* but also must do so in accordance with its own institutional processes.

What has also added to this expanding currency bubble is the fact that liquid currencies are no longer backed by the gold standard. Where once bank notes could be converted at the banks for gold coins (a procedure often suspended during times of war), this

---

*I am grateful to Chris Martenson's "Crash Course" for providing the background. See chrismartenson.com.

gave paper money a well-trusted unit of value. Global currencies—
especially the reserve currency of the U.S. dollar—were backed by
the unit value of gold. However, the end of the gold standard was
heralded in 1971 when the dollar was stripped of its gold backing,
allowing it to peg its own value. This also meant that money could
be printed at greater rates, since it was not tied to any fixed gold
price. The amount of *created money* now in circulation is astounding.
Trillions of dollars/sterling pounds/Euros are effectively in existence
today, supplying debt relief and credit. Only they are not in existence.
It is nothing more than *an illusion of artificial debt*. Yet the illusion is
very real and very painful.

It has become painful because the social matrix has now successfully tied almost all individuals into this false cage where they are
not so much physically enclosed but have become instead entangled
within a digital prison of credit and debt. Credit makes humans
work for the bank, while debt often can never be repaid. In other
words, money and credit are themselves forms of debt masquerading as false wealth. Credit is a socially constructed form of slavery,
an assault on the human spirit, while the world is built on a debt
that can never be repaid. Credit cards too are extensions of this
symbolic debt environment and form part of the armory of *silent
weapons* that wage a *quiet war* against the conscious being of each
individual. Also, these global institutions—international banks and
multinational corporations—now exist beyond (and often above)
nation-states as the global stage is being reorganized for a new level
of management and control.

In a social-*technique* matrix processes of digitization serve to enmesh
the individual within control systems that perpetuate his own dependence. Just as modern societies are shifting from paper money to digital money, personal worth is being valued by binary digits on a screen.
New technologies are dictating how finance flows, and thus how we
increasingly organize and structure our lives. Personal independence is

being undermined by stripping people of their physical assets, as was evident during the 2008 financial crash and the ongoing instability of liquid-currency markets. And the power of human consciousness is being undermined by the constant production of fear and chaotic scenarios (see chapter 5). Yet as the later chapters of this book will show, the evolution of human consciousness is entering a period of heightened stimulation and expansion. This is also perhaps why the control mechanisms of the social matrix are intensifying through the advancing capacities of digital technologies and databasing.

DIGITAL NETWORKS OF CONTROL

It is no exaggeration to suggest that societies within the Modernity Project are shifting toward a type of *digital Orwellianism*. In mirroring the scenario described by George Orwell in *1984* the more powerful social matrixes are developing ever more draconian measures of civilian surveillance. These measures will then be further consolidated within these societies in an effort to control and contain the increased social unrest that is likely to erupt in ensuing years. The social *technique* now in play will have an increased dependency on "databasing" the individual, with most lifestyle choices (travel, purchases, insurance, health, and so forth) being digitally tracked and traced. This scenario relies on the various technologies of closed-circuit TV (CCTV) cameras, data-mining software, biometric security, integrated digital databases, and Radio Frequency Identity (RFID) implants to track objects and people. It is also possible that micro-chipping will later be introduced into populations to further track and monitor behavior and movement. This would seriously limit the freedom to walk, drive, or even move without being recorded. These infrastructures within the social matrix will be designed to create increased dependency and to further strengthen already existing power structures and control institutions. Examples include exploiting private information, such as the rise of private-credit database companies such as Experian and

ChoicePoint. Already computer software is being utilized to cross-reference information databases automatically to discern queuing and congestion times for premium and nonpremium customers. Callers are thus categorized and left waiting according to their postal codes and assumed incomes. In this context physical location influences the priority status of the caller and his access to services.

Such digital networks are likely to be expanded to cover the smooth running of most technocultures. This could mean that the near future of social life will involve the increased use of the "digital identity" of each individual. For example, India, with its billon-plus population, is now planning to set up a new unique identification of individuals (UID) digital database that will contain all ten fingerprints, an iris scan, and a photograph of the person. The government claims that this establishment of citizenry biometric information is used to help identify beneficiaries of welfare schemes, children between ages five and fifteen for educational purposes, and the country's large rural population. This ambitious digital-databasing project was first rolled out in late 2010 and aims to shift a largely cash-strapped populace into digital-banking access (the credit/debit trap). Although these measures are characteristic of authoritarian control it will seem to most people living within these environments that this is the natural progression of social technologies that serve to bind efficiency and reliability. Of course, there will always be those privileged few who will receive priority treatment. Those not privileged, meaning the majority, will be required to undergo rigorous data checks before and during most activities (such as travel) or before being granted access to essential services (health, insurance, and so on).

Yet in some ways we are already close to such a scenario; we are already living in a highly monitored and surveyed world. Under the banner of a post–September 11 world, many intrusive technologies are being (and will continue to be) rapidly introduced. The UK government's Information Commissioner has stated that people in Britain already live in a surveillance society.[18] Britain has about five million CCTV cameras, one for every twelve people—more cameras than any other country. A 2007 report by the Royal Academy of Engineering (UK) said that travel passes, supermarket loyalty cards, and mobile phones could be used to track each person's every move. On March 15, 2006, the European Union passed Directive 2006/24/EC, which made it mandatory for all European Internet service providers (ISPs) to hold details on the data traffic of all their customers for at least two years. This includes every website visited, every e-mail sent, and every transaction conducted online for every EU citizen with access to the Internet.

Dataveillance is behind the surge in megadatabases emerging both in nations, economic blocs, and international networks. For example, the UK has plans for a decentralized National Identity Register (NIR) that will be spread across the national insurance, asylum, and passport databases. Europe has the TECS (The Europol Computer System), and the Visa Information System (VIS), as well as the new Schengen travel database, the SIS II, which shares personal data with a range of other organizations. Similarly the U.S. has been working hard to network its state data systems so interstate sharing can be achieved (see their earlier attempt: MATRIX: Multistate Anti-Terrorism Information Exchange). For our part we have been increasingly acclimatized to the need for technological infrastructures. Computers and data technology have been designed to be user friendly in order to pacify people to their presence and use; a type of function-creep toward a ubiquitous environment of pervasive data flows.

These practices of social management and institutional control are the result of activities structured around the "organizing principle" of modern societies. Also, modern state bureaucracies, with their emphasis on increased rationalization and efficiency, are institutions that push citizenry ever further toward being placed in databases and social cataloging. The phase underway now is for the increased militarization of the civil sphere, collapsing the once fixed notions of friend/ enemy and civil/military. Within the all-embracing social matrix the civil sphere is fast becoming the operations field of the military in which every citizen is deemed a potential terrorist. This construction of a technological cage is part of the Modernity Project's drive toward an acceptable form of social quarantine. It is a "scientifically rational" move toward social ordering in which the system is able to cope with and manage the expanding human population and range of human activities. This may or may not be the "inevitable" drive of advancing technologies. This is not a discussion on technological determinism. Instead what it does show is that power structures— such as advanced state militaries—seek to exploit these *control and containment* possibilities.

As manifestations of this "containment drive" the U.S. military-industrial machine is attempting to construct a system of total information awareness to cover, track, and gaze omnisciently over all physical movement and transactions. This is a deliberate move toward erecting a *total system:* an attempt to gain a devastating degree of control over physical and informational "freedoms." As part of this project the U.S. military commissioned a report called the Information Operations Roadmap.* According to this document the term *information operations* includes employing electronic warfare, psychological operations, and military deception in order to "influence, disrupt, corrupt or usurp adversarial human and automated decisions-making." The document continues by outlining how the U.S. military needs to secure a future electromagnetic capability "sufficient to provide maximum control of the entire electromagnetic spectrum, denying, degrading, disrupting, or destroying the full spectrum of globally emerging communication systems, sensors, and weapons systems dependent on the electromagnetic spectrum."[19]

---

*This document was declassified by the Pentagon and made public by the National Security Archive on January 26, 2006.

Clearly the goal here is to develop the capacity for full and complete dominance over all globally emerging telecommunications and thus their users. This is all part of the U.S. military's objective to secure a dominant Global Information Grid (GIG). And the U.S. military is not alone in these developments, as other state powers, such as China and India, are securing similar capabilities. The global world is no longer a terrestrial environment; it is now a virtual and non-terrestrial (space) arena. For example, the new generation of surveillance satellites launched since 2005 will allow those who operate them to gain precise information not only of alleged enemies but also of the movements of almost any individual on the planet, at almost any time, anywhere. This is a dangerous project toward the containment of our physical—and virtual—human global system. And it doesn't stop there. The aim is also to gain dominance over natural Earth processes.

The Interagency Working Group on Earth Observations* has recently published their Strategic Plan for the U.S. Integrated Earth Observation System, which discusses a vast range of geological integrated monitoring systems. Their vision is to discover, access, collect, manage, archive, process, and model earth geological data in order to better forecast flows such as weather, energy resources, natural resources, pre- and post-disasters, as well as a host of other integrated processes.[20] This indicates a disturbing shift in utilizing emerging technologies as an authoritarian strategy for Earth monitoring. This pattern is likely to accelerate once governing power structures begin to fully exploit "Earth changes" as a human security issue as well as a resource necessity. Such technocultures are moving toward developing monitored environments in which information is processed and geographical data secured. Increasingly relationships between humans, technology, and the environment are being merged with or steered toward a new construction of social life that embeds the individual,

---

*This group is backed by the National Science & Technology Council within the Executive Office of the U.S. President.

as a digitally rendered identity, within a global informational digital-social matrix. This outlines how the management of social control is being established—a *form of quarantine* both physical and mental. Most importantly, however, is that such a matrix actively seeks to stifle the expansion and manifestation of human consciousness and to marginalize those individuals who seek (without permission) to operate beyond its strictures. As the later chapters of this book will explore, however, this containment of consciousness is a failed project. The Modernity Project will be unable to contain and control the energetic increases that are gradually occurring on this planet.

I contend that we, as a global civilization, are moving through a crucial transition period. And within this period we are also likely to experience an instability phase as potential futures are played out between the rise of global human consciousness and those social power structures and hierarchies that seek to keep humanity "socially managed." We are already in the midst of a momentous shift, perhaps the most important transformational shift our current civilization has ever witnessed. This may turn out to be a struggle on the one hand between those who wish for humanity to move into a digitally contained and controlled global environment, and on the other the natural and inevitable evolution of human consciousness that will break into unprecedented areas of perception.

The transitional phase, however, will open the way for the manifestation of conflicting possibilities. Already the human mind is being messed with, and the Earth's natural electromagnetic environment is being polluted to an extreme degree (chapter 4). Some of this "mental molesting" comes from the natural growth of our global communication technologies. Yet there are also indications that suggest that the human mind is being bombarded with "interference" and "polluting static" by deliberate means. After all, this book has suggested that societal forces do indeed target the human mind in an effort to distract, influence, manipulate, and exploit its use.

Further, much material has come to light that indicates that specific regimes are experimenting with land and space-based technologies that have the potential to beam electromagnetic pulses and vibrations upon virtually any chosen spot on the Earth. The potential here for mass mind-control strategies is severely unnerving, as will be discussed in the next chapter.

4

UNDUE INFLUENCE
Playing Games with the Mind

I once put it rather pungently, and I was flattered that the British Foreign Secretary repeated this, as follows: . . . namely, in early times, it was easier to control a million people, literally it was easier to control a million people than physically to kill a million people. Today, it is infinitely easier to kill a million people than to control a million people. It is easier to kill than to control. . . .

ZBIGNIEW BRZEZINSKI,
NOVEMBER 17, 2008, CHATHAM HOUSE SPEECH

Control is the principle concern of those forces that are tightening the social matrix. The minority have always felt obligated not only to control the majority but also to keep them well away from realizing significant truths. This strategy to *keep people from themselves* may be behind all the social behavioral institutions and modern forms of entertainment and consumerist distractions. We are literally being kept away from our own minds for fear that people may begin not only to listen to themselves but also to begin "working on themselves"—something that American psychologist Abraham Maslow called *self-actualization*. This possibility for increasing numbers of people to self-actualize is becoming more likely as more and more people are becoming politically and culturally aware. The citation at the beginning of this chapter (from ex-U.S. National Security Advisor Zbigniew Brzezinski) recalls a time when the masses neither knew nor cared about politics and could be controlled simply by force of arms and economic coercion. Under those conditions, controlling people was easier, he says. Now, however, the technical capacities for large-scale destruction are an easier choice than covert strategies. Yet there still exists a fine line between the perception of freedom and the management of social control. The covert way still seems to be the preferred option in these modern times, as long as most people do not suspect any undue influence in their lives.

As discussed in earlier chapters, mechanisms of social conditioning exist from birth in the forms of social institutions (family, school, religion, media) as well as social norms that restrict certain fringe beliefs and thoughts. These conditioning programs are shameful in that they seek to not only discredit expression of the human spirit but also to deny the existence of nonmaterial realities. In the words of biologist Ludwig von Bartalanffy:

> Man as a machine that can be programmed; all those machines identical to automobiles coming off the assembly line . . . reducing man to the lower levels of his animal nature, manipulating him into becoming a feeble-minded and consumeristic automaton, or a marionette of political power, systematically dulling his brain through a perverse system of education; in short, dehumanizing him ever further by means of a sophisticated psychological technology. The effects of this manipulation we see everywhere . . . when mass persuasion became scientific, using psychological mechanisms and techniques. Then its power, because it was not imposed from outside but was internalized, became unlimited and nearly impregnable; aided by mass media whose barrage has no limits in space and is nearly continuous in time.[1]

Human behavior has long been understood to be largely shaped by outside influences, from early childhood experiences to secondary reinforcements. In more recent times social conditioning has been taken out of the hands of "natural forces" and, in more technologically developed societies, become a scientific procedure. The end goal is to produce happy citizens content to play their role within the industrial-military-political establishment—the social matrix.

The end result is also that the human mind has become distracted through modern static, dissonance, and disharmony. The need to turn inward, to dwell on our inner thoughts and intuitions, has been replaced by an artificial pull to turn outward. Yet the human being has always had a need to turn to the inner spirit, to connect homeward toward a source of the self. This has been evident in spiritual manifestations throughout history, from buildings and structures (temples, sacred sites and stones, statues) to rituals (meditation, prayer, fasting, pilgrimage) to people (healers, prophets, seers, shamans, and so forth). Humankind has a built-in spiritual impulse that can either be diverted into other expressions such as art or pleasure, or suppressed (as is the case in many overt materialistic societies). Yet there is a further extreme of suppression that comes in the form of harassment (undue influence). Such harassment can take the form of indirect electromagnetic interferences as well as direct electronic interference (such as in various forms of electropollution). This chapter will address some of these concerns; namely, how specific technologies are being employed in the human environment in order to interfere with the human mind and consciousness.

According to the research of Robert O. Becker (now a retired professor of medicine), "The human species has changed its electromagnetic background more than any other aspect of its environment . . . the density of radio waves around us now is 100 million or 200 million times the natural level reaching us from the sun."[2] Becker has no doubt that the greatest polluting element in the Earth's environment during our present era is the rapid growth in electromagnetic fields. Environmental factors are changing at a pace that may be too fast for us. Industrializing nations have an immense need for and use of energy that has radically changed the total electromagnetic field of the Earth. Most of us are unaware of this change in our environment because we are unable to directly perceive it with our senses. Whereas before the twentieth century the Earth's electromagnetic field was composed of natural fields, today we are drowning in a sea of man-made electrical currents and discharges. Biological organisms on Earth have evolved over geological time within the electromagnetic (EM) fields that were inherent in the basic magnetic field of the Earth, as influenced by the sun. Now all this has suddenly changed. The Earth's magnetic field is said to be roughly 500 milligauss, and remains fairly steady, only oscillating slightly depending on the time of the day and solar influence. Our global communication frequencies, while in a lower range, are oscillating at greater rates. Dr. Becker's research, along with others', shows that our human bodies and immune systems are being negatively affected by man-made electromagnetic fields: such as from power lines, satellites, and mobile phones. And those of us who live in the richer nations are especially swamped by a world of electrical appliances. The rapid rise in mobile-phone usage worldwide has contributed significantly to our exposure to EM energy above and beyond our normal limits. Some mobile phones operate in the megahertz range, others in the gigahertz range, which is billions of cycles per second. This means that the EM radiation is oscillating at extremely rapid frequencies. And the higher the frequencies, the higher the energy radiation.[3] It is almost impossible these days to go anywhere where there is no EM pollution from human activities and technologies.

There have been numerous studies (not all of them published because of commercial pressure) that indicate that there are definitive effects of low-strength oscillating electromagnetic fields on human brain function.[4] The other question here is whether such EM increases have had or will have a negative effect on the human nervous system. The Independent Expert Group on Mobile Phones (IEGMP)* concluded that there was enough scientific evidence to suggest that there may be biological effects from exposure to mobile-phone radiation below existing governmental standards. The group thus recommended "that a precautionary approach to the use of mobile phone technologies be adopted until much more detailed and scientifically robust information on any health effects becomes available."[5] The chairman, Sir William Stewart, also publically announced that children under eight should not use mobile phones at all. Other findings include the work of the National Research Council in Bologna, Italy, which reported that radio waves from mobile phones could promote the growth of cancer cells. Further, Tsuyoshi Hondou, a physicist from Tohoku University in Sendai, Japan, currently working at the Curie Institute in Paris, calculated that in a typical Japanese railway carriage "with mobile phone users surfing the net, the radio waves rebounding from the metal wall of the carriage would give an electromagnetic field that could exceed the maximum exposure level recommended by the International Committee for Non-Ionising Radiation (ICNIRP), even when the train is not crowded."[6] These are but a few examples from the numerous studies that show a link between mobile-phone radiation and public health. The fact that few of these ever find media exposure is not surprising; the media telecommunications industry (which includes mobile phones) is a global billion-dollar industry. In 2010 the world's richest man (on the annual Forbes "rich list") was Carlos Slim, who made his fortune mostly from controlling the mobile telecommunications industry in Latin America.

Now that mobile phones are a way of life for billions of people it is hard to imagine a modern "connected" life without them.† The

---

*Chairman Sir William Stewart, FRS, FRSE. The Expert Group was set up in 1999 and reported in May 2000.
†According to Market Intelligence Center, an information and communications technology-industry research institute, global mobile phone subscribers are expected to reach 4.5 billion by 2012.

problem with research on the dangers of mobile phone use is that at least ten years are required in order to build up a reliable data set. And so the debate is likely to rage on. However, the question still remains: What are the ongoing effects of the thousands of mobile antennas/masts and base stations (and related communication masts) on our physical and spiritual well-being? It is not my aim here to delve into the extensive research available on this topic, as it would require a whole book in itself.[7] It is reasonable, however, to suggest that the bioelectric energy bodies of human beings are being unduly influenced by the increasingly high amounts of electromagnetic exposure in the environment.

There is little doubt that social behavior, in the Western nations at least, has become increasingly erratic, with a rise in a variety of modern diseases such as attention deficit disorder (ADD). Yet the fact that the human being is susceptible (and possibly vulnerable) to the influence of varying EM frequencies, both natural and man-made, is not a new discovery. That such technologies of influence exist is verified by what Zbigniew Brzezinski (again!) wrote more than twenty-five years ago:

> Political strategists are tempted to exploit research on the brain and human behavior. Geophysicist Gordon J. F. MacDonald, a specialist in problems of warfare, says accurately-timed, artificially-excited electronic strokes could lead to a pattern of oscillations that produce relatively high power levels over certain regions of the earth. . . . In this way one could develop a system that would seriously impair the brain performance of very large populations in selected regions over an extended period.[8]

The use of directed frequencies for the impairment of brain function is a worrying prospect. And the fact that military/political analysts were discussing these possibilities at least a quarter of a century ago makes them all the more real. Actually, if people are willing to delve into military reports they will find that the use of frequencies for military purposes has been talked of openly. There is a well-established scientific and military awareness of the susceptibility of the human body to harmonic interference. This leads one to ask: Are modern technocultures moving toward a type of psychocivilized society?

A PSYCHOCIVILIZED SOCIETY?

Technologies are now being researched that seek to penetrate and, to a degree, intervene in the brain's neural functioning. While some have termed this positively as a future "neural society,"[9] I consider whether this is not shifting dangerously toward the type of social governance where greater emphasis is placed on social control and covert influence. The background to the research of these technologies may have its origin during the Cold War between the then USSR and the U.S. The United States' Project Pandora* was set up to specifically research programs on the health effects of microwave exposure following the Moscow Embassy incident. From 1953 to 1976 the Soviets directed microwave radiation at the U.S. embassy in Moscow from the roof of an adjacent building. While this clandestine microwave targeting was allegedly known for some time by U.S. officials, the event was not made public until 1976 when the U.S. State Department finally accused the Soviet Union of bombarding the U.S. embassy with microwave radiation for illicit purposes. It was initially reported as a harmless procedure for charging Soviet spy bugs and jamming embassy-based U.S. electronic monitoring of Russian communications.[10] However, the U.S. State Department soon indicated that, in addition to interference, the microwave radiation could have serious adverse effects on the health of the occupants of the embassy. Soviet studies in the area of electromagnetic microwave radiation reported psychological

---

*This project was organized and administered by the psychology division of the psychiatry research section of Walter Reed Army Institute of Research (WRAIR).

symptoms in human subjects that included lethargy, lack of concentration, headaches, depression, and impotence.[11] *Time* magazine reported in March 1976 that the U.S. State Department launched a medical investigation of the thousands of U.S. diplomats and their families who served in Moscow since the early 1960s. In the wake of the microwave disclosures former embassy employees and their families have recalled suffering strange ailments during their tenure in Moscow, ranging from eye tics and headaches to heavy menstrual flows. Some point out that former ambassadors to Moscow Charles Bohlen and Llewellyn Thompson both died of cancer, and five women who lived there have undergone cancer-related mastectomies— although no medical authorities attribute these deaths and illnesses to radiation.[12]

U.S. officials and military personnel, long before the public exposure, were aware and concerned about the consequences of microwave bombardment of civilian and military targets. In 1972 the U.S. Defense Intelligence Agency (DIA) released an internal report that had been previously prepared by the U.S. Army Office of the Surgeon General Medical Intelligence Office titled "Controlled Offensive Behavior—USSR" (1972).* The report's authors believed the Soviet research to be in the area of "reorientation," suggesting that the U.S. was worried over concerns that the Soviets may be planning a mass zapping of U.S. citizens with the hope of brainwashing them into a new ideological outlook. The 174-page report is extensive, with much material about various forms of beamed energies and remote strategies. On the opening section on electromagnetic energy the report concludes:

> Super-high frequency electromagnetic oscillations (SHF) may have potential use as a technique for altering human behavior. Soviet

---

*The report was later declassified through the Freedom of Information Act (FOIA). See www.dia.mil/public-affairs/foia/pdf/cont_ussr.pdf for a list of declassified reports.

Union and other foreign literature sources contain over 500 studies devoted to the biological effect of SHF. Lethal and non-lethal
aspects have been shown to exist. In certain non-lethal exposures,
definite behavioral changes have occurred.[13]

During this time the U.S. establishment was not naive to the potential
of conducting at-a-distance experiments upon the neurological functioning of human behavior.

In the 1970s José Manuel Rodriguez Delgado was a controversial
figure in neuroscience. A professor of physiology at Yale University,
he was an acclaimed neuroscientist. In 1970 the *New York Times
Magazine* hailed him as the prophet of a new psychocivilized society whose members would alter their own brain functioning. For
decades Delgado had been experimenting with the implantation of
electrodes into animal brains. For example, Delgado's most famous
experiment took place in 1963 at a bull-breeding ranch in Córdoba,
Spain. Delgado implanted radio-equipped electrodes, which he
termed "stimoceivers," into the brains of several fighting bulls and
stood in a bullring, attempting to control the actions of one bull at a
time by pressing buttons on a handheld transmitter. In one instance
Delgado was able to stop a charging bull in its tracks only a few feet
away. The *New York Times* published a front-page story on the event,
calling it "the most spectacular demonstration ever performed of the
deliberate modification of animal behavior through external control
of the brain."[14] In 1969 Delgado described remote brain-behavior
modification and its implications in his book *Physical Control of
the Mind: Toward a Psychocivilized Society.*[15] Delgado's research during this time was supported not only by academic grants but also by
the U.S. military's Office of Naval Research. This research is now
nearly half a century old, and much has happened in the interven-
ing decades. Technologies that can remotely transmit information
to the human mind have been in covert development since the Cold

War years, and in several high-ranking establishments. The capacity to target human minds within the electromagnetic spectrum has immense potential for remotely influencing masses of people, if not whole nations.

Igor Smirnov* of the Russian Academy of Sciences, has been conducting research into behavior modification via remote transmissions. Smirnov's laboratory in Moscow (the Institute of Psycho-Correction) uses electroencephalograph scanning (EEG) to measure brainwaves, which are then computed to create a map of various relations between human impulses and their correlating brain waves. This data can then be used for experimenting on brain-body modification at a distance. Asked in a 2004 interview whether it was possible to defeat terrorism Smirnov replied:

> Only informational war is capable of defeating terrorism completely. And we possess this weapon. Peoples' actions can in fact be controlled by unnoticed acoustic influence. Look—it's easy. All I have to do is record my voice, apply special coding, which converts my voice to mere noise, and afterwards, all we have to do is record some music on top of that. The words are indistinguishable to your conscious; however, your unconscious can hear them clearly. If we were to play this music over and over again on the radio for instance, people will soon start developing paranoia. This is the simplest weapon.[16]

Smirnov's capabilities were apparently demonstrated to U.S. observers as far back as 1991 when infrasound—a very low-frequency transmission—was shown to be able to transmit acoustic messages via bone conduction.[17] Military researcher Timothy Thomas has publicly stated that "examples of unplanned attacks on the body's data-processing capability are well-documented."[18] Thomas also states that Russian military intelligence has declared that "humanity stands on the brink of a 'psychotronic war' with the mind and body as the focus." Similarly,

---

*Smirnov was referred to by a *Newsweek* article as a "subliminal Dr. Strangelove."

the Air Force Research Laboratory (AFRL) brief on this subject, titled "Controlled Effects," also noted the power to use the electromagnetic spectrum for remotely interfering with human subjects' thinking and behavior.[19] Other military reports that have surfaced on the operational use of electromagnetic energy sources to interfere with conscious thinking include the U.S. Air Force Scientific Advisory Board's 1996 report titled "New World Vistas." This Report discussed the potential to "control emotions (and thus actions), produce sleep, transmit suggestions, and interfere with both short-term and long-term memory."[20]

Research in this area of covert intervention and mental manipulation has sought to exploit environmental impacts—electromagnetic, acoustic, or similar energy waves—as a means of influencing and even managing human behavior.

> In this new systemic approach the human communicates with, and can communicate with, the environment through information flows and communications media. By this understanding military thinking has begun to openly declare that "one's physical environment, whether through electromagnetic, gravitational, acoustic, or other effects, can cause a change in the psycho-physiological condition of an organism."[21]

This ties in with what was said earlier about covert governmental funding of academic communications research. Subsequent investigations into the sociological discipline of communications research, which crystallized in the U.S. in the early 1950s, shows that it was financed and mentored by governmental psychological-warfare programs. This covert funding indirectly shaped mass communication research, and thus developments in communication would be specifically funded and encouraged.[22] Documented and declassified evidence shows that what may have begun as a program in standardized propaganda and psychological warfare has now developed into research on remote targeting and psychocivilized control practices. In such cases there is concern that the human mind has no "firewall" and may be vulnerable to unwanted or rogue interventions. In this sense the human body, its mind and consciousness, may increasingly be a victim of unwarranted psychological interference because we have neglected to protect ourselves. How could we? We didn't know! The control strategy of interfering with human consciousness with the intent of remote influencing is a deep secret. The knowledge of such practices has always been withheld from public information and consumption. Of course, who would believe it anyway?

These findings indicate that a shift is occurring (or has already occurred) in how the human mind is now a valid target over and beyond strategies of propaganda and persuasion. Because of the rapid rise in the expression of human consciousness over the twentieth century it is now considered imperative—by controlling forces—to utilize more potent means to distract and confuse the human mind. That this is evident can be seen by the shift toward developing social, leisure, and commercial applications that specifically operate through exposing the human body-mind to remote sensors. For example, in recent years there has been a considerable rise in commercial gaming applications. While some of these have actually helped to keep a user's brain active with complex online solving skills it now seems the latest frontier is the arrival of "sensory gaming." Technologies have been developed that use a form of EEG scanning to interpret electrical signals emitted by the brain and to convert them into actions on a computer. In this way the user/gamer is able to direct actions in the online environment via their thoughts. One such commercial company with a working product is Emotiv. In one of their press releases they stated that they had created "the first brain computer interface technology that can detect and process both human conscious thoughts and nonconscious emotions."[23] The technology, apparently, is able to detect and mimic a user's expressions and respond to his emotions. Similar gaming companies now have on the market products that use "brainwave pickup" technologies.

On the extreme side of this, wireless acoustic transmissions have been developed to "stop" people from over-gaming—in other words, as a treatment for gaming addiction. In some high technocultures, such as South Korea and Japan, teenagers are spending an unhealthy amount of time at their computers in gaming environments. There have even been instances where gamers have died after extensive sessions in front of a computer without a break, such as in MMORPGs (Massive Multiplayer Online Role-Playing Games). For example, in 2005 a young South Korean man collapsed in an Internet café in the city of Taegu after playing the game StarCraft almost continuously for fifty hours. He went into cardiac arrest and later died in hospital. In response to this, South Korean company Xtive, established in 2005, spent a year researching a system of acoustic sound waves that act as subliminal transmissions during the gaming experience.

> We incorporated messages into an acoustic sound wave telling gamers to stop playing. The messages are told 10,000 to 20,000 times per second. . . . Game users can't recognize the sounds. But their subconscious is aware of them and the chances are high they will quit playing.
>
> . . . Game companies can install a system, which delivers the inaudible sounds after it recognizes a young user has kept playing after a preset period of time.[24]

These developments in using remote waves and acoustic sounds to target a person's bioneural brain functioning are only the tip of the iceberg. Further advancements in these technologies are likely to be introduced into the commercial-social sphere. Also, if these applications are commercially available, then it leaves us wondering what capacities have been developed in military/covert areas of operation. The corporate attraction here is understandable—the human brain is a large market. Gaming giant Sony Corporation has been granted a patent on a device for transmitting sensory data directly into the human brain. Sony's patent describes the device as firing "pulses of ultrasound at the head to modify firing patterns in targeted parts of the brain, creating 'sensory experiences' ranging from moving images to tastes and sounds."[25] This is based on a technique known as transcranial magnetic stimulation, which activates the nerves by using rapidly changing magnetic fields to induce currents in brain tissue.

Similarly in 2004 Microsoft was awarded U.S. Patent 6,754,472, titled "Method and apparatus for transmitting power and data using the human body."* In this patent Microsoft is granted exclusive rights to a technology that envisages using human skin's conductive properties to link a host of electronic devices around the body, from mobile phones to microphones. Other examples of how the human body and brain are being deliberately targeted for the new wave of "information flows" within the social matrix include patents 4,395,600 and 5,507,291. Patent No 4,395,600 is titled "Auditory subliminal message system and method" and is geared toward subliminal messaging to influence consumer shoppers.

> Ambient audio signals from the customer shopping area within a store are sensed and fed to a signal processing circuit that produces a control signal which varies with variations in the amplitude of the sensed audio signals. A control circuit adjusts the amplitude of an auditory subliminal anti-shoplifting message to increase with increasing amplitudes of sensed audio signals and decrease with decreasing amplitudes of sensed audio signals. This amplitude-controlled subliminal message may be mixed with background music and transmitted to the shopping area.†

In a similar manner, patent No 5,507,291 is called "Method and an

---

*See Google Patents 6,754,472.
†See Google Patents 4,395,600.

associated apparatus for remotely determining information as to person's emotional state." This application comes very close to what has been discussed on military uses of information warfare.

> In a method for remotely determining information relating to a person's emotional state, a waveform energy having a predetermined frequency and a predetermined intensity is generated and wirelessly transmitted towards a remotely located subject. Waveform energy emitted from the subject is detected and automatically analyzed to derive information relating to the individual's emotional state.*

Whether or not these actual patents have—or will—ever make it into production and use we may never completely know. The fact that these patents exist and that people have worked on these applications points to some of the incredible interest in appropriating technologies for influencing human functioning, and that the majority of these technologies seek to unduly influence people remotely— that is, at a distance. Thus, these developments in recent innovative technologies offer serious implications for social privacy and mental liberty.

Almost everyone who went to see the popular feature film *Minority Report* will remember the notion of precognition; namely, the ability to know a person's actions before those actions are committed. This sci-fi scenario is worryingly close to the truth. A team of neuroscientists has developed a technique that can scan a brain and learn from the patterns of neuronal activity what a person is thinking or intending to do. This research is the culmination of recent studies where brain imaging has been used to identify particular brain patterns pertaining to behaviour such as violence, lying, and racial prejudice.[26] This is the first acknowledged instance of judging whether people

---

*See Google Patents 5,507,291.

have the intention to commit a criminal act regardless of actual hard physical evidence of the crime. The danger is that this type of *mental processing* might become compulsory within strict control societies. And since this technology is very new there are no current ethical or moral debates on this issue, and the implications for its civil use are disturbing. If developed this type of *technique* may be used for future forms of social management, from criminal interrogations to airline security checks, and exploited by social authorities, marketers, and employers.

A hypothetical situation in the future might place these scanning devices within regular x-ray machines at airports. On passing through to the passenger lounge all travelers will be scanned not only for potentially dangerous physical objects but also for *dangerous intentions*. Yet who has not had a dangerous intention? In this manner all travelers will have to safeguard their thoughts at all times; who knows whether such scanning devices are embedded in the walls of the airport lounges and/or the walkways, or in the toilets on board the airplane? This uncertain and somewhat dystopian scenario is one that could shift highly technologized states (technocultures) into psychocivilized societies. The ultimate social matrix of control and technique may well be one where thoughts and intentions become part of regular monitoring and state management. As the previous chapter discussed, the manufacture of social control that is creeping in through a rational "logic" of technology will likely represent a form of quarantine not just physically but also mentally.

The aspects discussed here and in previous chapters represent the encroachment of physical control infrastructures and strategies on the human individual. They represent a developing trend but not an inevitable future. My intention is to describe and make known these processes not because I feel they will be our certain global future, but the very opposite. These are the physical barriers that aim to pull back humanity from its rightful conscious evolution, and in this context they will be overcome. They will be surpassed through a combination of increasing individual awareness of the nature of social matrixes and the influx of energies seeding the Earth (to be discussed in later chapters). In order to move forward it is necessary, I feel, to gain an understanding of our present predicament. The potential of the human mind and consciousness is staggering. So immense that the few elite players in control of global processes are in a rush to bring in strategies of containment while they feel they still have a chance. The future will be a *future of consciousness:* of vision, understanding, and foresight. In the meantime, however, we have to deal with distracting forces, which are highlighted in these opening chapters. Further, in a global world of evolving technologies it is inevitable that these constraining forces will be introduced through the seemingly innocuous social uses of technology.

Already our "natural" environments are saturated with informational flows in various spectrum bandwidths—we are constantly walking through TV programs, mobile-phone conversations, and even military broadcasts. Yet we are not decoding these transmissions. However, the human body and mind act as a biological antenna, which makes the human nervous system vulnerable to exploitation. Some may see this as a great opportunity for creating an "efficient" future, such as foreseen in the following scenario.

> Inside the hatband is Sharon's communication center and intelligent assistant, which has scanned and sorted the 500,000 e-mails she received overnight. By the time she reaches the car, it has beamed the 10 most urgent ones and her travel schedule to her visual cortex. The text scrolls down in the bottom of her field of vision. . . . At the airport there is no ticket check-in or security line. Sharon simply walks through the revolving door, which scans her for dangerous items, picks up her identity, confirms her reservation, and delivers her gate number, all in the space of a second.[27]

Developing trends in technology predict a future that is wholly immersed in an informational digitized environment. It is also likely that the major technology for the future will be neurotechnology, as there is currently much research under way in this field, with large government/military/industrial funding. Although neurotechnologies are likely to be put to therapeutic and medical uses, such as for improving emotional stability and mental clarity, they also invite obvious opportunities for intrusive strategies of control and manipulation.

Much of what has so far been discussed in this chapter may seem fanciful or like science fiction. However, these technologies are very real and, for the most part, operational. The possibility exists for such invasive technologies, based on the control of remote wavelengths, to shift our present societies further toward psychocivilized society.* By this I mean a society that manages and controls social behavior predominantly through nonobvious methods of psychological manipulations, yet at a level far beyond that of the "normalized" social manipulations of propaganda and social institutions. What I refer to are the technological methods (*technique*) of psychological interference and privacy intrusions that encourage a docile and constrained society. It appears that technologies are racing ahead of us in order to better get into our heads.

Yet not only artificial technologies are affecting human brain waves. The Earth too acts on our minds through electromagnetic vibratory frequencies.

OUR ENERGETIC ENVIRONMENTS

Recently there has been a rise of interest in the relationship of brainwave frequencies to the Earth's naturally circulating rhythmic signals, known as Schumann resonances (SR). In the early 1950s German physicist Dr. W. O. Schumann calculated that global electromagnetic

---

*I have used José Delgado's phrase here.

resonances were present in the cavity formed by the Earth's surface and the ionosphere. Schumann set the lowest-frequency (with highest-intensity) mode at approximately 7.83 Hz, which is in the alpha-brain-wave range. This range has also been co-opted by the military to be used for extra-low frequency (ELF) signals for submarine and military communications. So put together, the Earth's surface, the ionosphere, and the atmosphere form what could be seen as a complete planetary electrical circuit. This planetary circuitry acts as a "wave guide" that handles the continuous flow of EM waves. In fact in 1905 Nikola Tesla speculated that this atmospheric circuitry of global EM resonances could be utilized for the creation of worldwide wireless energy transmission.

These SR frequencies are important because all living biological systems are known to function within electromagnetic field interactions. In fact, electromagnetic (EM) fields are what connect living structures to resonant energy patterns (or morphic fields).* The SR cavity formed between the ionosphere and the Earth produces oscillations capable of resonating and "phase-locking" with brain waves, since the human brain is also an EM receiver and transmitter. EEG measurements have found that the brain has the following four frequency bands: delta (up to 4 Hz), theta (4 to 7 Hz), alpha (8 to 12 Hz), and beta (12 to 30 Hz). The Earth's SR waves have been observed by experiment to emerge at several frequencies related to brain waves, such as in deep meditation.[28] In particular states a resonance is possible between the energy field of the human being and the planet. In such a state of resonance it is speculated that a mutual "information-sharing" energy field is created. This is hardly surprising since the human body (both physically and energetically) evolved over eons of geological time as part of Earth's own evolution. The human species is thus a product of the Earth's environment, and must have built up an energetic relationship to surrounding atmospheric EM oscillations. As Earth is surrounded by an ionosphere (a layer of electrically charged particles),

---

*See the work of Rupert Sheldrake, especially his book *A New Science of Life*.

natural fluctuations in frequency thus impact the energy field within and around the human body. It is reasonable to assert that the frequencies of the Earth's naturally occurring EM waves have shaped the development of human brain-wave signals. If the frequencies of human brain waves evolved in response to Earth's own wavelengths, then there is every likelihood that variations in the Earth's oscillations will result in reactive changes in the human body and mind. Such changes could be categorized as behavioral and mental.

That the EM field around the Earth impacts, resonates, and influences the human body is not esoteric nor conspiracy theory. At all times our physical bodies act similar to how lightning rods ground energy (or send it to the earth). The well-documented human biofield thus binds us closely to the ionospheric and EM fields of planet Earth.[29] The human brain likewise is a source of extra-low-frequency signals that communicate with the body via the nervous system. As in a full physical-energetic circuit the body is closely interwoven with the Earth's fluctuating energy fields, which to some degree help to regulate our body's internal clocks and circadian rhythms. The Earth's electromagnetic frequencies are also known to be affected by the activity of the sun as well as global weather patterns and Earth changes. The emergence of increased solar-flare activity and geophysical disturbances can affect human behavior through fluctuations in wavelengths received by the brain. Instabilities in human biorhythms have been known to cause various diseases ranging from obsessive-compulsive disorder to aggressive behavior, panic attacks, and narcolepsy.[30] However, these have been attributed to abnormal fluctuations. What some sources indicate is that for decades the overall measurement for the Earth's Schumann resonance was roughly 7.8 cycles per second (Hz), but that is now changing. It appears that the SR has been gradually rising and remaining constantly at higher rates. This is speculated to be the reason behind the constant remodification of military and civilian aviation satellite and communication technologies. Science doesn't yet know why this is the case, nor what to make of it or even if these reports are credible. While this speculation is still controversial to many, it may indicate that there are "frequency changes" under way in our natural environment.

The year 2010 started out turbulently. On January 12 a magnitude-7 earthquake* struck the island of Haiti just west of its capital, Port-au-Prince. Then on February 27 a magnitude-8.8 earthquake struck just off the coast of Chile and close to Concepción, the second-largest city. This earthquake was five hundred times more forceful than the Haiti earthquake and the seventh-strongest earthquake ever measured. In addition to these two major quakes there were a multitude of lesser earthquakes all over the world in the first three months of 2010, including in Japan, Indonesia, Turkey, and California. Such Earth movements create an enormous amount of energy, which is released into the environment. As well as physical destruction there is a huge cost in the mental health of people affected by earthquakes—stress, anxiety, fear, tension. Such geophysical events also create sizeable disturbances in the electromagnetic spectrum, which can have "resonating" effects, which are in turn picked up by the human brain and translated as states of nervousness and anxiety. Such states are easily interpreted by the human body, similar to how a person can feel "bad vibes" or a threatening presence in certain locations or circumstances. With a dramatically unstable Earth and accompanying Earth changes there are significant disturbances in atmospheric wavelengths, pressure, and EM radiations. How this will influence the human mind, especially those who are in close proximity to the centers of energetic disturbances, is uncertain. That it does have an effect is quite certain, since the human body has evolved over time in resonance with the Earth. Yet flows are often two-way, and thus the opposite may also be true.

Since there is a correlation between the human mind and the external energetic environment it is highly likely that human states of

---

*This is calculated using the moment magnitude scale, which is currently used by seismologists to measure the size of earthquakes in terms of energy released.

mind will likewise reflect their frequencies back into the environment. While these may be minor fluctuations or influences, we should consider the exponential affect of many minds. The majority of people are unaware of these processes of reciprocal energetic exchanges, yet human energy fields radiate out as well as receive. And the power of the mind is no small matter. As this book suggests, humanity's sight is veiled to the true magnitude of the mind's capacity. Human consciousness is truly a slumbering wonder. Yet even unconsciously the human mind has great force; thus the huge efforts invested by minority powers to manipulate and influence how people think. If each individual is emanating thoughts/feelings of stress, worry, fear, and anxiety, then there is surely a reciprocal affect (fluctuation) within the energy spectrum of the Earth. If this occurs on a mass scale then the effects could become noticeable. There is the popular view that the unstable state of the world actually reflects the current state of global human consciousness: unbalanced and fearful. Earth and her inhabitants are not separate entities but are a unified living field. Thus we all reflect parts of each other: one body.

What this picture lacks, however, is the nonmaterial element. The physical realm manifests through materiality, yet nonvisible energy is in fact the glue that binds all. This understanding is not mysticism but science. Atoms may be the building blocks of the physical world, but delve deep enough beyond atoms and we find quarks, the fundamental constituents of matter. And what lies beyond quarks? Energy and more energy. The energetic realm permeates our world and the universe. The current cosmological model states that dark energy accounts for 74 percent of the total mass-energy of the universe. Energy resonates with energy, and the human body is in a constant interaction not only with its environment but also with each person's thoughts, emotions, and other subconscious processes.[31] With the increasing global levels in fear and stress that we now see, as a consequence of both natural disasters and human fear mongering, there is every chance that these fluctuations are having an effect on the collective energy field that permeates our quantum reality. Keeping the human mind distracted—and disturbed—lowers the possibility that human consciousness will evolve to new levels of perception. The evolution of human consciousness is paramount to the survival of the human race; yet lethargic, unfocused, undernurtured minds are a symptom of the deliberate conditioning of our control societies. This is why we literally need to *take back our minds* away from physical and mental structures of containment and undue influence.

In this chapter I have tried to examine some of the concerns over unwarranted and potential harmful interferences with the human mind. Some of these have come from advances in sensory technologies (such as in gaming). Others, however, are more malicious and concern the research undertaken by military bodies to develop and test apparatuses that target and molest the human mind. That these technologies exist is itself worrying. Whether they are actually employed we will perhaps never be sure. Yet there are thousands of individuals worldwide who attest to being the victims of mental molestation. Some of their accounts are highly credible and are supported by practicing psychiatrists.* However, I have dealt with this subject only briefly, for it would need a whole book in itself (of which there are already many). What I have tried to say is that humanity lives within an artificial hostile environment. Further, that the "rational logic" of the techno-culture is designed for greater efficiencies of management, control, processing, and ordering. That these social structures are exploited by an elite minority is my main argument. Such technologies could likewise be liberating if handled in an appropriate manner. Yet so far the liberating uses are playing second fiddle to the exploitative strategies. Thus there is a pattern of nation-states creating a *social matrix* that seeks to "better manage" their populations. This is, of course, a euphemism for societies of control. And within such societies there is a conditioning of behavior and thought. It is time that humanity

---

*For an example, see the Colin A. Ross Institute for Psychological Trauma.

collectively—and individually—frees itself from these constraints. In order to walk into the future we need a full expression of the human mind and an energetic consciousness. *Change is coming*. But first we need to surpass what is perhaps our greatest barrier: FEAR.

The overabundance in our societies of manipulated fear is a subject to which I now turn to in the next chapter.

5

CONSTRUCTIONS OF FEAR
The Armageddon Meme

Humans detest uncertainty. Uncertainties produce anxieties. To reduce anxiety, if no factual structure is readily available, humans will simply invent one or accept a ready-to-wear media reality structure. . . . These perceptions, of course, are fictional constructs.

WILSON BRYAN KEY

Reality is an illusion, albeit a persistent one.

ALBERT EINSTEIN

Our deepest fears are the dragons that guard our greatest treasures.

RAINER MARIA RILKE

We are living in a different world in the twenty-first century. The first decade of this new century has been characterized by uncertainty and instability. It wasn't the much-hyped "Millennium Bug" that changed the world stage; it was the fateful September 11, 2001, which put our planet on a different footing. The opening years of the twenty-first century have thus been characterized by new levels of security and safety fears. Much of the world has now been plunged into a postmillennium state of insecurity. And these insecurities have been heightened by the breakdown of old and familiar dualities such as democracy versus Communism, and friend versus foe. Media-sponsored fear mongering has helped to turn each individual into her own social spy. For example, the so-called War on Terror in the West has been used to shift "the enemy" from someplace outside society to now dwell within. What this means is that all civilians can effectively be categorized as a potential terrorist. Not only does this assist nation-state antiterrorism laws in that citizens forfeit their rights if they are suspected of being a terrorist (or harboring terrorist tendencies), but also it encourages social distrust and community disharmony. As discussed earlier in the book, a breakdown in community cohesion serves the social matrix as it decreases the effectiveness of organized social unrest. People are being coerced to spy on their neighbors, to keep a watchful eye on suspicious behavior. In the UK the Department of Education has organized conferences to train teachers how to identify students who may go on to be suicide bombers or other types of terrorists. Such measures are not only worrying for civil liberties but act to bring unease and paranoia into people's everyday lives. And this is exactly the point—to further infiltrate the mental/emotional space of people's daily lives; in other words, to really bring the terror home. This cleverly orchestrated movement within the social matrix of modern states (at this point mostly Western) confirms that civil space is increasingly becoming the new battle zone. Such dystopian trends further create an environment where human behavior is increasingly governed by processes outside individual control. Further, the presence of fear, anxiety, and distress, as they permeate the fabric of a society, can weaken the mental and emotional resilience of people.

This chapter addresses a fundamental issue in the supremacy of human consciousness: the age-old mythological battle between dark and light. This is the struggle between forces that perpetuate negativity, apprehension, and fear, and energies that seek to bring about harmony, balance, and a natural conscious order. The manufactured and sustained "War on Terror" that rages through our media channels and through the public consciousness is now a major player in this struggle between the energies of control and those that favor evolutionary development. I believe that the real danger we face as the global order rearranges itself through geopolitical maneuvering is not physical insecurity but mental/emotional impacts. The invasion of Iraq, for example, was surely about the need to secure physical resources—in this case, oil. Yet this is part of an outer agenda—a material-control strategy. Such material-control strategies include controlling the flow of global resources, including oil, food, and money. This great game on world resources constitutes only the outer history, the smaller picture. The other part is what may be referred to as the *secret history,* the hidden (or occult) reasons for particular actions. These acts generally impact the nonmaterial realm wherein lies the flows of energy and consciousness. That such occult strategies operate behind physical events may be a new and unfamiliar notion to many people. Yet any serious investigation into history will reveal that monarchs, governments, and ruling parties have utilized nonmaterial forces in tandem with (and often behind) the perpetration of physical acts. This may appear in benign forms such as the use of court astrologers and seers to the more elaborate uses of arcane rituals. These traditions stretch back as far as antiquity (for example, Babylonia) and as recently as the British government using occult forces during World War II. As I have repeatedly stressed, there are powers that operate within the global order and that oppose human development. When launching a major operation such as the invasion of Iraq, why not kill two birds with one stone? The hidden agenda behind this cruel strategy is, in my opinion, to also wage a war against human consciousness.

Much of the world has been plunged into a state of mental and emotional warfare since the heightened activities of the global War on Terror. This might be more appropriately named a War in Terror, as it perpetuates the rising tension of fear, anger, and bloodthirsty hatred. The escalation of the global terror situation is not limited to the West and its very specific foes. This is a war with no definable enemy, no definable strategy, no definable end, and an almost impossible goal of securing a "terrorless" world. Yet through its actions it has helped to further catalyze anti-Western tensions and ideologies, as well as fueling once-lesser fractured parties. Splintered groups throughout the Middle East and developing countries have been united against a common enemy (the "evil West") and this has resulted in a more polarized world. While this may first appear contradictory to a globalizing Modernity Project that seeks to develop ever grander systems of control, it actually plays into this process. We must remember that things that appear contradictory or opposite on the surface are often working together on other levels. Networks of resentment, terrorism, and violence now stretch, tentaclelike, throughout the world. They also reach inward into communities, since terrorism is no longer "out there." With potential terror networks now brought into the everyday world (women suicide bombers, sleeper cells, and so forth), the social-control strategies can be further increased as "security measures" needed to better protect people's freedoms (especially in the "freedom-loving" West). While these measures are being put in place for our benefit, we are also being made to feel more vulnerable in an insecure world where even our own streets, our buses, our places for social congregation are not safe.

Also, in those countries suffering the interventions of Western forces (such as Iraq, Palestine, Afghanistan, and so on), there is the daily barrage of fear, death, violence, military control . . . the list goes on. Most people have a difficult enough time securing their daily living. The thought of being conscious objectors, or of considering issues of moral, ethical, and spiritual evolution just does not enter into such lives. What does enter the lives of millions of people is the bombardment of waves of negativity, fear, and anxiety. Much of this is by way of media channels that bring the visuals, the stories of ongoing "attacks" into our living rooms. Take the Twin Towers event as an example; this was the defining moment of terrorism brought into our homes. It just so happened that video cameras were filming at both moments of impact. So for days, months, and now years, we have seen the images repeated, again and again, of the impacts and the towers falling. This is a visual bombardment of our minds. The public collective consciousness has now been conditioned with these images, and with the seeds of an endless global war—both overt and covert. After all, fear is the strongest weapon; when it pervades a person's consciousness it weakens their harmony and introduces a *dis-ease*. The human collective consciousness, I would argue, has been polluted with the seeds of fear. Further, these seeds of fear have been deliberately planted within our minds and our societies as part of a larger agenda of control. Fear as a consciousness suppressant also works highly effectively on a subconscious level when people are unaware that the fear is even operating. Yet it can make us more suspicious, more possessive, and less hopeful for our global futures. Fear resonates at an extremely dense level and, in line with how resonance operates, actually serves to bring our own human vibratory level down. We often sense this in our lives: days when we feel lighter, when everything is possible, and we are infused with inspiration and motivation. These are the finer energies of positivity that infuse our bodily energetic systems. Yet at other times, when we feel negative, we feel "down" and our energies are heavier, like a stone.

The orchestration of global events has created polarized energies; fear, stress, and tension create disruption in the unity of human energy. *We are being distracted by deliberate design.* Part of this strategy for distraction is for the system to create problems that do not correspond to the reality but are made to appear as if they do. The minds of the people are then focused on what they feel is the "reality problem," which may then become a new form of social reality for a temporary span of time. This strategy is in play through the media, which infuses the mind of viewers with a perpetual state of tension and paranoia over what are deemed as domestic insecurities. Now that our global world has been injected with rising fear and negativity it is imperative that these forces are not allowed to penetrate our consciousness. The present state in world affairs is, I emphasize, very much about a war—not a war on terror but a *war on human consciousness*.

For this reason I discuss the "injections of fear" into our societies and cultures as representing an *Armageddon meme*. A meme can be anything from cultural artifacts (films, songs, myths, fairy tales) to social laws and "truths" and belief systems divine and/or dogmatic. In other words, a meme pool is a repository of ideas from which any given culture can extract and use—or be used by. Ideas also are memes, and similar to biological viruses they can spread through a social/global body. Some memes are natural to our global body (conscious evolution), while others act as invaders (fear, hate, suppression). A particularly dangerous meme now infecting global consciousness and acting as a depressant is that of terrorism. War, then, is not only about resources (such as oil) or concocted territorial disputes; it is also about releasing an active depressant within the collective psyche of humanity. For this reason our global world has been maneuvered into a permanent war economy.

A PERMANENT WAR ECONOMY

There is no better way to construct societies of control than through the notion of a *terrifying peace*.* What this expresses is the notion of peace as constituted through the presence—and potential—of terror. In this way peace does not exist on its own merits but as a state of (in)security in defense against terror. The UK government, in line with EU statutory law, manifested this *terrifying peace* when using the precautionary principle for suspected terrorists residing in

---

*I am grateful to my friend and colleague Manabrata Guha for many discussions on this theme.

the UK. This means that the state can arrest people for what they believe they may do in the future. If the state has a suspicion for future guilty acts they are lawfully able to protect against this by locking away those who may be guilty in the future. The irony here is that once locked away the suspected person is no longer able to perform what they have been suspected of. This is similar to an old folk story of the wise fool who arrives at the door of the king's castle to be told by the guard that the king has decreed that anyone who tells a lie is to be hanged. Then upon asking for his destination, the wise fool replies, "I am going to be hanged." "I don't believe you!" exclaims the guard. "You are lying." "Very well, then. If I have told a lie, hang me!" "But if I hang you," replies the guard, "then you would have told the truth and I shouldn't have hung you!" "Exactly," replies the wise fool. "This is your definition of truth."

The paradigm of prevention that the precautionary principle instigates is a dangerous precognitive precedent that is veering dangerously close to the thought-crime practices of Orwell's *1984*. It allows the power structures to imagine the worst without any, or little, supporting evidence. What is worse is that politicians in the EU are now using this "lawful tool" in displays of power, exaggerating fear, and instigating a wave of terrifying peace. These public constructs are the fantasies of fear, a phantasmagoria projection of fearful images. Such state behavior shows us how the politics of fear operate: it is fear of an imagined future. It is the "lawful" instigation of *their truth*. This type of "logical reasoning" is an inherent part of the Modernity Project's scientific rationalism. Again, as the famous philosopher Bertrand Russell states:

So long as there is imminent risk of war it is impossible to escape from the authority of the State except to a very limited degree. It is mainly war that has caused the excessive power of modern States, and until the fear of war is removed it is inevitable that everything should be subordinated to short-term efficiency.[1]

Russell goes on to explain how, throughout history, the chief source of cohesion has always been warfare. Not only does it catalyze technological development but it has succeeded in consolidating the power of larger states and power blocs. For example, World War I gave us the League of Nations, which, following World War II, was upgraded to the United Nations. War has been utilized by governing power structures to consolidate social cohesion domestically (nationalism and rationing), while simultaneously strengthening larger international power blocs. What is even more worrying is that Russell notes how if there were no successive wars, population control would have to be orchestrated through more deliberate technical means: "If there is not to be an endless succession of wars, population will have to become stationary throughout the world. . . . This will require an extension of scientific technique into very intimate matters."[2]

Warfare, and the state of warfare, performs multiple functions. It is not solely the case that nations enter into territorial disputes and thrash it out on a world stage. There are many levels of maneuvering taking place (on both outer and hidden levels) that involve power, money, resources, and—above all—control. A permanent war economy is a feature of how governments are now tightly aligned with the powerful infrastructures of both the military and industry. This "iron triangle" relationship is now referred to as the military-industrial complex (MIC). This term was popularized in the farewell address of President Dwight D. Eisenhower when he warned of the insidious power of this complex: "In the councils of government, we must guard against the acquisition of unwarranted influence, whether sought or unsought, by the military-industrial complex. The potential for the disastrous rise of misplaced power exists and will persist." This misplaced power now permeates most governmental infrastructures and often works above and beyond national governments. This complex is what some commentators refer to as the shadow government, as its military-industrial dealings operate irrespective of national borders and state policies. I would now refer to this conglomerate as the military-industrial-entertainment complex, as all these strands are interrelated in their dealings. I referred to this previously when I spoke of "militainment" in the crossover (or merging) of the military and entertainment industry. This Leviathan of power has cooperated together to shift (or co-opt) the world toward a "total war"—a permanent war whereby terrifying peace has become the norm rather than the exception. This state of affairs is counterproductive to the forces of conscious evolution and human development.

Such manufactured agendas within the global system serve to create waves of insecurity that reverberate within the human global consciousness. Moreover, the usual response to such "insecurities" is to develop greater social securities, which further deprive people of their civil liberties and extend the technological cage of control that negatively influences the expression of individual consciousness. This is the social construction of fear and learned helplessness, which results in greater dependency on the old structures of top-down governmental control. We want to feel safe—we need our governments to protect us from perceived enemies who wish to destroy our way of life. We thus ask for powerful state protection—yet it always comes at a price. Part of this price is our subjugation and the handing over of our authority to others—to external dependencies. Yet just this act of expecting others to be responsible for us has a powerful psychological effect of disempowering us. Not only do so many people hand over their physical responsibilities and power, but also, perhaps more importantly, they give away and relinquish their spiritual, inner power.

Most of the global interventions to extract power (primarily from the Western nations) have established a "perpetual war for perpetual peace" that is without end. Inside this web of warfare, played out by the military-industrial complex, is an ever greater stranglehold on human consciousness and natural development. Humanity has thus been hampered by a power grab that has been referred to as the Anglo-American Establishment,[3] and even in some circles as the Anglo-Saxon Mission. This has been orchestrated through economic warfare as well as physical wars. The controlled mainstream media has always played its part in duping the masses into believing the orthodox accounts of history and world events and to distract people into mass passivity. Yet now that the power elite are fearful of a rising consciousness from within (an increasing wave of awareness from its own citizens), the war gets turned inward into every living room and every mind. This specter of fear is now pervasive not only through nation-states but also on a global scale: the phantasmagoria of Armageddon has arisen. The end of the world is nigh . . . prepare for the end. Oh, and by the way, be very, very scared. . . .

DECODING THE ARMAGEDDON MEME

Human development is a spiritual process; by failing to connect with this realization, people are further kept in a material, glitzy ignorance. We are literally kept in the dark from realizing that an act of inner understanding has the potential to generate great outer change and transformation. However, by various means social realities have largely been governed for centuries (if not longer) by levels of fear. As stated in an earlier chapter, societies were once mainly controlled through visual fear and public torture. Still today some developing countries rely on physical violence, intimidation, and even rape as a means of suppressing the people. Today's more modern societies utilize a complex system of institutions to disseminate conditionings of fear and worry. The more successful channel is that of communication: films, books, Internet, and so forth. In this way the *fear memes* can more effectively be deposited within the mass collective consciousness. Earlier examples of this were the 1950s Hollywood movies of alien invasion, which were symbolic (and subliminal) metaphors for the invasion of Communism (alien = Reds). Similarly, today many fear China as the new "alien invader." We are told in celluloid and in MS media to fear the terrorist, and now we are being told to fear for the end of the world. The Final Judgment is upon us, and our world will soon crumble. These are all ingredients in a *fear vibration* that affects the reality around us. Similar strategies (such as hellfire sermons) have existed within our cultures for many generations. These ploys all serve to lower social vibrations by exploiting people's mental and emotional energies. Fear perpetuates fear, locking humans into a lower vibration level. The choice is to fear or not to fear: *Any person who makes a choice not to fear is worth a stadium filled with those who choose to fear.*[4]

Much of this saber rattling can be placed under the heading F.E.A.R. = False Evidence Appearing Real. It is thus necessary to distinguish when a situation is being fantasized out of proportion (or sometimes out of thin air) by the MS media and when it belongs to manipulated but very real physical events. For example, a range of global stresses are now coming into play that can have potentially series consequences. They include, but are not limited to, financial woes, food shortages, health issues, global pandemics, and so on. In terms of finance, global rating agencies (such as Moodys and Standard & Poor) have already between them downgraded several major U.S. and UK banks, as well as downgrading several EU countries such as Greece, Portugal, Ireland, Italy, and Spain. Social cohesion is also under threat from rising food prices (especially when wages are stagnant) and various periodic flu pandemic scares (swine flu, bird flu, and so on). When under such stresses the human mind is open to being converted to new sets of beliefs. In other words, any new regulations presented by the ruling powers, regardless of their austerity, might be submissively accepted. Such conditioning behavior was demonstrated as part of the famous experiments with Pavlov's dogs. Pavlov found that once extreme stress was induced in the dogs they could be made to give up their old conditioning and take on the new set of responses regardless of how strong the old conditionings were. Further, the dogs would then adopt the new set of conditionings as firmly as the old and resist losing them.[5] Stresses, it seems, are useful tools in creating compliance within populations. And fear, when internalized, becomes our own worst kind of WMD (weapon of mass destruction), as it distorts and scrambles not only our emotions but also our body's potential to protect itself. States of mind have been proved, through the placebo effect, to have an influence on the immune system and the body's ability to heal itself. Fear, as a debilitating emotion, can lead to a weakened immune system as well as a weakened state of mind. This is exactly why we should be careful of the new rampaging virus: the Armageddon meme.

Collective human consciousness has been *expecting something* for thousands of years. In ancient civilizations it was the return of the gods, then came the messiah, and for the last epoch of Christian civilization there has been the expectation of either the Second Coming or the final battle of Armageddon. Whichever way we look at it there has been an expectancy meme running through our collective consciousness, whether we adhere to these notions or not. What this does is build up energy upon the planet, like a spiral or a coil being wound. Evidence of end-of-the-world expectancy has shown up in psychological studies. Dr. Kenneth Ring, a professor of psychology, has made extensive study of people's prophetic visions during the near-death experience (NDE). In a research paper he describes how there was a strong correspondence in people's visions while in this state.

> The future scenario, however, is usually of short duration, seldom extending much beyond the beginning of the twenty-first century. The individual reports that in this decade there will be an increasing incidence of earthquakes, volcanic activity and generally massive geophysical changes. There will be resultant disturbances in weather patterns and food supplies. The world economic system will collapse, and the possibility of nuclear war or accident is very great. . . . All of these events are transitional rather than ultimate, however, and they will be followed by a new era in human history, marked by human brotherhood, universal love and world peace. Though many will die, the earth will live.[6]

These studies were performed prior to 1982 but still contain elements immediately recognizable in events transpiring today. However, Ring is quick to point out that such prophetic visions should not be taken at face value, as they bring a message that reinforces the myth of cultural renewal and regeneration. They also mirror many of the prophecies of Earth changes made famous by various wisdom traditions as well as by modern seers such as Edgar Cayce and Gordon-Michael Scallion, among many others. In recent years there has been a tremendous build-up of prophecies and visions that foretell of coming dramatic Earth changes. These prophecies have found a large global audience through modern communication technologies such as the Internet. What should be noted here is that prophecies as such have a twofold potential. On the one hand they serve to warn people of the possibility of coming dangers so that they can be prepared; on the other they offer an opportunity for people to view the "possible future" if nothing is done, therefore stimulating action for creating change. Prophecy thus outlines the possibilities and not the actualities. However, many of the prophecies now circulating (or being recirculated) or taken at face value by many people are becoming absorbed into the collective psyche (our human collective consciousness) and create a foreboding.

The subconscious foreboding of coming disasters and world cataclysms are feeding an energy build-up that seeks to "nourish" itself with further social fears. The Armageddon meme I spoke of earlier is thus self-replicating in that it spreads itself, much like a virus, through the many minds of its carriers. And these carriers can be found all over the Internet, with various doom websites offering last-minute strategies for survival. Feeding into this social hunger for the Armageddon meme are various big-budget Hollywood films. Films such as *The Day After Tomorrow* and *2012* affect the human subconscious by encouraging fears about the end of the world and near-total destruction. In the U.S. the History Channel launched its own "Armageddon Week," full of dramatic documentaries about end-time prophecies and possible near-future destruction of the planet. They also aired a program titled

Apocalypse Island (January 4, 2010) about an island in the middle of the Pacific Ocean where the gods supposedly would come to watch the final minutes of civilization. Much of this hyped new interest in end-time prophecies has been sparked by the controversies surrounding the Mayan calendar.

The Mayan calendar indicates that the Age of Jaguar, the thirteenth *baktun,* or long period of 144,000 days, will come to an end with the fifth and final sun on December 22, 2012. That date, according to the Mayan system, will mark the switch to a new era of planetary evolution, one that requires a radically different kind of consciousness. However, since the famed Mayan calendar actually ends at this date, it has been misunderstood by many to signify arrival of cataclysmic earth events. Combined with various mythic and current prophecies into a mixing bowl of beliefs, superstitions, and viral warnings, the end result is a smorgasbord of apocryphal end-of-world scenarios. Instead what the Mayan calendar may have been indicating was a cyclic procession of astronomical origin that coincides with cyclical Earth changes *of a natural order*. Parts of these changes are perceptual in nature; that is, the geomagnetic disruptions have an electromagnetic influence on the biological material (living bodies) of the Earth, affecting both evolutionary processes and consciousness energies. Change, which is inherent in all processes, is a natural feature of both human and planetary evolution. This does not mean that in the upcoming years—especially on or around 2012—we are going to have either global destruction or divine ascension to an awaiting fifth dimension; these are the two extremes of circulating beliefs. It may be that in these upcoming years we will witness increased disturbances in the human psyche. These influences could possibly occur through magnetic environmental impacts, such as from more extreme weather conditions, a decreasing of the Earth's magnetic shield, and the increase of sun-flare activity. As later chapters of this book indicate, there are indeed processes occurring on our planet right now that foretell significant changes for our human, social, and environmental systems. The choice we are faced with is how to consciously deal with these issues. Again, the central argument of this book is that our human futures rely on the direction human consciousness will take. During these transitional years, in which many social, political, and environmental changes will be occurring, it will be paramount for those social forces aiming to retain their physical control to manipulate human consciousness. This manipulation will not only concern the lower end of the spectrum such as propaganda, consumption, and social norms (as discussed previously) but also ever increasing levels of human social awareness. The greatest weapon to afflict the power and growing awareness of human consciousness is fear: False Evidence Appearing Real. Doom is, and will continue to be, big business. If we fear the future, we limit our own possibilities. We also drastically weaken ourselves—mentally, spiritually, and emotionally.

One example occurred in October 2009. Prior to this month there was a rapid increase in psychic and metaphysical information, a great "buzz," on the Internet all pertaining to "something big" coming. In an instant the Internet was throbbing with radio chat shows interviewing self-proclaimed prophets who spoke of dreams of immense destruction: whole cities destroyed, nuclear explosions, biological warfare, and so on.

The Internet phenomenon of Web bots* started going all crazy with linguistic predictions of upcoming doom. What was predicted as possible late-October events included a rapid collapse of the U.S. dollar, Israel bombing Iran, possible martial law in parts of the U.S., and extreme-level pandemic of the H1N1 flu virus. Other sources began predicting the arrival of UFO mother ships over the planet, forced bank closures, global infrastructure breakdowns, strange atmospheric conditions, and so forth. Even several futurists came onto the scene and sent out newsletters to warn clients/readers of a potential

---

*In this context Web bots refer to the Web Bot Project, which is an online software program that claims to be able to predict future events by tracking keywords entered on the Internet. See www.halfpasthuman.com.

upcoming "October instability." In the end nothing happened. Yet it did create considerable Internet chatter and many worried people who had received e-mails, heard partial news on the radio, received warnings from friends, and more. Such memes spread quickly. As mentioned, not only are there real changes happening, but also there is a simultaneous buildup in human collective mental energies. Many people instinctively know or feel that something is coming or that changes are afoot. The danger here is that this uncertainty can be exploited by social forces into fear mongering, which can lead to anxious worry and perceived helplessness. The year 2012 is, in my opinion, being deliberately manipulated by the MS media in a bid to exploit its darker side. There are now countless preachers on digital and physical pedestals giving sermons on our coming catastrophes. This year has also been aligned with the "moment of Ascension," when millions of worthy souls will be transported to other dimensions, mirroring the religious doctrine of the Rapture.

Change is not something that occurs at a given minute in time; it is a continual process that is always in motion. And in these years of the early twenty-first century, rapid change is occurring both within our social systems and within our consciousness. These changes will continue to affect many of us; hence the importance of gaining authority over our thinking, emotions, and inner awareness. In these changing times it is necessary to not only take back the responsibility of our thinking—our consciousness—but also to increase our awareness of transpiring events. It is a time of growth, not of increased mental and spiritual repression. As part of decoding the Armageddon meme, I will briefly outline what some of the discussed predictions involve.

Ancient Mayan prophecies, it is said, are based on astronomical observations and knowledge, which the Maya arranged into their temporal cycles based on astrological movements. The final cycle is due to terminate on December 21, 2012, at the winter solstice. After this date there is no more calendar, which has been taken to mark the end of our present age. While this also suggests the transition to a new era of Earth history, many commentators are focusing on the chaos, upheaval, and destruction that will accompany this great shift. Why should such great disasters accompany this date? Well, coincidence or not, this date (thereabouts) also aligns with other potential events. These include:

1. Increased sunspots, sun flares (coronal mass ejections), and overall sun-peak activity. Over the twentieth century the sun has been becoming more active during its peak of its eleven-year sun cycle (during the Maunder Minimum). Solar physicists have predicted that the next peak of the solar cycle could indeed generate a very high degree of electromagnetic flux (perhaps record levels), which would impact the Earth, its infrastructure, and environment. After all, many of the powerful storms on the Earth are related to increased solar activity (sun storms). The 2005 Atlantic hurricane season (that is, Katrina, Rita, Wilma, Dennis, Emily) coincided with some of the most active storm weeks of the sun. Some Armageddon memes have portrayed the coming sun flares as possibly wiping out all human life on Earth (such as Alex Proyas's film *Knowing*). Other memes that abound on the Internet say human life will be thrust back into the Stone Age. These catastrophic themes play on the idea of the Earth's weakening magnetic field.

2. In December 2008 NASA announced that the THEMIS project had detected a massive breach in the earth's magnetic field and that in the near future this would allow large amounts of solar plasma to enter the earth's magnetosphere.[7] Similarly scientists in South Africa have already measured cracks in the Earth's magnetic field the size of California.[8] In the past we have always relied on Earth's magnetic field to protect us from solar storms and coronal mass ejections. With our primary defense shield down we may be vulnerable to harmful solar radiation.

Some Armageddon memes suggest that the Earth could be undergoing a magnetic pole reversal, which could drastically affect all human life. During the course of this reversal the Earth's magnetic field will become even weaker, increasing the danger farther from solar and stellar radiation. Catastrophe pundits have referred to the fact that in 2007 the NASA THEMIS satellites found evidence of magnetic "ropes" connecting the Earth's upper atmosphere directly to the sun, providing stronger evidence to confirm the theory of solar-Earth electromagnetic interactions. This could prove significant if the sun were to become even more volatile, as is suggested by the following.

3. Russian geophysicist Alexey Dmitriev and his colleague Vladimir B. Baranov, using data originally gathered by *Voyager* as well as more recent data, believe that the solar system has entered a more highly energized region of space. And this extra "donation" of energy is creating "excited energy states" in all planets in our solar system, including the sun. This turbulent region, it appears, is making the sun hotter and stormier and has already caused climate changes on several planets.[9] The scientists write that the exposure to an increased energized stellar region will affect our planet's own energetic capacity for growth, as it will result in some of Earth's systems being in a highly charged and excited state. Uncertain environmental weather patterns could result, as well as electromagnetic disturbances both in natural and biological systems. Some commentators prefer to think this increased energy will bring utmost chaos, not just disturbances. This passing of "energized space" would reach a peak between 2010 and 2020, with the pivotal date in 2012. Now tie this in with the next piece of news.

4. The Yellowstone supervolcano is said to erupt, with catastrophic consequences, every six hundred thousand to seven hundred thousand years. Now it is overdue for another eruption. Speculations are rife throughout the Internet about an

imminent supereruption (as depicted in the film *2012*). These rumors have been spread because of that spate of small earthquakes under Yellowstone, which began after the January 2010 Haiti earthquake. Between January 17 and February 1, 2010, 1,620 small earthquakes were recorded, with the largest of the shocks measuring 3.8.

5. With these physical signs occurring over the planet, the "Armageddonist" movements of various religious sects are, through their various sources, predicting that a religious war will bring about the end times in 2012. There are even scholarly interpretations of the Bible that predict that the Earth will be destroyed in 2012.[10] Some people are pointing out the present environmental disruptions and Earth changes as harbingers of the end times. Others in this camp prefer to support a Rapture scenario in which the faithful will be transported away from the Earth and be saved. The Left Behind series of books first published in the U.S. support the popularity of this topic.

6. This is where things can get a little dramatic. Various Internet groups, forums, and individuals are all predicting that a large hitherto unknown planetary object will enter our solar system and thus create gravitational disturbances on our Earth. More fundamental believers say that the unknown planet—Planet X, or Nibiru—will create a pole shift on the Earth, which could wipe out most of humanity. And the timing? Well, despite some variations, the most common, since the popularity of the Mayan calendar, is around the end of 2012.

7. The pole shift is a popular 2012 scenario. Some predictions state that the shifting/wobbling magnetic poles are indicative of a complete Earth pole reversal, as has occurred previously in Earth's geological history. Some theories suggest that this will happen when the Earth and sun come into exact alignment with the center of the galaxy. This is also predicted to occur in or around 2012. More hard-core theories continue to suggest that

the pole reversal will create gigantic earthquakes and tsunamis that will bring down all of our buildings, structures, and cities, leaving nothing standing. Continents will shift thousands of kilometers and great tidal waves will come in to leave billions of people dead. Extreme.

In the end, we just don't know. And these are only *some* of the ideas being talked about in reference to 2012. Rather than considering this date as a marker to surpass in the evolutionary journey many pundits are using this as an end date. It verges on the ridiculous, in my opinion, that human life will be wiped out or the world will stop turning at an extremely specific hour in the human calendar. There are also many more theories, ideas, predictions, and prophecies that I have not touched on. As one recent thinker wryly noted, "People today are in danger of drowning in information; but, because they have been taught that information is useful, they are more willing to drown than they need be. If they could handle information, they would not have to drown at all."[11] And this, I feel, is part of the ploy of messing with our minds: to distract us by mixing information with misinformation and disinformation. What we end up with is a whirlwind of information circling the globe at ever increasing speeds. Many of these Armageddon themes are then seized on by the mainstream media and hacked into popularized, and often vulgar, treatments. This serves only to validate the rest of the apocalyptic material circling the information airwaves. People are susceptible to information in the media because they have no other sources with which to corroborate the information. They also have few inner resources by which to assess information. Timothy Leary, the wisecracking cultural philosopher, once said that everyone needs an inbuilt Bullshit Detector. Unfortunately, most of us do not possess this, so we are gullible when it comes to external sources of information. It is imperative, then, that as individuals we each begin to take responsibility for ourselves. This entails responsibility for the ingestion of daily information. Time to put increased trust in our intuition and to *feel* what sits right with us, and to spurn what seems to be a mishmash of propaganda or misinformation.

These are transitional years that humanity is moving through. We are approaching a cusp of consciousness and awareness. There are increased energies pouring into the Earth and the danger here is that the varied social matrixes in which many people live will flood the mental airwaves with increased images of catastrophes, apocalypse, and perpetual warfare. The Armageddon meme will be likely to work overtime in the upcoming years as social strategies for containment and control seek to increase their share. When individual consciousness tries to manifest it is ridiculed by mainstream society—these are the social institutions that have been carefully established to nurture and support a selected census of thought and conditioning. *Yet we must not be afraid to think out of the box.* The dominant worldview of scientific realism or materialism (matter-realism), has strained for centuries to keep the spiritual/metaphysical paradigm debased and suppressed. I repeat: In whatever guises they operate and however ridiculous this may sound to some people, there are forces operating in our world today that seek to counter human evolution. There are retrogressive social factors built into the fabric of our societies (our institutions, our conditioning) that work to suppress our natural tendency—especially at this time—toward accelerated conscious evolution. Each of us should be mindful not to be attracted to forces/energies that hinder, distort, and disrupt the human spirit. The less work we do in this area of personal responsibility, the more license we give to these hindering forces to act on us, and in our name. The more aware and awake we become to the distorting factors in our cultures and societies, the less we become powerless under their sway. And with the taking of each conscious act, we give courage and support to our own growth.

The energy of human consciousness is a tremendous force, more powerful than we can imagine in our present condition. Humanity has been granted incredible gifts of directed intention and will to develop and to use *with conscious expression*. If we fail to use these gifts wisely, we may be in danger of opening the doors to other malignant forces. And this is a key element: the planet we live on is a planet of choice. We choose, and have always chosen, what to accept as a part of ourselves. The human spirit abhors strategies of force; physical coercion will always be met with resistance. Subtle persuasion, however, is a very different tactic. If we can be made to believe, and hence accept, something then we naturally and easily assimilate it into our personality and belief systems. As a species we are then much more malleable, manageable, and maneuverable. And this is the trap of consciousness: we are enmeshed in a matrix of belief systems and conditionings that map our lives out for us. From this we need to break away.

As examples, warfare, fear, insecurity, and materialism are social forces put in play to retrograde our individual and collective spiritual and conscious evolution. The forces behind our various social matrixes understand this and thus create strong materialistic events in a bid to halt humanity's development. These forces wish to keep humanity absorbed and distracted within the present material cultures and its attachments so that people fail to reconnect with a spiritual side. Because human development is a spiritual process, by failing to connect with this realization people are further kept in material distraction. A simple act of awareness, of inner understanding of these processes, can work with great effect to bring about personal change and transformation. We must each act, in whatever small way, to understand the events and happenings in the life around us. At first the insights may not seem profound, yet the focus of intention and awareness will set the ball rolling.

When we perceive the world as life-threatening instead of life-promoting we inhibit our natural capacities for health and development. Each of us needs to break out of this straightjacket of thought and perception. We must withdraw our consent from the fear being activated around us and directed at us. The winter of dormant consciousness is coming to a close and the spring is now upon us.

It is our responsibility as a sentient race of physical-spiritual beings to win the war of minds that we have unknowingly been thrust into. We do not live in a world of threats and insecurities but a world of opportunities and transformations. We shall go beyond all fear barriers. Our answer, as individuals, to the question of increased indoctrination should be—will be!—our own conscious, willing choice for breakthrough, transformation, and evolution.

Change is coming, and everything is possible . . . there really is nothing to fear.

6
WINNING THE WAR OF MINDS
Changing the Mental Game-Play

Who looks outside, dreams; who looks inside, awakes.

CARL GUSTAV JUNG

There is a correlation between the state of the collective human mind and the affairs of the external world. Both are related and are energetically entwined. Of course, our educational and scientific establishments tell us (not teach!) that mind and matter are separate things and that there is an "out there" and an imaginary world "in here": *East is East, and West is West, and never the twain shall meet.** Yet despite these material admonitions our political and entertainment industries continue to ply the public with heavily layered propaganda, subliminal messages, and signifiers in a bid to influence and manipulate how people think. Clearly, the mind and *how we think* is very important to our world at large. Viewing our current human epoch, with its varied ideological and political conflict, mental conditioning, and strife among peoples and nations, it appears that collectively we are in a state of global psychosis. The positive and creative power of human thought has largely been veiled to us throughout the successive ages, from reli-

---

*Famous lines from "The Ballad of East and West" by Rudyard Kipling.

gious monopoly to class structures, industrial work constraints, educational biases, and now media dumbing down. Knowledge has more or less trickled down to the average person through heavily filtered channels, and most often has been doctored, amended, and/or edited. The end result has been not knowledge but consensus information, or "allowed" information. To put it more crudely, the human mind has been drip fed for far too long. Human consciousness, individually and collectively, is in danger of losing out to evolutionary growth because of arrested development.

The social structures of human life have paid little or no attention to the requirements for conscious evolutionary growth. Many of us have been brought up within a social structure that demands we become a "productive" member of our society; thus much emphasis is placed on developing individual skills so that we can compete with each other for survival. Inherent in this is a residual fear that if we open ourselves too much to others we may lose our competitive edge and defined sense of individuality. We have been partially programmed to play the role of victim or fighter, externalizing our troubles and our blame. Yet the responsibility has always lain within us. Similarly we have been taught to believe that what passes for consciousness is simply a by-product of our mind's complexity and is purely an extra feature, and further that it is something that we should manipulate for our physical survival. And the spirit? Well, that has never been proven, has it? But if it makes you feel better, and if it adds to the quality of your life, then what's the harm? Well, the harm is that many of our modern "rational" societies have developed in detriment to conscious evolution.

Western science, which for the last millennia has asserted itself as a dominant force, has been at pains to stress that matter is primary and that consciousness is secondary to our reality. This emphasis on the primacy of matter promotes a materialistic lifestyle. After all, if this is the only life there is (as we are led to believe) then why not live it to the max in sensual gratification and extreme consumerism?

This level of consciousness creates the game-play reality that is ideal for ongoing social control. The modern worldview, which denies the primacy of consciousness, is fostering forms of human alienation, both psychological and social. Human beings are in need of meaning and significance as much as they are in need of air to breathe and food to eat. It is a great paradox that modern science has produced a view of the cosmos that has no room for consciousness. In these shifting years it is important that each person not only recognizes the primacy of consciousness but also begins to acknowledge the energetic potential of this reality.

Our distant human ancestors saw the world around them very differently. For them, life existed as a vibrant matrix of connected, living energies. Each stone, flower, buzzing insect, played a role. Each spoke to everything else. All matter, organic or inorganic, was in correspondence. The line between living and nonliving was blurred. There was a sense of communion virtually nonexistent today. Nowadays the average person is unaware of the affinities that bind the interior and exterior realms. In one way the physical world used to be softer and less defined. Life was permeated by a mosaic of energetic affinities and correspondences. Biology was not restricted to within the membrane of bodies but was bound to the heavenly movements. Human patterns mirrored their cosmic counterparts. Their rhythms were joined in fusion, influencing human function. Today we know such correspondences as bio-rhythms, such as the twenty-four-hour circadian rhythms. It is said that humans breathe an average of 25,920 times per day, the same number of years for a full precession of the equinox (the number of years it takes for the sun to complete a full cycle of the zodiac). Similarly the average human life span of seventy-two years contains the same number of days. Our ancient ancestors knew of such biological interconnectedness. They knew too of the interrelatedness of consciousness and mind: of how the field of consciousness acts as an extended mind and thus how thoughts connect species and groups. Further they knew that thoughts are not so much created within an individual mind but are impressions received from the interpenetrating collective mind. Living in such a reality where consciousness was primary meant that no thought or action was separate or without consequence; all of life was inextricably woven together.

Many ancient teachings have revealed that universal order is a mind-before-matter manifestation. In other words, Mind (or consciousness) is the fundamental basis underlying Matter. Connection with the mental universe, through internalized affinities and correspondences, was taught to be vital for a harmonious relationship with the external physical world. Matter could be approached through the sphere of the Mind. Creativity was inherent within the power of the imagination.

The tragedy of humankind is that we have almost no suspicion about the powerful conscious energies inherent in our collective psyche. The present collective fear about Armageddon and end times (as discussed in the previous chapter) may itself be a manifestation of the deterioration of our energetic collective psyche. This tremendous energy source has been tapped into through deliberate and cunning use of media manipulation of mythological images, collective stereotypes, and subconscious signifiers that play on our collective vulnerabilities. The result is that we have now arrived at global critical times, with all focus and attention placed externally onto physical trappings, material gains, and security fears.

Any society or civilization, which makes the material world its sole pursuit and object of concern, cannot but devolve in the long run. Such misappropriation of energy has been partly responsible for creating the present chaotic situation of our world. It is imperative that humankind attains its evolutionary target at any cost. The alternative of not doing so would be a blow both to Nature and the survival of our species. As philosopher and mystic J. G. Bennett has written:

Man didn't come into this world for nothing. Man is an extraordinary achievement that has required long and difficult preparation. This achievement is not complete. It would be quite a considerable cosmic disaster if this experiment with man on this Earth were to fail, and for this reason much is being done to prevent this experiment from failing—not because man deserves to survive, but because he is really needed.[1]

It is therefore imperative that people begin to break away from the conditioning enslavement of our social matrixes and make intentional efforts to participate in our own conscious experiences. We need to make our mental focus and conscious potential a part of our everyday experience. This includes being conscious of the type of impacts we receive, and to avoid those impacts and influences that are negative. Since like attracts like it is important that we each encourage ourselves through exposure to more positive forms of influence. For example, true words encourage us and give us strength, because we instinctively recognize truthfulness—our bodies react to this, even if indirectly as through galvanic skin response, pupil response, or electrical nerve responses. In short, our bodies *feel* the essence of what impacts us, and negative or false information weakens us. This concept was researched scientifically through testing muscle strength. Dr. David Hawkins has written extensively on how muscle testing shows that various impacts create either strong or weak reactions from the body. In his work he relates how people who listened to lies exhibited a weakened muscle reaction, while those who listened to positive words and statements showed a strong muscle response. According to Dr. Hawkins:

We have at our fingertips a means of accurately distinguishing truth from falsehood, workable from unworkable, benevolent from malign. We can illuminate the hidden forces, hitherto overlooked, that determine human behavior. We have at our disposal a means of finding answers to previously unresolved personal and social problems. Falsehood need no longer hold sway over our lives.[2]

In his work Dr. Hawkins further mentions the lower-energy attractors that serve as negative, energy-depleting emotions such as shame, guilt, apathy, grief, fear, desire, anger, and pride. Higher-energy attractors are the welfare or positive emotions such as courage, neutrality, willingness, acceptance, reason, love, and joy. However, he also notes that more than 99 percent of humans calibrate below the level of joy. Now, this is something which surely needs to be changed.

We should not be afraid to say no to insane conditions and demands. We need to accept the possibility of self-evolution and the larger potential for conscious evolution, to work on our inner feelings and perceptions, and to shift toward a positive understanding of the capacity and potential of our human resources. In other words, to feel empowered and not powerless, to possess an inner confidence that allows us also to work in our external environments in the ways most appropriate. The art of living with a vibrant human consciousness is about bringing the creative energy and perspective of the inner world of spirit into a specific and positive focus on the external world of global needs.

Many of our social institutions discourage us from finding our own personal center; we are distracted from ourselves and coerced to focus on the material, external world and its disturbances as well as its petty invasions. However, it is often the case that during moments of cultural and social breakup and/or disturbance the human mind works with an energy and intensity not manifested when social patterns are stable and monotone. At such dynamic periods there can be the realization that no individual is isolated, that each person is interwoven into a vibrant network and web of psychological, emotional, and spiritual mutual exchange and interrelation. Such realizations can be heightened during periods, such as now, when it appears that human consciousness is moving through a transition time of potential change and growth.

The growth of human consciousness has been speeding up not only over the past decades but for centuries. This is partly why the social matrix has upped its mechanisms of control, from discipline to surveillance societies, overt security threats and terrorism, and cultural programming of fear and the Armageddon meme. Now, however, collective human consciousness is close to reaching a tipping point. Subtlety is giving way to new ways people are manifesting awareness and intuitive understanding. There are instances of breakthroughs in the new sciences, in consciousness studies, in the popularity for mysticism and esoteric teachings, and so forth, all of which indicate that a new spurt of evolutionary growth is at hand. It is interesting to note that according to the research of Dr. David Hawkins, human consciousness was dangling below the 200 level (190)* for many centuries before it suddenly rose to its present higher level some time in the mid-1980s. The overall average level of human consciousness stands at 207 (as of mid-1990). Hence, many past predictions and prophecies of doom may have been avoided because they relate to a time when human consciousness was below the 200 level. The world staying at levels below 200 over a prolonged period of time would, says Dr. Hawkins, cause a great imbalance that would likely lead to the destruction of humanity. When one's consciousness falls below 200 at any given moment a person begins to lose power and thus grow weaker and more prone to be manipulated by one's surroundings, says Hawkins. Now, however, human consciousness is on the rise, and as it rises it has the capacity to affect—or infect—other minds. A chart in Hawkins's book *Power vs. Force: The Hidden Determinants of Human Behavior* summarizes the following:

The power of the few individuals at the top counterbalances the weakness of the masses:

---

*This is Dr. Hawkins's scale for calibrating the level of human consciousness according to his Map of Consciousness.

1 individual at level 300 counterbalances 90,000 individuals
   below level 200

1 individual at level 400 counterbalances 400,000 individuals
   below level 200

1 individual at level 500 counterbalances 750,000 individuals
   below level 200

1 individual at level 600 counterbalances 10 million individuals
   below level 200

1 individual at level 700 counterbalances 70 million individuals
   below level 200.[3]

What this tells us, very meaningfully, is that as human consciousness rises it has an exponential capacity to affect others like an expanding energy wave. No wonder there has been so much effort to restrain the rise of human consciousness—it is an exponential field of force!

In effect what is occurring is that there are now parallel movements taking place: the *upward* shift toward accelerated conscious energies, and the *downward* pull toward global control and containment of the human spirit. It is literally a tug-of-war—what I have referred to as the war for human consciousness. That is why it is essential that as a collective species we win this war of minds. And it is my full understanding that we will win. Why do I say this? Because it is part of our evolutionary trajectory, and there are many signposts indicating this.

We have spoken of the 2012 Mayan calendar date and its attendant cultural baggage. It may well be that 2012 will act as a signpost: a signifier of the future. For when we pass this date—and we will pass it—we will know, collectively, that there is a future awaiting us. Further this future will require our conscious participation, especially since we will have been relieved of some of the fear baggage. This relief that 2012 passed without global Armageddon is likely to release a new wave of energies. Despite the efforts by manipulative social forces to turn 2012 into a focus of fear, it may serve instead as a catalyst for change.* This could well mark the beginning of change, as peoples' minds respond to the ongoing manipulative forces by changing the mental game play. The state of human consciousness may then be directed toward efforts to raise and assist the energies of our Earth. Our conscious energies may then fully utilize our immense potential for connection, collaboration, and creativity.

A PLANETARY EMERGENCE

The social philosopher Marshall McLuhan was an early pioneer in understanding how our communication networks could enhance our global consciousness. His now-famous phrase *the global village* refers to how McLuhan envisioned the world transforming into a global nervous system, connecting each individual into a distributed web of conscious sharing. This would be the beginning of a new social mind that would converge into a shared global consciousness. This expansive *neural net* would be a catalyst for how people begin to realize their depths of involvement with one another as a connected human community. McLuhan even went as far as stating that the basis for evolution would dramatically shift away from a Darwinian involuntary process toward being a part of collaborative human consciousness.[4] To some degree we have witnessed this in how people globally have been using the Internet to form constructive social networks in order to question and protest against social injustices and abuses of power. This was displayed most effectively in the antigovernment protests that began in the Arab world within the first month of 2011. As if the smell of revolution was in the air protestors in Tunisia managed to successfully oust their president and his corrupt regime, followed by huge demonstrations throughout Egypt against the regime of Hosni Mubarak. These Egyptian protests were so

*This would in fact be closer to the Mayan significance of 2012; that it marks passage to the "yellow sun" energy, a cycle of higher vibrations.

potent and organized that the Egyptian ruling regime suspended all national Internet and mobile-phone operations. Similar antiregime protests also began to erupt in Jordan, Syria, Bahrain, and Yemen. In this sense the increase in human interactions facilitated by these global communication networks are concentrating and multiplying human mental and psychic energies. Many people have referred to this increasing phenomenon as the Global Brain. Peter Russell was an early indicator of how this accelerated connectivity could catalyze an awakening within human consciousness and our neuronal structures.[5] Some, like Russell, have speculated that this could then lead toward a form of global-social *superorganism*. Another way to look at this is that by stimulating the nervous system into receiving and processing ever-increasing amounts of energy, it will act as a precursor to how humanity is prepared to utilize increased vibratory energies. Of course, not everyone uses such communication networks. Also, as I discussed earlier there are caveats in doing so; it leaves us wide open to abuse such as the dissemination of misinformation as well as disruptive signals (such as explicit sexual imagery).

My response to this would be that there are multiple forms that our next evolutionary phase can utilize and put into play. The important point here is that change will come *through our social and cultural forms* and not by avoiding them. Part of winning the war of minds is by creating a conscious (mental and psychic) shift from within our daily lives and within our social matrixes. We thus make use of the tools that are already available to us. The appropriation of communication networks comes at a time when increased energies are already impacting the Earth, as I discuss later in this chapter. All these impacts play a part in our next evolutionary stage of development, which I have termed neurogenetic evolution (see chapter 7).

Similarly the Jesuit priest Pierre Teilhard de Chardin explored through various works how the increased complexification of social organisms (specifically human life) would eventually converge to form a mass formation or "planetization." De Chardin felt that a stage would be reached whereby a global species could no longer develop except through an intense form of social "interpenetration."[6] The core of de Chardin's work was the creation of a noosphere, a term coined in 1925 that envisioned, in contrast to the biosphere, a global interrelated system of organized thought and consciousness. This noosphere (a term now very popular on the Internet, for obvious reasons) was seen by de Chardin as being a synthesis of mind obtained by a global uniting and as part of the patterned development of evolution. In other words, it represented what is nowadays referred to as conscious (or psychic) evolution; as such it signals the neurogenetic path of evolution necessitated by the ending of the biological-cultural evolutionary stream. As de Chardin noted in the first half of the twentieth century:

> It may well be that in its individual capacities and penetrations our brain has reached its organic limits. But the movement does not stop there. From west to east, evolution is henceforth occupied elsewhere, in a richer and more complex domain, constructing, with all minds joined together, mind. Beyond all nations and races, the inevitable taking-as-a-whole of mankind has already begun.[7]

De Chardin is clearly describing here a collective, unified soul of humankind, which he has referred to as a conspiracy of individuals who are intent on developing forward through the evolutionary journey of humankind. It takes enough minds to break away from conditioned thought, the relics of old energy systems, and to allow, in de Chardin's words, for the universe to be raised in and through the human species. By a process of mindful growth it may come about that the "world's evolution towards spirit has become conscious."[8] This is, if nothing else, part of our globally shared mythologies.

Indeed, we need to once again reengage with our mythological mind, to the thought processes of our collective unconscious, and to be more open to our intuitions. We have entered and passed through a historical period of collective amnesia whereby our minds have been subjected to stunted growth. We can look upon this time as a form of psychic arrested development. It is a shame that so few of us ever question the information that is deliberately fed to us throughout our lives. Do we really believe that this planet, our Earth, has only been home to a six-thousand-year-old history of civilization? Are we to accept that the early Mesopotamian cultures, such as Sumer, were the only precursors to civilization? Or that humans are the only sentient creatures to have roamed this terrestrial domain? Why do we ridicule people who attempt to put forward an alternative history? Why do our "experts" decline and even mock those anomalies that lie outside our accepted histories? In short, why have we, as a collective species, grown so shortsighted and fundamental in our thinking? We have suffered too long this tragedy of a collective myopia—a state of species amnesia conditioned into us through the social systems that bring us up and supposedly nurture us. We have been bred to forget and to comply, consume, and play ball.

A *planetization* may be under way that utilizes global channels of communication as a medium for catalyzing and sensitizing the collective mind. This "sparking" of the global mind has been hinted at during, for example, various transpersonal meditation practices. Christopher Bache, a transpersonal psychologist, has made intriguing investigations into the collective psyche of humanity. Bache's many and varied investigations during transpersonal sessions led him to the revelation that humanity, in facing an environmental and species catastrophe, will be catalyzed into a "great awakening." The focus of this transformative process, Bache tells us, is not individual but applies to our entire species and signifies a shift toward a unified field of awareness. Bache experienced this revelatory event as both something to be accomplished and something already accomplished. In this sense the evolutionary transition is established as inevitable; the question is rather how we, as individuals, respond and cope with the transition.

Bache sees this shift as a quantum jump in our evolutionary status that will lead to a sudden reorganization of global culture. It signals "a turning-point that would forever divide the human story into the before and after of THE GREAT AWAKENING."[9] Up until now people (the masses) have been deliberately isolated and shielded from the knowledge about this shift that is set to occur within our species. However, we are not totally blind, as we are endowed with intelligence that will guide and prepare us for the shift ahead. Bache sees this collective conscious awakening as a unified field becoming more aware of itself. He visualized this as a network, or web, of flashes beginning to stabilize and connect.

> I repeatedly saw extended webs of energy suddenly contract and explode in brilliant flashes. In the past these flashes had not endured long and had been swallowed by the inertia of the collective unconscious of our species. Now, however, the flashes were beginning to hold their own. Not only were they not dissolving, but they were beginning to connect with other flashes occurring around the planet.[10]

Bache reveals that this is a stage of purification for our collective species; a period when humanity is required to become more consciously aware and to rid itself of negativity and psychological trauma. In other words, we must collectively cleanse ourselves in order to bring in the more refined energies.

It appears that there are emergent signs of many people on our planet now beginning to wake up to the situation of our collective control and the suppression of our conscious faculties. Despite the vast resources being employed to put humanity under a collective hypnosis through the manipulation of fear, negativity, disinformation, and distraction, an emergent awakening is under way. There is now an exponentially increasing mass of us who are waking up, and in many and varied ways. Recent destabilizing events in our financial and political spheres have drawn people's focus to the corruption, exploitation, and lies that are being perpetrated against us in a bid to preserve power and dominate through greed. Even the global upsurge in religious fundamentalism has drawn people's attention not only to the deficit of spiritual values in our major religions but also to how religion is being used as a tool for furthering social, psychic/spiritual, and emotional control. There is a definite turning of the tide under way, a shifting of our minds as more and more people wake up to the "reality" that we are living within a false construction—a matrix of deception, denial, and distraction. And that this has led us, on this planet, to a serious imbalance and disharmony with our relationship to natural and psychic forces. This trancelike grip on our collective consciousness is being rapidly stripped away as an energetic force—an evolutionary pulse—enters our present time-space locality. People are awakening to the possibility that there is so much more to our lives than a materialistic and consumer-based lifestyle. Perhaps the magic is returning to reengage humanity with our mythological selfhood. Social philosopher and thinker William Irwin Thompson describes this metaphorically as similar to how a higher intelligence may attempt to communicate with a lower form of intelligence through the disruptive, yet energetic, periods that mark the ending and beginning of social-cultural cycles.

Imagine that you have just discovered a civilization as small as a DNA molecule. You want to establish contact, but since your dimensions prevent you from entering the same space-time envelope, you must search for other means of communication. From observing the civilization closely, you find that there is an informational class that seems to carry messages back and forth among parts of the society, and you observe further that these messengers are actually enzymes of a structure that is isomorphic to one of your own patterns of information. Since you cannot talk directly to the members of the civilization, you decide to talk through a patterning of the bits of information the enzymes carry back and forth. Unfortunately, the very act of trying to pattern an enzyme alters its structure so that a part of your own message is always shifted. It seems that the only time the enzymes are able to carry a high proportion of your own message is when their civilizational structure is either breaking apart or just about to come together again. Fascinated by the problem, you choose your opening and closing epochs carefully and begin to carry on an extended conversation with the civilization.[11]

As the energy of the "old civilization" of power, control, corruption, and deceit begins to fall apart, new forms of consciousness arise that have the capacity to catalyze a global awakening of minds. In other words, a planetary emergence is taking place that is a crucial step in winning the war of minds.

In this next phase of our psychic growth it is important that spiritual values not be shrugged away or brushed under the carpet. No longer shall it be necessary to hide the expression of spiritual thought within coded texts, cloaked gatherings, or embarrassed whispers. Such compassionate inner energy should be once again released into creative forms and shared experiences, as did our shamanic forefathers. People who lock their psychic energy into dying, rigid forms will find it difficult to accept and adapt to the new pulse of life. Such people will be attracted and attuned to the Armageddon meme and dragged into negativity and fear. This age-old system of psychic terror has been practiced for eons, as testified, for example, by the practice of Aztec human sacrifice. It is said that the Aztec priests would deliberately prolong the human sacrifice in a dramatic manner in order to build up the astral emanations of the victim and the entranced spectators. This sacrificial display would climax in the ripping out of the human heart and flinging it down the pyramid steps in an act to seal the collective conscious of the people in a state of awe and fear of the ruling priesthood. In a similar manner Nazi Germany utilized such collectivization through terror and public propaganda to seal their occult and political authority. Such collectivization of terror—as described in previous chapters—has been an ongoing strategy for power and control over the burgeoning masses. Yet this, I contend, belongs to the old energies and is a dying system. Because of this, the power systems entrenched in our global societies are fighting and struggling for one last, ultimate grasp for power. Like a flailing fish out of water they are struggling for a last breath. As Professor Needleman so aptly remarked, "The esoteric is the heart of civilization. And should the outward forms of a human civilization become totally unable to contain and adapt the energies of great spiritual teachings, then that civilization has ceased to serve its function in the universe."[12]

It may be that new necessities also bring into being new functions. And it just so happens that the universe appears to be shifting into new and heightened dynamics, a stage of excitability that may just stimulate the terrestrial human mind into accelerated activity and wakefulness.

A PERIOD OF ENERGETIC EXCITABILITY?

During Solar Cycle 24 (2009–2020) scientists are expecting an increase in sun activity, coronal mass ejections (CMEs), and solar storms. It is also likely that during this cycle there will be a noticeable increase in magnetic fluctuations arriving on Earth. Exactly what the implications will be for the biosphere and the human body are unclear. Those who are more energetically sensitive may experience an increase in intensity during this period. And if the magnetic interference becomes markedly increased, as it may well do over the next decade, then many people could become consciously affected by the changes, albeit not fully knowing or understanding why. According to some reports we could be heading into a period of heightened excitability both for the solar system and for humanity.

As mentioned, geophysicists Alexey Dmitriev and Vladimir B. Baranov have indicated that the solar system has entered a more highly energized region of space. And this extra "donation" of energy is creating excited energy states in all planets in our solar system, including the sun. This turbulent region, it appears, is making the sun hotter and stormier and has already caused climate changes on several planets.

> Effects here on Earth are to be found in the acceleration of the magnetic pole shift, in the vertical and horizontal ozone content distribution, and in the increased frequency and magnitude of significant catastrophic climatic events. There is growing probability that we are moving into a rapid temperature instability period similar to the one that took place 10,000 years ago. The adaptive responses of the biosphere, and humanity, to these new conditions may lead to a total global revision of the range of species and life on Earth.[13]

The authors write that the exposure to an increased energized stellar region will affect our planet's own energetic capacity for growth, as it will result in some of Earth's systems being in a highly charged and excited state. This also infers that the human body as well as the human psyche will come under increased "charged and excited" impact. Yet this is not all; it now appears that the human mind is affected by being aligned with the black hole at the center of our Milky Way galaxy.

At the very center of our galaxy there is what astrophysicists call a supermassive black hole that rotates every eleven minutes. As is synonymous with the name, the density of this black hole is so great that not even light itself can escape. The gravitational energy of the supermassive black hole is so great that it actually flattens out to form an energy plane, almost like a disk. This energy center, together with its spin and radiating energy plane, immerses the Milky Way with pulses—or bursts—of energy. Much of the fabric of our galaxy, solar system, and Earth is affected by these energy bursts. There has never been a time when this energy has not influenced life on Earth. Some palaeontologists have speculated that fossil remains indicate moments of sporadic evolutionary bursts that could have resulted from increased cosmic radiations. Scientific researcher Paul LaViolette goes further and explicitly states that the energy core at the center of our galaxy emits huge gamma-ray bursts in cyclic durations, and that these pulses have been responsible for historical cataclysms and major Earth changes.[14] What this indicates is that aside from whether our solar system is currently moving through an energized stellar region or not, there are powerful cyclic energy forces that may have incredible influence over our sun and our solar system's planets. This in turn will affect the conditions of life on Earth. Since all forms of life are themselves patterns of energy (matter is formed from condensed energy), then this suggests there may be unknown impacts on the collective psyche of the human species. We don't need to have a Ph.D. in space science to know that in winter months many people suffer from light deficiency, which causes depression, lack of energy, and a lapse in attention spans. Similarly in summer months there is an increase in creativity, energy states, and motivation. As to the link with the galactic energy core, this is, I do admit, more a case of speculation. There is, however, emerging scientific study that is now validating these hypotheses.

Researcher Dr. James Spottiswoode discovered that ordinary people become more psychic during the time when Earth is aligned with the galactic center. This occurs during a moment of local sidereal time (LST), which measures the Earth's movement in relation to the position of the stars and their twenty-six-thousand-year vernal equinox. Spottiswoode discovered this during twenty years of research of laboratory studies of the phenomena of extra sensory perception (ESP). In an existing database of 1,468 free response trials, he found a 340 percent effect size increase for trials within one hour of the peak time of 13.30 local sidereal time. This is apparent evidence of a causal connection between psychic capacity and the orientation of the receiver, and the earth and the fixed stars/galactic center.[15] While this does not suggest that the masses are making a radical jump into a psychic population, it does infer that there are incoming energies/radiations that affect the psyche of humanity. This further indicates that there may be periods in which the psychic development of humanity is aided and supported by cosmic circumstances. During these periods we should take advantage of such "energetic excitability" to increase our own mental awareness and participate in creative change. Or at the very least to be aware of the controlling forces in our lives and to make active decisions to separate from such imposed social somnambulism.

Psychiatrist and teacher Maurice Nicoll often stated that most people do not realize that they are invisible. Instead we are living in a world of invisible people, most of whom are blind to their inner lives. The Russian philosopher and mystic P. D. Ouspensky (a friend and colleague of Nicoll) was more explicit in saying that

> . . . man as we know him is not a completed being; that nature develops him only up to a certain point and then leaves him, either to develop further, by his own efforts and devices, or to live and die such as he was born, or to degenerate and lose capacity for development. Evolution of man . . . will mean the development of certain inner qualities and features, which usually remain undeveloped, and cannot develop by themselves.[16]

The social matrix that has formed within modern technocultures has stunted and made more difficult these processes for developing a person's inner life. The construction of credit-debt-ridden societies indentured to a virtual economic system has also, whether directly or indirectly, contributed to the lessening of developmental influences. The potential, and capacity for further growth along a path of conscious evolution has been smeared with a massive amount of disinformation and false paths. It has served the elite power structure well that in general people have not awakened to the understanding that humanity possesses incredible capacity and inherent resources for creative development and evolutionary expansion. This struggle over the conscious mind of humanity, which has been going on in various forms for eons, is coming to a crux in our present generation as varying external influences are manifesting that will have an "activating" effect upon the human psyche. Some of these impacts will be in terms of solar/galactic radiations and fluctuations in the electromagnetic spectrum of Earth.* Other impacts will affect our world, such as further breakdowns in social structures and increasing civil unrest. Already in 2011 we saw the Arab Spring revolutions, the many people protests in European countries (such as the *indignados* in Spain), and the Occupy protests that began in the U.S. and have spread worldwide.

The fracture and breakup of some social systems (as seen in the global financial markets) represent a stage whereby humanity has need of overcoming—rather, growing beyond—past structures of conditioning and management. These signals indicate that new ways of awareness, consciousness, function, and organization are required in relation to an evolving path rather than a path of stagnation and halted growth. Social knowledge systems have failed to inform the people that inner evolution is a built-in human mechanism, and as such is an essential part of us. Thus Nature brings us only so far—it is up to us to continue the journey of inner development. The capacity to have intuitive understanding and perceptive thoughts is a functional matter; it has nothing to do with being rewarded or specially chosen. Inner growth is not something that a person "earns" (despite what various gurus might say); rather, a person becomes capable of receiving new perceptions (see chapter 9). As the Sufi mystic and poet Rumi wrote: "New organs of perception

---

*Earth changes and geophysical disturbances alter the EM spectrum of the Earth and also, solar gravitational forces. Remember: at this present time the Earth has a hole in its magnetic field the size of California.

come into being as a result of necessity / Therefore, O man, increase your necessity, so that you may increase your perception." Similarly, the English poet William Blake wrote: "If Perceptive Organs vary, Objects of Perception seem to vary / If Perceptive Organs close, their Objects seem to close also." Many of us have only a hazy sense of the inner self that mainly consists of conditioned images, beliefs, and allowed alternative thought streams. Part of the process of the struggle for our minds consists of slowly detaching from dependence on external forms of institutional knowledge (consensus information), materialistic distractions, convoluted and brain-draining forms of entertainment, and subservience to externally manipulated forms of fear. The transition includes developing a real and gratifying sense of personal strength, a sense of responsibility that lies within, an expanding awareness to the lies and manipulation of social institutions and bodies, and a growing realization that great change is needed both personally and on a worldwide scale. Rather than not even considering the possibility of inner development, it should be a question of us not being able to avoid this primary core requirement. Again quoting Rumi:

> There is one thing in this world that you must never forget to do. If you forget everything else and not this, there's nothing to worry about; but if you remember everything else and forget this, then you will have done nothing in your life. It's as if a king has sent you to some country to do a task, and you perform a hundred other services, but not the one he sent you to do.

As we recover the recognition (or burning intuitive sense) of needing to assist in our personal task of inner growth, we are likely to feel more resistance to any external structure that attempts to have control over how we think. We will come to realize that manipulation of our consciousness is a much more insidious and menacing action than the more overt methods for controlling our physical, external lives.

* * *

As discussed earlier regarding the psychoanalytical background to propaganda studied by Edward Bernays, insidious control also operates on a subconscious level, such as by means of instilling fear into people through economic uncertainties. Our awareness of these machinations must, as Rumi reminds us, come through the awakening of our own *organs of perception*. These are not necessarily literal organs of flesh and blood but rather are our capacities for recognition and understanding of spiritual realities that can further lead to a rise in conscious awareness. In other words, the best defense against these forces is knowing about them: "If you know about them, you are protected. . . . But you must not be idle about acquiring real knowledge of these things."[17] Our real power against controlling forces is to remember that *we become what we think*. Another way to consider this is through the New Testament's idea of "repentance," which, rather than referring to a confession of one's sins (which is an ecclesiastical ritual based yet again on dominance) instead refers to the notion of *metanoia*. This purer notion asks a person to work toward changing her thinking; literally, to change one's mind by moving beyond present preconceived notions and limiting patterns of thought.

This ongoing war against human consciousness is aimed toward showing the human being as an unfocused, fearful, weak entity that has no inner vision of strength. This manipulated reflection will serve to further weaken people as their social environments experience periods of disturbance and breakdown—economic, social austerity, security issues, and so on. By understanding these underhanded and coercive processes each of us can sustain our own sense of meaning—*of spirit*—in the face of these uncertain times. We must be on our guard against the encroachment of negativity. This is another control mechanism: to introduce negativity within our lives in order to weaken our thought processes. To allow negativity to roam within our minds will result in the deterioration of our will to move forward and develop. Negativity is another meme—or rather a *virus*—that takes away our self-confidence and creative energies for defying the fear-fueled world around us. Rather than being offered alternatives to the path our societies are moving on (materialism/rationalism/dominance) we are ceaselessly being told there is no option but to operate on old habits of competition and force. These distractions serve to turn people's minds outward onto external concerns and back to the tooth-and-claw struggle for survival—our social Darwinism. This diversion away from our inner knowing sustains a "reality" based on continual fighting, aggression, inequality, and hierarchical power structures that we willingly submit to. Change will just seem too grand a concept for our weak selves to cope with. In other words, leave change for the authorities to cope with, and we will accept their just decisions. This is *not winning the war of minds*.

The violence, suffering, and destruction that have plagued human societies for eons are results of an imposed way of life that has for far too long been viewed (and even accepted) as the norm for our post-Neanderthal species.* This has led to the breakdown of connections and communications within modern social communities, and even among humans worldwide as well as between humans and Nature. However, as this chapter has been explaining, global communications have been shaping a new empathic global mind. I hope that as our decentralized communication networks continue to connect our diverse cultures the younger generations will grow up with a catalysed, empathic mind-set. It may also be the case that newer generations are born with enhanced psychic capacities (as will be explored in chapter 7). As it stands, our youth learn and grow by observing and copying; that is, they mimic their elders and peers. Modern societies know very well how to produce adults without security or self-esteem, to dull the natural intelligence, creativity, and vision of individuals. The result is too many people with limited capacities of selfhood and inner authority. Yet the tide has been turning for some time now; only it has taken

---

*Researchers in Germany have discovered recently that modern humans share some of their DNA with the ancient Neanderthals.

until relatively recently for these changes in human consciousness to manifest both within our external structures as well as in our internal perceptions. Many of us are feeling a sense that something is amiss, that something is badly out of shape, but we can't quite put our finger on it. Until now, that is.

REVITALIZING THE HUMAN MATRIX

The limitations imposed on human consciousness have served to shut down whole areas of brain functioning and to block the intuitive and inner perceptive faculties. This has largely been achieved through an educational/institutional conditioning that strengthens the left side of the brain (linear, rational, mechanistic, and competitive) while subduing the expression of the right side (creative, abstract, cooperative, and visual). However, now that the Earth is celestially moving into a different cyclic part along our precession of the equinoxes, it appears that different energies (solar/cosmic radiations) are impacting our planet. These energetic shifts may lead to electrical influences upon the human nervous system that thus affect our quantum consciousness (to be discussed in chapter 7). On a physical level it appears that these impacts have already influenced our social structures in that those that are aligned with the older energies are finding it increasingly more difficult to sustain themselves during this transition period. As these structures—economic, political, and social—begin to show their corrupt underpinnings, the realization of the veil that has been pulled over us will become clearer. This realization will help to speed up and catalyze the human awakening to the "terror of the situation."* By affirming the new reality of change we can not only minimize the disruptions to our personal lives but also we will align to the universal law that *nothing endures but change.*

---

*This is the well-known phrase used by the mystic G. I. Gurdjieff. Similarly, we might also add Kurtz's final words, "The horror! The horror!" in Conrad's *The Heart of Darkness.*

Everything is BECOMING and CHANGING. Nothing stands still. . . . There is no reality, enduring quality, fixity, or substantiality in anything—nothing is permanent but Change . . . a constant action and reaction; inflow and outflow; building up and tearing down; creation and destruction; birth, growth and death.[18]

As with the changing seasons we can prepare for springtime on planet Earth. With positive feedback we can filter our mental energies back through our worldwide decentralized communication systems in an effort to shift from a competitive to an empathic global civilization.[19] That is, we can begin to utilize our global forms of communication to usher in a new model of human consciousness.

Communication is our new global energy. The first industrial revolution was made on the discovery of coal and steam. This fired up our Western industries and ushered in new forms of social containment (urban) and controls (the factory, scientific management). This top-down hierarchical revolution was central to fueling the dominance of Western imperialism. The second industrial revolution can be said to have been the development of electronics in the latter half of the twentieth century, which culminated in the Internet. This revolution, which has given the world mobile computing, is distributed but dominated by corporate giants of media (see chapter 3) and creates an intricate global web of surveillance and databasing. The third industrial revolution, which is now emerging, will be a convergence of distributed communications (based on bottom-up open systems) combined with the new energies of a globally aware "planetary mind." This is very likely to open the way toward a form of distributed consciousness. Already the human brain is wired differently today, as each new revolution creates a rewiring of the brain. Distributed communications will foster increased stimulus for the right side of the brain that will help to diminish linear thinking and replace it with a connected, collaborative consciousness. Worldwide control and containment strategies/institutions will be opposed through an emerging planetary empathic nervous system that will see a different planet within two generations, perhaps less. Humanity already contains the seeds of these conscious potentials.

Along with the spread of a globally emerging empathic consciousness a natural acceptance of spiritual realities may also manifest. A focus of one's mind and mental energies will help us to not take things so personally or to be overidentified with personal attacks or distractions. Part of the ongoing smokescreen has been to irritate and fluster the masses in general by a variety of external impacts. However, we must learn how to focus on events at hand without being shut off to the world around us. This change occurring over the next generation will usher in a fresh dynamic energy that will dismantle many people's conditioned passivity and fears. We can refer to this as a type of mental transmutation whereby each person actively takes a creative role in changing and transforming her own mental state. After all, according to ancient Hermetic teachings the "Universe is mental."[20]

The mental game play is changing, and we will witness increased frenetic activity on the part of the ruling powers to maintain their social matrixes of fear, suppression, and coercive forces. A healthy relationship with our immediate environments—our family, friends, and community—will be beneficial during this period as we turn away from materialistic self-indulgence, selfishness, and isolated individualism and toward badly needed cooperative and co-creative relationships. Our mental faculties will be taxed as they shift away from the "safe shelter" of fear-ridden false securities. As historian Lewis Mumford has noted:

Every transformation of man . . . has rested on a new metaphysical and ideological base; or rather, upon deeper stirrings and intuitions whose rationalized expression takes the form of a new picture of the cosmos and the nature of man . . . In carrying [human] . . . self-transformation to this further stage, world culture may bring about a fresh release of spiritual energy that will unveil new potentialities, no more visible in the human self today than radium was in the physical world a century ago, though always present.[21]

It is likely that accompanying these perceptual and cultural changes will be a new and deeper appreciation of humanity's position in the cosmos in the ongoing journey of our species evolution. In a manner similar to Mumford, British historian Arnold Toynbee referred to the possible transfiguration of modern society into some kind of *re-spiritualized* form. As our global society goes through the tumults of a reorganization—or a transfiguration—I consider it likely that fresh energies will not only filter into cultural and social forms but will also radiate into the global collective human consciousness. We are, in one way or another, about to enter into a period of neurological rewiring. During this process the attacks against human consciousness (our thinking and emotions) will dramatically increase, as mentioned previously. However, the arrival of heightened perceptions within increasing numbers of people will significantly alter our social-cultural relations as well as people's relations with Nature. People will learn to adjust to this as their energies begin to stabilize and perceptions adjust into greater alignment with more empathic and creative forces. Our relations with social and political institutions will necessarily undergo a major change as people will instinctively know/feel when they are being lied to.

At present it is as if humanity is looking out at the world and the cosmos with one and a half eyes closed. We are on the verge of stepping into a new era of human consciousness but as yet our current levels of thinking are not adequate to take us into this renewal. However, just as each new evolutionary leap in human progress has been accompanied by a parallel leap in human thinking, so too will there be a shift in our collective consciousness. Our "primitive" ancestors did not perceive the same world that we perceive today with our senses. We perceive so little of our world, constrained to a tiny part of the electromagnetic spectrum, and further within this limited segment we have been conditioned through ideology and dogma to accept particular sets of thought and behavior. Yet variability can work both ways; just as the human mind is vulnerable to manipulation and programming, so too is it sensitive and responsive to catalytic stimuli that can assist in its developmental rewiring. How the mind is rewired affects our very image of the universe and all phenomena observed. Our position, both within life and within our universe, is thus a creation of our mind; as such these perceptions and understandings morph in relation to the perceptive capacities of our minds. Continued evolution carries within it the inherent capacity for transfigured mental, emotional, and spiritual perceptive faculties/organs within the human species. At each stage we manage material energies and create our view of the cosmos. It is somewhat a tragedy to realize that there have been a minority of players in this evolutionary drama that have attempted to spoil it for the rest of us by their manipulations. Much indigenous tribal wisdom—from Shamanism to oral knowledge—has existed for many generations to pass on our human heritage. Yet the Modernity Project, with its greed for control of material progress, has eliminated much of such knowledge and its transmission lines. It is as if a hoax has been played on human consciousness, placing it within quarantine. Now, however, the winning of this war of minds has come to our side.

A transition of human consciousness is badly needed. Without one we may be coerced into further material constraints: a world tied into diminishing resources, increasing insecurity and fears, economic depressions and financial woes, territorial aggression and ideological tensions. All these are distractions orchestrated as part of a great game to keep the lid on rising human consciousness. Our present social matrixes only serve to blunt the sensibility of human consciousness and lower our resistance to polluting forces/influences that stunt our continued development. As one mystic recently put it, the human brain is "so sensitive to the environment, so perceptive of the ills in a society and so acutely conscious of the wrongs and inequities done, at this present stage of evolution, that a sweeping change must occur in ever sphere of human life to keep it healthy and sound."[22] We must ensure that the controlling forces operating through our various global societies and networks no longer have the means whereby they can nullify and pacify the majority of people by material distractions and coercive conditioning. Humankind has achieved incredible things and scaled great heights—yet we have failed to adequately explore within ourselves and to wake-up to the *dis-ease* of our times. We must no longer succumb to this tyranny of consciousness.

A revolution in human consciousness is approaching whereby not only will humanity be receiving new impacts through physical changes/disruptions but also energetic impacts upon our physiology. It is very possible that such impacts will affect the human nervous system and catalyze a shift in the perceptual and consciousness faculties of our species. It is these issues that shall be explored in the next chapter.

7
OUR EVOLUTIONARY FUTURES
Agents of Mutation

It is vain to be always looking toward the future and never acting toward it.

JOHN FREDERICK BOYES,
ENGLISH ESSAYIST (1811–1879)

Homo non proprie humanus sed superhumanus est. *(To be properly human, you must go beyond the merely human.)*

The human being has to become what he thinks himself to be.

RUDOLF STEINER

Recent science informs us that we each carry around with us a 100-billion-cell bioelectric computer that creates our realities. Almost

---

An earlier version of this chapter was published in *World Futures* by Kingsley Dennis (2010), "Quantum Consciousness: Reconciling Science and Spirituality toward Our Evolutionary Future(s)," *World Futures* 66: 7, 511–24.

all of its 100 billion neurons were established the day we were born, with around 250,000 neurons created every minute while our bodies were forming in the womb. Still, this phenomenal "reality shaper" has undergone monumental perceptual change over our evolutionary history. However, when compared to the skeletal remains of prehistoric human beings there appears to have been no observable change in human anatomy for at least a hundred thousand years. In comparison, our human mind has taken leaps from its earliest cave-art beginnings. This suggests that we have shifted from a biological- to cultural- to a neuroevolutionary path and that further advance involves the development of the human nervous system and our consciousness. Evolution, for humanity, is as much a psychical and psychological adaption as it is physical. What is required, at this significant juncture, is another catalyst of consciousness change. In other words, new circuits need to be activated, and these depend on both internal and external impacts. As I have alluded to previously, the next step that is required will be a neurogenetic evolutionary shift. Neurogenetic evolution will be a necessary step in order to move beyond the limitations of our current developmental impasse. Civilizations in our historical past (and perhaps also in our unknown past) have collapsed as they evolved to the limits of their material resources without there being a parallel development in human consciousness. At such vital transition periods it is essential that a conscious energy force be introduced into the stream of human life in order to catalyze the next spurt in evolutionary growth. Without such conscious energy the material systems are in danger of either running out of control (as is the case now) and/or breaking down—which may also be the case in the near future. Such a conscious energy force needs to serve as an impulse to help catalyze people toward striving for their own modes of self-knowledge and understanding (self-directed actualization).

Such a pivotal step not only involves the human mind/brain and consciousness but also the human nervous system and our genetic blueprint: DNA. Such a mutational change requires a coherency between our biology—our human physiology—as well as our energetic field of consciousness. Because of this, we could say that we are at the edge of a possible *quantum evolution* of the human species. Just what is meant by this will be examined throughout this chapter. I will also allude to the occurrence of evolutionary agents of change; that is, the minority of people who are already manifesting symptoms of mutational transformation. As in any evolutionary leap there appear among the species the initial beginnings of such transformation before the change becomes more widespread. The changes that are occurring within humankind herald a new epoch for human consciousness. Humankind has an evolutionary target to attain—and it must be reached. The alternative of not doing so would be detrimental, to say the least, both to Nature and to the survival of our species.

Throughout this book I have stressed how our inner faculties and mental capacities have been kept in a form of quarantine by social forces. That is, certain faculties of perception, consciousness, and inner intuition have been stifled in order to keep the majority of humankind "manageable." This hypothesis may not suit everyone, and each of us is free to make up our own minds about our current situation (or predicament!). What I suggest is that not only is it time to literally take back our minds—our powers of self-directed thinking—and to work toward the raising of our consciousness, but also it is time for this energetic shift.

Our mode of life and our perceptual faculties now need to be orientated in favor with the potential evolutionary transformation of human consciousness. In recent years our societies—the conditioning social matrixes—have developed in detriment to conscious evolution. This is one of the major reasons behind the cultural failings of our critical times. There has been virtually no preparation—little discussion and research—into how humanity, both physically and mentally, can deal with a world in energetic change, or how a shift in the vibrations of human consciousness will affect the energy systems and nervous system of our bodies. As has been noted, the "maturing of the nervous system and the brain is a biological process, depending on a host of psychic and material factors."[1] It can be said that the inner stirrings of self-awareness within people have been strategically diverted into cultural indulgences such as religious conversion, pseudospiritualism, and a range of degenerative cults. A great amount of our unconscious energies have been channeled into wrongly directed material pursuits and as such have been instrumental in creating an unstable and radically polarized world. Yet within the collective consciousness of humanity exists a powerful and rising energy that strives to propel our species forward on an evolutionary trajectory. To stem this force would be akin to plugging up Earth's volcanoes, and could very likely lead to the disastrous scenario being dispersed through the Armageddon meme (see chapter 5). Our collective evolutionary force, in the worst-case scenario, could face a process of devolution. My contention, however, is that this will not be the case. Part of our dilemma though rests in our blindness over how our mental and perceptual faculties operate.

The human brain as a collection of nerve cells operates as a multilayered frequency receptor. Due to initial conditionings early on in life (see chapter 1) each receptor becomes wired to perceive a particular wave frequency. As the brain's receptors tune in to a particular pattern of frequency waves a pattern-recognition response is received by the brain and interpreted according to the perceptions allotted to the frequency. In other words, the act of tuning in involves picking up familiar frequency patterns out of the ocean of frequencies that surround us constantly. By tuning into the same patterns again and again we are reinforcing a particular reality set. We are thus unconsciously tuning in to a consensus reality pattern and forming our perceptions continually from this. Unfamiliar patterns often get ignored since they do not fall within our receptor remit. Perception is thus dynamically created moment by moment as the brain constantly scans the bands of frequencies that surround us. However, if this pattern-recognition behavior does not evolve over time our perceptual development is in danger of becoming stalled. The result is that we become fixed—or trapped—within a particular reality. This is why human development requires that we move through various paradigm shifts,* in order to evolve our collective thinking/perceptual patterns.

The vulnerability is that we become too accustomed to particular perceptual patterns and ignore other sensory inputs or influences. Also as a species we have been collectively uninformed about methods obtainable to shift among various frequency bands and patterns. This knowledge has been available within various wisdom traditions (such as shamanism and occult and mystery schools) yet kept out of the public domain. The end result is that we become fixed and dogmatic in our sensory "beliefs" and cling desperately to the small section of reality we perceive as the whole. Yet in truth each individual has the capacity to choose how they receive and filter these frequency waves. The human brain and nervous system are flexible enough to shift between frequency patterns and to interpret "realities" beyond the consensual pattern. This information has been guarded through the eons in order to keep humanity within a locked reality. In past generations many mystery schools considered humankind too immature to undertake such training—hence the need for rigorous and strict initiation rituals and testing. This embargo on human consciousness has been taken to extremes in recent generations, to the point whereby the mass of humanity has lost touch with their inner capacities and developmental traits. The result is that we have clung to an irrelevant objectivity, rigorously supported by our sciences, and dismiss subjective and intuitive impulses and experiences. However, it has now become an evolutionary necessity that this fault—or embargo—be lifted in order to rejoin the path of our required development. This next stage of human development is that of a neurogenetic "mutation," which using present terminology aligns with a form of quantum consciousness.

---

*See Thomas Kuhn's *The Structure of Scientific Revolutions* for information on paradigm shifts.

QUANTUM CONSCIOUSNESS

The human body is a constant flux of thousands of chemical/biological interreactions and processes connecting molecules, cells, organs, and fluids, throughout the brain, body, and nervous system. Up until recently it was thought that all these interactions operated in a linear sequence, passing on information much like a runner passing the baton to the next runner. However, the latest findings in quantum biology and biophysics have discovered that there is in fact a tremendous degree of coherence within all living systems. Extensive scientific investigation has found that a form of *quantum coherence* operates within living biological systems through what is known as biological excitations and biophoton emission. What this means is that metabolic energy is stored as a form of electromechanical and electromagnetic excitations. These coherent excitations are considered responsible for generating and maintaining long-range order via the transformation of energy and very weak electromagnetic signals. After nearly twenty years of experimental research, Fritz-Albert Popp put forward the hypothesis that biophotons are emitted from a coherent electrodynamic field within the living system.[2] What this means is that each living cell is giving off, or resonating, a biophoton field of coherent energy. If each cell is emitting this field, then the whole living system is, in effect, a resonating field—a ubiquitous nonlocal field. And since biophotons are the entities through which the living system communicates, there is near-instantaneous intercommunication throughout. And this, claims Popp, is the basis for coherent biological organization—referred to as quantum coherence. This discovery led Popp to state that the capacity for evolution rests not on aggressive struggle and rivalry but on the capacity for communication and cooperation. In this sense the built-in capacity for species evolution is not based on the individual but rather living systems that are interlinked within a coherent whole.

Living systems are thus neither the subjects alone, nor objects isolated, but both subjects and objects in a mutually communicating
universe of meaning. . . . Just as the cells in an organism take on different tasks for the whole, different populations enfold information
not only for themselves, but for all other organisms, expanding the
consciousness of the whole, while at the same time becoming more
and more aware of this collective consciousness.[3]

Biophysicist Mae-Wan Ho describes how the living organism,
including the human body, is coordinated throughout and is "coherent
beyond our wildest dreams." It appears that every part of our body is
"in communication with every other part through a dynamic, tuneable,
responsive, liquid crystalline medium that pervades the whole body,
from organs and tissues to the interior of every cell."[4]

What this tells us is that the *medium* of our bodies is a form of
liquid crystal, an ideal transmitter of communication, resonance, and
coherence. These relatively new developments in biophysics have discovered that all biological organisms are constituted of a liquid crystalline medium. Further, DNA is a liquid-crystal, lattice-type structure
(which some refer to as a liquid crystal gel), whereby body cells are
involved in a *holographic* instantaneous communication via the emitting of biophotons (a source based on light). This implies that all living
biological organisms continuously emit radiations of light that form a
field of coherence and communication. Moreover, biophysics has discovered that living organisms are permeated by quantum wave forms.
Ho informs us that

the visible body just happens to be where the wave function of the
organism is most dense. Invisible quantum waves are spreading
out from each of us and permeating into all other organisms. At
the same time, each of us has the waves of every other organism
entangled within our own make-up. . . . We are participants in
the creation drama that is constantly unfolding. We are constantly

co-creating and re-creating ourselves and other organisms in the universe. . . .[5]

This incredible new information actually positions each living being within a nonlocal quantum field consisting of wave interferences (where bodies meet). The liquid crystalline structure within living systems is also responsible for the direct current (DC) electrodynamic field that permeates the entire body of all animals. It has also been noted that the DC field has a mode of semiconduction that is much faster than the nervous system.[6] If biological living systems are operating within a nonlocal interwoven field of resonating energy, then perhaps it is possible to see this manifesting in physical behavior?

Mae-Wan Ho describes how coherent excitations in living systems operate in much the same way as a boat race, where the oars (people) must row in step so as to create a *phase transition*. This indicates that there is an inherent tendency in Nature and in living systems to resonate in sync as a way of maintaining order and coherency. This type of behavior serves to reinforce the relationship between the individual and the collective that before had been thought random. This discovery is important in that it lends validity to the emerging paradigm of the global brain and of the growth of a planetary empathy—the third revolution (as discussed in chapter 6). Each person is thus not only in an empathic relationship with others but also *entangled*. This view has recently been corroborated by neuroscience with its finding of mirror neurons.

A mirror neuron is a brain neuron that is activated (fires) when a living being (such as a human, other primates, or mammal) observes the action of another. In other words, if an individual watches another person eat an apple, then the exact same brain neurons will fire in the person observing the action as if he were performing the act. Such neuron behavior has been found in humans to operate in the premotor and inferior parietal cortex. This phenomenon of mirror neurons was first discovered by a research team in Italy in the 1990s when studying the neuronal activity of macaques. This discovery has led to many notable neuroscientists to declare that mirror neurons are important for learning processes (imitation) as well as language acquisition. In more modern general terms we might also say that this capacity is what ties a person in sympathy and empathy to another's situation. It may also explain why people become so emotionally attached to events on television, and even cry in response to watching someone crying on the screen. In this way we are emotionally *entangled* through a mirroring of brain neuronal firing. When we also consider that our bodies are entangled through a quantum field of electrical biophoton resonance, it explains how we are affected by and from others—via wave/field interference. This information is significant when considering a shift toward heightened empathy between people both near and at a distance (via digital communications) as well as the potential for catalyzing future abilities for telepathic communication between individuals.

Neuroscience, quantum biology, and quantum physics are all beginning to converge to reveal that our bodies are not only biochemical systems but also a sophisticated resonating quantum system. This helps us to understand how the body can be efficiently coherent, as well as explaining how we feel drawn to others, especially when we use terms such as *good vibes, good energies,* and *we just seem to click.* Our bodies, then, as well as our brains appear to function like receivers/decoders within a constantly in-flux information energy field. This explains how the human brain is able to store a lifetime of memories and experiences* as a wealth of data may well be stored within the informational field that encompasses the brain, and indeed the whole body. This new understanding of the quantum human informational field also gives credibility to the existence of extrasensory perceptions (ESP) and related abilities. Human consciousness is not only empathic, in a "wave-interference" relationship with other mind fields, but also is

---

*Eminent mathematician John von Neumann calculated that during an average lifetime of seventy years we accumulate some 280 trillion bits of information.

constantly transmitting and receiving information. If this is indeed an inherent aspect of human functionality then we can see why the power hierarchies maintained by a minority have been active in suppressing its operation. As children we are told/conditioned from very young age to dismiss our fantasies—to grow out of and grow up from such illusions and get with the "real world" (whose world?). Early educational and social-peer conditioning serves to wire our brain neurons into a particular set: a fixed pattern of receiving and interpreting the world. Thus we are literally hardwired into a specific reality paradigm and social operating system. Within this paradigm any thought of extrasensory perceptions are sneered at as childish nonsense (manufactured social peer pressure). Many of our early expressions of intuition are thus suppressed and stifled and replaced with "normal" thoughts and perceptions. Imaginative insights and visions are usually left to the eccentric artists, mystics, and fringe creative innovators. Much of our modern minds have been denied their left-right brain full function and pulled into a tight left-brain rational functioning that operates as mechanical, linear, competitive, and narrow.

The Modernity Project has fashioned a mind-set that is a highly focused and logical narrow-band receiver. This arrangement has been further strengthened by modern social institutions in order to suppress visionary and creative insights and our intuitive capacities. The abstract right brain, with its magical world of creative visionary thinking, has been sidelined. Much of this right-brain activity was the source for indigenous wisdom, shamanic practices, and similar traditions that modern materialism has mercilessly eliminated over the years. We have been conditioned to think of such "magical practices" as primitive, barbaric, and worthy of little more than Western colonialism and imperial rule. The social institutions in our modern materialistic age act to influence us to reject anything extrasensory as a load of nonsense, wishful thinking, or New Age delusion. Thus with our left-hemisphere-dominated brain we live in the everyday world of matter: of material objects and external attractions. We are shown to exist as separate forces, as islands in a chaotic sea of physical and natural impacts, and at the whim of random neutral influences. Yet we now know that this is not the case.

To recap, quantum biology has shown that the body displays an incredible degree of *quantum coherence,* and that a quantum consciousness field exists throughout the human DNA and thus the human nervous system. Our biochemical structure is composed of a confluence of energies in complete entanglement and that operate as a nonlocal field within and outside the human body. Further DNA is a liquid-crystal, lattice-type structure that emits biophotons, which are light based. What this leads to is a new understanding that human DNA operates also as a quantum field. In other words, we can begin referring to DNA as *quantum DNA.* Therefore the 97 percent of human DNA that is not involved in protein building is active within a quantum state. It may well be that a future manifestation of quantum consciousness will come from part activation of the 97 percent quantum DNA that so far has baffled our scientists with its function. This quantum DNA activation may likely be related to the state of human consciousness and has remained dormant in response to human consciousness not being sufficiently prepared, or made ready, for its manifestation. This field "life force" may be similar to the pervasive pranic energy that, as Gopi Krishna states, forms the impulse for evolutionary growth in the human nervous system.

An ever-present possibility, existing in all human beings by virtue of the evolutionary process still at work in the race, tending to create a condition of the brain and nervous system that can enable one to transcend the existing boundaries of the mind and acquire a state of consciousness far above that which is the normal heritage of mankind at present.[7]

This transcendental stage of consciousness that is depicted above as being a part of our natural evolutionary heritage is connected with the human brain and nervous system. We now know that we have a DNA quantum field activated within our bodies. Some biophysicists are already discussing whether quantum behavior may not be a common denominator for all living processes. As such a quantum informational field throughout the human body will determine the coherence of our light (biophoton) resonance as a vibratory rate. If human consciousness begins to shift its vibratory rate then there is every likelihood that DNA—as a quantum field—will likewise undergo a resonance shift, bringing into activation parts of its 97 percent hitherto "inactive" capacities. This may or may not be linked to the increase in electromagnetic frequencies now impacting our solar system from the galactic core. Is there a possibility that a phase step in the "engine of evolutionary energies" is under way?

The Russian biophysicist and molecular biologist Pjotr Garjajev, who has studied human DNA with his research team in Moscow, found that the 97 percent "inactive" DNA actually has complex properties. Garjajev discovered that the DNA, which is not used for protein synthesis, is instead actually used for communication—more exactly for *hypercommunication*. In their terms, hypercommunication is a data exchange on a DNA level. Garjajev and his group analyzed the vibration response of the DNA and concluded that it can function much like networked intelligence, and that it allows for hypercommunication of information among all sentient beings. For example, the Moscow research group proved that damaged chromosomes (such as those harmed by x-rays) can be repaired. Their method was to capture the information patterns of particular DNA and then transmit these patterns, using focused light frequencies, onto another genome as a way of reprogramming the cells. In this way they successfully transformed frog embryos to salamander embryos simply by transmitting the DNA information patterns. Garjajev's research shows that certain frequency patterns can be "beamed" (such as with a laser) to transfer genetic information. This shows how DNA operates through resonance and vibratory frequencies. It also shows that human DNA can be modified—or altered—through the impact of external frequencies. This may also help to go some way toward validating the existence of such phenomena as remote acts of healing and other psychic attributes. It also suggests that DNA is a living, fluid, and dynamic "language" that as a quantum informational field is responsive not only to laser waves (as in the above experiment) but also EM waves and sound, given that the correct frequencies are applied.

The knowledge that human DNA can be influenced and modulated by frequencies (sound, light, language, and thought) is likely to have been known to various spiritual traditions, mystics, and teachers over the ages. This is perhaps why a variety of exercises have existed that utilize thought focus (prayer), sounds (music, chanting, singing), light (both natural light and produced light, such as in stained glass), and language (specific recitations such as a mantra and zikr). DNA appears to function not only as a protein builder (the minority function) but also as a medium for the storage, receiving, and communication of information. Somewhat more controversially, Garjajev and his Russian colleagues also found examples where DNA could cause disturbing patterns in a vacuum, resulting in the production of what seemed to be magnetized wormholes.* These wormholes appeared to function as connections outside our normal fields of time and space (which hints at interdimensional communication). This phenomenon is indeed worthy of further analysis and experimentation. Yet it does seem probable that DNA is involved with various forms of hypercommunication of which, at present, we know very little about. However, there are examples of hypercommunication at work in Nature. For example, the organization of ant colonies appears to make use of this distributed form of communication. When a queen ant is separated from her colony, the worker ants continue to build and construct the colony as if following some form of blueprint. Yet if the queen ant is killed, then all work in the colony ceases, as if the blueprint had suddenly been taken offline. This suggests that the queen ant need not be in physical contact to continue

---

*For more information see the work of Grazyna Fosar and Franz Bludorf.

to transmit the blueprint, yet upon her death the group consciousness ceases to operate within a hypercommunicative informational field. We can thus refer to these forms of hypercommunication as quantum-field consciousness, or simply as *quantum consciousness* (since quantum implies nonlocal field effect).

At-a-distance human phenomena such as remote healing, remote sensing, and telepathy may work along comparable lines. On a more basic level we could say that many of us experience this as the sense of intuition and moments of inspiration. We may even be receiving these forms of hypercommunication when we are asleep. There are count-less examples of people, artists, and designers who gained inspiration for their work in their dreams. One example is the Italian composer Giuseppe Tartini who one night dreamt that a devil sat beside his bed playing the violin. The next morning Tartini wrote down the piece from memory and called it the Devil's Trill sonata. Not only do these experiences seem to be increasing (or perhaps people are more open to speaking of them?), but newer generations of children are manifest-ing a higher level of clairvoyance and other extrasensory capacities. In recent times they have been referred to as indigo children, or the "new children." These developments may indicate that a higher form of group consciousness is emerging within humanity and that these abilities are now finding greater expression. This does not, however, deny the presence of negative influences against collective quantum consciousness since stress, fear, and similar impacts (see "Decoding the Armageddon Meme" on page 126) all serve to disrupt awareness and manifestation of quantum states. In this context we would do well to return to those practices recommended for centuries by spiritual traditions and teachers, that is, mediation, reflection, watchfulness, and mindfulness. Einstein was famous as a daydreamer throughout his life, and he often claimed that his greatest inspiration came to him when in such states. Enhanced connectivity between humanity may thus be served by each of us paying more attention to our inner states and striving for harmony and balance in our lives.

QUANTUM STATES AND THE AKASHIC FIELD

Materials for enhancing these inner (or quantum) states can be found within many traditions, whether from the major religions (Christianity, Islam, Judaism, Sikhism) or from other streams of wisdom such as Buddhism, Taoism, Sufism, and various meditative practices. There are also many written materials (books, tales, poems) that function to stimulate right-hemisphere activity. This is the case with many Sufi stories (such as the Mulla Nasrudin tales* and the famous "The Thousand and One Nights") as well as poems by Jalaluddin Rumi (which are now bestsellers in the West). Many of these traditions also encourage group meditation as a way of stimulating group consciousness (and thus quantum connection). Practiced meditators can achieve an extremely high level of cross-hemispheric synchronization. Similarly people who mediate together have been discovered to synchronize their brain activity. Through the use of EEG brain scanning, brain-wave activity has been found to synchronize among participants of such a group. We can now speculate that this is a result of resonance occurring between the various quantum fields, as described by biophysics. To some extent this has been replicated by the vast array of hemispheric audio material that is now available on the mass market (at various quality levels). These stimulants act to induce an altered state of consciousness—what some practitioners have referred to as transpersonal consciousness. In these states people have experienced very profound connections with the collective consciousness. Philosopher Ervin Laszlo refers to this collective information field as the *Akashic Field*.[8]

There is now reason to speculate that this so-called nonlocal Akashic Field is in fact a part of our shared (and overlapping) quantum fields of consciousness. If this is so, then this leads us to further question whether DNA, which emits biophotons and exhibits interdimensional properties, may not itself be the seat of quantum

---

*See the corpus of tales from Idries Shah.

consciousness. Modern science has for a long time considered the human brain the center of consciousness, yet this belongs to materialistic and linear thinking that posits consciousness as a product of complex matter. The brain is indeed our most complex neurological arrangement consisting of the most intricate network of synapses. Yet it is more likely that the brain functions as a receiver and transcriber of electrical signals that are emitted from the quantum DNA. In this way the trillions of parts of our human DNA act as a coherent quantum field to regulate every part of our body in each moment. The human body is thus a resonating quantum field (which may also have interdimensional properties hitherto unknown and/or dormant). Our reality is thus provided by the work of the brain that transcribes signals into perceptions, yet it is the DNA that is a living intelligence. This idea of DNA being a living intelligence is not new to many indigenous-wisdom traditions. For example, as anthropologist Jeremy Narby pointed out, shamans who undergo trance states often seem to be communicating with DNA as a means of acquiring knowledge about plants, healing, and spirit worlds.[9] Subsequently Narby explored how Nature is also imbued with this form of living intelligence, which acts as survival patterns to enable evolutionary growth.[10] Shamans, intuitives, and others who are able to tap in to this living intelligence find a *design* or blueprint behind all physical structures, which points to a quantum field of living intelligence that acts as an evolutionary impulse within all living systems.

We can thus speculate that human DNA, as a quantum energy field, may likely be the seat of human consciousness. Further, it is possible to say that this *quantum consciousness field* is the very same as what has been referred to as the Akashic Field. Moreover, DNA is receptive to particular external influences such as can be manifested through prayer, meditation, and specific sounds/vibrations. This offers startling possibilities for our well-being and evolving selves if we are capable of some form of communication with our own living intelligence (our own "higher selves"?). We may even have the potential to interact with our physical cellular structure through focused minds and directed intentions. The implications of this are profound and even infer that humanity may have a future opportunity to be in a relationship, through quantum consciousness, with its own DNA and living design. Further, if resonance/vibratory patterns of quantum consciousness can be passed between generations, then it may be that the new generations now being born will exhibit different consciousness patterns. These may be the initial signs in the neurogenetic evolution of humanity. New generations will be the evolutionary agents that will lead the way through a social-cultural-human renaissance and renewal.

EVOLUTIONARY AGENTS
Our Next Quantum Leap?

Quantum consciousness—living field intelligence—could well represent the next stage in human evolution; that is, evolution of the global mind of humanity. Various mystics and consciousness researchers have alluded to this by a variety of names, ranging from *cosmic consciousness,* to *superconsciousness, transpersonal consciousness, integral consciousness,* and more. All these share a common theme: namely, the rise of intuition, empathy, greater connectivity to the world and to people, and a sense of *knowing* about what each given situation demands. Further, such a form of quantum consciousness would likely instill within each person a sense of the greater cosmic whole: the realization that humanity exists and evolves within a universe of intelligence and meaning (perhaps even interdimensional). This would serve to impart within humanity a more profound and acknowledged spiritual impulse.

We can speculate that a variety of factors could in some way result in increased wave patterns (vibrations) entering into the quantum DNA field and catalyzing a shift in the consciousness of humanity. These include a shifting of the Earth's geomagnetic forces (as is already occurring), varying solar radiations from each sun cycle, galactic pulses from the center of the galaxy, and our solar system moving through a more "energized" portion of interstellar space. The bridge that divides us at present from another level of living intelligence is in essence a vibratory shift. If such a vibratory shift is a potential means of catalyzing quantum consciousness, this could then lead to increased intuitive faculties and extrasensory phenomena not only becoming an important part of our lives but also to opening up access to greater creativity and inventive capacities for participating in our own human futures. The rise of these attributes in a critical mass could be the key to our next *evolutionary leap*. Forms and intimations of these new consciousness patterns are already emerging in the world, but as yet they have not become a part of mainstream research. Such evolutionary "mutational" agents include visionaries, mystics, artists, psychics, intuitives, spiritual teachers, and what have been termed indigo children. These children (called Indigo because of their purportedly colored auras) are described as possessing increased empathy, creativity, curiosity, and will. They are also reported to be spiritually inclined from a young age and to exhibit strong intuitive capacities. Because of their natural and inherent resistance to authority they are seen as distracted, rebellious, or alienated in the conventional school system. Yet this is nothing new, as throughout recorded history social revolutionaries have felt impelled and inspired to resist authority and instigate change.* As such, many of the individuals who have felt an awareness of this have been caught up in revolutionary events or have been involved in social-cultural upheavals as a way of facing and responding to the confines and constraints of their control societies. These human efforts, Krishna notes, come from evolutionary impulses.

> I can safely assert that the progress made by mankind in any direction, from the subhuman level to the present, has been far less due to man's own efforts than to the activity of the evolutionary forces at work within him. Every incentive to invention, discovery, aesthetics,

---

*See James Billington's *Fire in the Minds of Men*.

and the development of improved social and political organizations invariably comes from within, from the depths of his consciousness by the grace of . . . the superintelligent Evolutionary Force in human beings.[11]

This suggests that efforts to try to manifest such impulses within the physical realm have met with opposing materialistic and power-centered external forces. However, each of these attempts—or movements—has helped to prepare the "mental soil" for a new consciousness to slowly seed and grow. On the whole social/cultural/material forces have been slow to react to the need for an evolving human consciousness. On one hand there is the seeping of spiritual knowledge into physical life, increasing people's awareness of spiritual matters, which is essential, and has been occurring over long periods of time. On the other hand there have been various processes at work that have attempted to suppress the spiritual impulse in humanity by forcing a materialistic paradigm as the ruling consensus reality. Such a reality, as has been explained, stifles the innate capacities of human nature and interferes with the necessary pattern of human evolution and consciousness.

However, at particular periods there are moments during which humanity becomes ready for the activation of particular faculties and/or evolutionary traits. I believe that humanity is moving into a time now where aspects of consciousness will be opened up and developed, leading to new creative and inspired capacities. This is a significant time for humanity during which various external power forces will attempt to reinforce structures of control, confusion, and fear while human consciousness and even human DNA begin to evolve/shift beyond the present paradigm. This period of our species' neurogenetic evolution represents the time for challenging the now outmoded social structures that have held us back for so long. Within this struggle for our minds—our ways of thinking—lays so much confusion, distraction, and conflicting energies. However, the old energies inevitably must give way to the new, and it may only be a matter of time before new generations move into evolving consciousness and its physical expressions.

During this transition, wherein the struggle for dominant thought patterns will be more marked, it is important that people are aware that a conscious spirituality lies beyond the threshold of our daily consciousness. If we fail to make the effort to bring conscious awareness more to the fore then we are liable to remain vulnerable to degenerative forces that may lead to an evolutionary dormant state. We can realize this from our very cultures and our social establishments, which appear as obstacles to true and genuine spiritual ideas and states. Thus it is critical that an understanding of spiritual matters begins to permeate our everyday lives and to counteract the drive of our materialistic cultures. In this regard an alert mind is one that is aware to how external circumstances come into being. Not only should we be alert to how material distractions try to placate and pacify our minds, but also how events enter into our lives. There are a great many interventions occurring at all levels in human life; to this end we should watch closely for those events that attract our attention—it might be a hint for us from unknown sources. Also it will help if we are aware to notice how people are influenced, and by which means. To see the nature of influence in operation will help us to become more attuned to its ways and hopefully less vulnerable to its machinations. It is important in these years ahead that we try to develop a consciousness that is both open to spiritual impulses and simultaneously aware and attentive to degenerative and/or manipulative forces. Which set of forces dominate this next stage—be they materialistic forces or those of the spiritual impulse—will largely determine how the evolutionary trajectory of humanity develops. Again as Krishna notes: "Material objectives would continue to dominate the thinking of mankind, leading to a stultification of the evolutionary impulse and atrophy of the evolutionary mechanism, the vicious precursors of degeneration and decay."[12] The environmental forces of contrived fear, escapism, distortion, and distraction all add to keeping human consciousness in a dormant state.

Our general lack of knowledge and awareness about the power, capacity, and potential of human consciousness and its role in our evolutionary development, has brought humanity to a critical threshold. It has allowed confrontational and conspiring forces to bring our planet into unbalance and disharmony. Our inability—or unwillingness—to bring conscious spirituality to the forefront of our lives has fostered a collective state of passivity and even apathy. A revolution in human consciousness is now required not only in order to break the spell of our ignorance but also because it is our inheritance. Now that we have the capacity to engage with spiritual impulses, environmental impacts are being supplied that have the potential to catalyze in us new patterns of consciousness, with emerging faculties of heightened perception and understanding. Such new energies may also assist in opening up transcendental patterns of thought that would bring humanity into a more direct relationship with intelligent cosmic forces, thus breaking the collective coma of our cosmic isolationism. It is possible that a new state of quantum consciousness will allow humanity access to an unimaginable *energetic field of information* (both cosmic and interdimensional). This would then open up new vistas of creative intelligence that are hitherto closed to us because of our lower vibratory/energetic state of consciousness. We would literally be able to break out of our quarantine and take back our minds.

To summarize, humanity as a global species may be in the throes of passing through a transition toward a different state of consciousness. This new state may likely be characterized by quantum properties such as coherence and nonlocal field information. Because of this I have termed this new state a *quantum consciousness field*. Knowledge and understanding of this consciousness field could greatly transform how we relate to other people, the world around us, and our cosmic neighborhood (so to speak) as well as other perceptual realities. It could also catalyze other hitherto underdeveloped human faculties such as increased intuition, telepathy, and ESP (extrasensory perception). Some of these features are already appearing within younger generations that are born into a world that bemuses them and makes them feel out of step with the events they see happening around them. This evolutionary development manifests a transition from biological and sociocultural forms of evolution to incorporating a new level: neurogenetic evolution. This neurogenetic phase is essential, I argue, to allow humanity to evolve to the next stage upon the evolutionary ladder. We should remind ourselves that we are living through vastly changing times. As one thinker recently stated:

> We live in changing times whereby humanity is undergoing a transformation. Our consciousness, which has a vast potential for further development, must undergo a release from old, binding structures, and break out towards a rapid expansion. This is thus a period for both profound change and great danger: thought systems are in battle, are colliding, and vying for control. We need to become more aware of what is happening around us, and to observe the machinations of a controlled, material life. We need to understand phenomena at deeper levels, and not just accept what we are told, or what is fed to us through well-structured social institutions and channels. We must learn to accept that our thinking is a great tangible spiritual force for change.[13]

If a person is not sufficiently prepared for these changing impacts it may cause imbalance and confusion. Personal responsibility means each person must seek to balance the energies of both his inner and outer lives—and to strengthen his connection to self-consciousness.

Let us not forget that we are in the midst of a battle for perceptions, and with the correct focus of mind we have the means to transform each daily negative into a positive. Yet we need to start thinking for ourselves and to see how the world around us actually operates. Too much reliance on the systems of controlled thought will serve only to instill fear and obedience into our stirring souls. We must stir ourselves into the opposite direction, toward creative and visionary growth and compassionate understanding. We need to know and to feel that we have the spiritual impulse running through us and that it runs through every aspect of our physical lives. By connecting with this we have the personal capacity to not only take back our minds but to move forward into a future of increased intelligence and wisdom. It is, in the end, a matter of how we perceive our worlds.

8

USHERING IN THE NEW LIFE

A Reenvisioning of
Society and Spirituality

*If the world is saved, it will not be by old minds with new
programs but by new minds with no programs at all.*

DANIEL QUINN

It appears that many signs now point toward humanity entering a
transition phase within an increasingly energized environment. This
changeover will see support for structures of the old energy and its
corresponding paradigm diminish. In short, we are moving into a new
energetic epoch and change is therefore inevitable on multiple fronts.
We must also realize that with all great change comes disturbance,
like waves of quantum interference, as the old and new energetic levels clash. There is no getting away from this as we work to replace
our present programming (our old programs) with new vision. As leg-
endary architect and philosopher Buckminster Fuller once remarked:
"You never change things by fighting the existing reality. To change
something, build a new model that makes the existing model obsolete." We should also remember that we have so many old programs
surrounding us that are supposed to make it look like everything

is working fine when in fact we are buffeted by a groundswell of illusions. Yet these old programs won't get us anywhere, as this little tale indicates.

> A man was found sitting in the middle of the desert in a contraption made of rocks, bits of lumber, and old, blown tires, which he was busily steering as if it were actually a vehicle in motion. Asked what he was doing, the man said, "Driving home." "You're never going to get there in this," he was told. He said, "If not in this, then in what?"[1]

We are also at the wheel of a junkyard banger (conditioned with old programs) that we tell ourselves will get us home—wherever "home" may be. This is not entirely our fault. Our situation can be likened to the allegorical tale of "The Islanders" by Idries Shah.[2] This longish instructive tale talks of how a once peaceful, purposeful, and meaningful society—an almost ideal society—had to leave its homeland because of deteriorating conditions and spent a period of time on another island. This exile to the other island required that the people acclimate to the new conditions, which included a heavier, coarser, level of perceptions and a tendency toward physical fulfillment and pleasures. Yet before the exile, a leader of the people devised a training program in order to keep alive in people's memory not only the existence of their original homeland but also how to acquire the means to return once conditions were right. He called this system the art of shipbuilding.

Slowly the immigrants began to settle down on the island under the new heavier conditions and learned to make use of local resources for all their needs. Selected individuals were taught the art of shipbuilding in order to keep alive the teaching of how to return to their homeland. Yet for the majority of people this teaching could not be kept in their consciousness because of the overriding difficulties of trying to adjust to the new circumstances. However, enough people with the knowledge were available for when the people needed it. These teachers made it clear to people that a certain preparation was required before anyone could learn to swim or to start building a ship. And for a while this situation progressed fairly well. Yet after some time a cunning person realized that he could gain some power by exploiting the situation of shipbuilding. He declared that there was no need for people to exert themselves in the art of shipbuilding because people were already completed and did not need to leave the island. After all, declared the trickster, how many ships and swimmers have ever returned to us? He asked for physical proof, which of course could not be provided. And so the masses rallied to the cause and shipbuilding became a scapegoat, with many shipbuilders hanged by the mobs. The new gospel was no longer one of shipbuilding but of free thought and rational thinking. Any ideas that went against the new ones were simply called irrational and thus bad or primitive. Any thought of shipbuilding had to be suppressed because it was beyond the rational. Thus to be rational one had only to adhere to the norms of the society of the immigrant islanders.

Life on the new island gradually became one of emotion and reason. Shipbuilding was generally viewed as an archaic and absurd leftover from earlier, more primitive, days, and the thought of leaving the island now began to fill most people with terror and insecurity. The island seemed to have been transformed into a prison without bars. Local cultures devised their own literature and "science" to debate and prove how new rational values and patterns have civilized all people. Plausible explanations could be produced for almost anything, and scholars, historians, and sociologists all began to see life as a natural pattern having occurred from the beginning of the island's history as if no prior time had ever existed. Of course, shipbuilders still existed and continued to teach the art of shipbuilding to the few who cared or were awake enough to care. Yet for the rest, they were allowed to indulge in their various expressions of ideas, opinions, differences, as long as it was not "absurd." And freedom of speech was allowed also, although it seldom was accompanied by a sense of understanding. After a time even bizarre mimicry cults of shipbuilding began to appear, advocating pseudoswimming and selling swimming lessons as entertainment promised as profound. These distractions were useful for many people in giving them a newfound sense of meaning in their lives, and helped them to feel much better about themselves and to give them a sense of superiority. This was followed by countless cults, groups, and exercises that exploited emotionality and encouraged people to consider such emotional attachments as a peak of achievement. Such emotional states were now considered to be deep and meaningful. Later on, various institutions were formed, such as universities, art centers, museums, stadiums, colleges, and so forth, and all served to indulge people in false satisfactions and both emotional and rational distractions. These magnificent and lauded facilities for indulgence became social and cultural icons. Many of them were also considered to be connected with the ultimate truth. . . .

Most people had now forgotten about shipbuilding; some had never even heard of it. Yet it continued, and ships carried on leaving and swimmers kept on swimming away. Those still concerned with the art of shipbuilding no longer resided in the public domain. Rather they preserved their art discreetly, appearing as normal to all the rest. Even those who tried to seek them out were often unsuccessful, ending up instead in one of the pseudoswimming clubs. So for most people the discussions on opinions, rationality, doubts, debates, scientific truths, and logical proofs all served to create a civilized modern island life. Yet now and again a person would manage to pass through the morass to find a real teacher of shipbuilding. Usually, though, the following conversation took place, as a way of bargaining.

"I want to learn to swim."

"Do you want to make a bargain about it?"

"No. I only have to take my ton of cabbage."

"What cabbage?"

"The food that I will need on the other island."

"There is better food there."

"I don't know what you mean. I cannot be sure. I must take my cabbage."

"You cannot swim, for one thing, with a ton of cabbage."

"Then I cannot go. You call it a load. I call it my essential nutrition."

"Suppose, as an allegory, we say not 'cabbage' but 'assumptions,' or 'destructive ideas'?"

"I am going to take my cabbage to some instructor who understands my needs."[3]

"The Islanders" by Idries Shah does, I think, speak for itself in quite a revealing way. On one level it mirrors the processes that have been outlined in this book—how cultural norms and conditionings begin to restructure society and social institutions (or the social matrix, as I have often referred to it). As this happens, the opinions, mind-set, and belief paradigms that are "modern" begin to ostracize and brand the ancient knowledge systems as irrational, unscientific, primitive, or even absurd. In simple terms, it brands them as bad thinking. This is reminiscent of Orwell's *Animal Farm* slogan of "Four legs good; two legs bad." Constrained and contained thinking is often a case of function-creep rather than an overt coercive gesture, hence so many people are unaware of how their patterns of mental thought are influenced and programmed. As one critic recently stated, "If we actually manage to survive here, it will be because we've moved into a new era as different from ours as the Renaissance was from the Middle Ages—and as unimaginable to us as the Renaissance was to the Middle Ages."[4] However, as was discussed in the previous chapter, there are already signs emerging of a changing environment and a possible neurogenetic evolutionary shift. With this in mind we can assert, to some degree, that as a planetary species we are being offered an energizing hand.

In chapter 6 I discussed how recent astronomical data suggests that our solar system is moving through a more energized region of space, and that this coincides with predicted increases in the sun's activity (solar flares and coronal mass ejections). I have speculated that these energetic events may have some influence over how evolutionary mutations occur. In other words, these energetic (electromagnetic) impacts may affect the human nervous system and DNA reproduction, leading to a neurogenetic mutation in the human species. The forerunners of this species change may, I speculate, be found in the emerging numbers of children being born with heightened sensitivity and psychic abilities.* For the rest of us the changes that may occur in our societies, as old systems and old mental programs appear increasingly dysfunctional, will require our own forms of preparation. Namely a shift in our social matrix will require more conscious energy from us. Let's be fair: most of us until now have been mentally lazy (admittedly not all our own fault!). Our present sources of knowledge, inspiration, and vision—such as our educational, media, and religious institutions—have been failing us for a long time. We therefore need to bring online a more energy-intensive source: our human vision and ingenuity, which can help to bring about an alignment between our spiritual/humanistic and materialistic forces. It may be that this confluence of energies we are passing through will catalyze some of these shifts.

We also need to recognize that the Modernity Project as a control society is in its final stages. Just as in Shah's "The Islanders," we have been fooled into thinking the art of shipbuilding no longer exists, or if its does it is either absurd or irrational. But it is neither of these: it is the art of developing our inherent capacities for visionary change and growth. We are maritime masters yet forgetful of our skills, having been moored for too long at the island of Circe,† where we have been transformed into our animal natures. We need to begin to take back our minds because we will need to be independently alert of the

---

*Many people refer to these new children as indigo children or even crystal children.
†A reference to Homer's *The Odyssey*.

coming sociocultural changes; our modern technocultures cannot be maintained for much longer because they are so energy intensive. Our interrelated technological social matrixes have managed rapid expansion (and accelerated control mechanisms) due to the abundance of cheap and plentiful finite energy reserves. Intensive and extensive control mechanisms have been (and continue to be) put in place as a way of managing the masses as many critical energy infrastructures also face breakup and/or interruption/disarray. Seed vaults and other such deep underground storage bases (and there are many of them placed strategically throughout the world)* betray the derisive agenda for resource control in a resource-depleted future.

Writer Philip K. Dick's novella *The Penultimate Truth* puts another twist on this theme by describing how millions of people are crammed into underground bunkers, believing that World War III rages on the surface above, only to eventually realize, of course, that no such thing is going on—it is just another lie. And speaking of monumental lies, here is a modern parable that is called "In the Image of the Gods."

At the birth of civilisation amidst the ancient rise of the dynasties there emerged a powerful race of beings who superseded all known life in their high intelligence and wisdom. They believed that their inheritance belonged to the stars and that they themselves were indeed a genetic offspring from deliberate breeding with alien intelligences that had arrived from the cosmos to visit their planet Earth in an earlier age: they considered themselves to be in the "image of their gods." To this order they built many domains of worship, and erected many centres of astrological significance to study the heavens, the knowledge of the operation of such centres being strictly limited to the higher brethren.

As a further act of worship and thanks to their creators of life, this elite passed a decree where at the ending of every month a human

---

*Some of these have been referred to as Deep Underground Military Bases (DUMBs), which are reported to be as large as mini cities.

sacrifice would be made as a show of their continuing devotion, and in the hope that their higher ancestors would one day return to view their work. These sacrifices were taken from the regular population of humanoids, as it was the elite wise that were required for the civilisation's constant progress. The choices as to who would be sacrificed were made at random. After a period of time however, the common populace began to grow disgruntled at this state of affairs and became restless at their unvoiced position below the ruling authority. This unease quickly grew and developed into a general state of unrest that was seen by the elite as both a danger to their own positions and to the equilibrium of their society's fabric. They became anxious that a remedy be quickly and effectively found. This question as to how to solve this unrest was sent out to all the great and wise that composed the elite, and to all the most respected and knowledgeable beings.

Finally, after much raised eyebrows, there stepped forward the figure of Jesuem Moham Rosencrantz who was regarded by most to be a highly intelligent individual and a gifted practitioner of magic. He declared that he had looked into this problem deeply and with his profound insight and practical knowledge had come up with the ideal solution. This consisted of hypnotising the common people into believing that they were immortal, and if they sacrificed themselves to the gods then their spirit or "soul" as Jesuem called it (so as to give it a mystical regal nomenclature) would ascend to the stars to be beside the throne of their gods and they would continue to exist within eternal peace. Jesuem proposed that this hypnotic trance would lead everyone to believe that the ruling elite were thoughtful and considerate beings who strived for the mutual good of all classes of beings. To add further onto this the populace would be hypnotised into also believing that their present position was a worthy and satisfactory one and that there was no need to strive for any knowledge or awareness of one's self since there would be no need for this as their sole purpose was to live for the community and reach heaven in eternity. This proposal of Jesuem Moham Rosencrantz was welcomed with mighty approval by all the other elite beings, and was soon put into action.

The general humanoid was thus turned into a walking automation, believing in their mundane life and looking towards death as a gateway into the realms of the holy. And so this ancient civilisation remained intact and continued to prosper for many generations, producing much intelligent thought and practises that are sadly lost to the world of today; known only to the wise few as secret knowledge. Sadly, the only remnants that have remained from this early order is their magic that has been passed through the genetic gene pools for thousands of years. The power of this initial trance state created by Jesuem was so intense that it has survived until this present day in the consciousness of virtually every human. Most people are still living within a diseased sleep, unaware of their state and their lack of knowledge. They still carry with them the idea that once dead their eternal "soul" will ascend to the land of the gods, and so while alive they maintain this slaved duty to the social order.

It is of interest here to also note that this notion of ascending to the stars has been expanded and developed upon through the ages to incorporate its opposite—namely that if a common man throws his life against the grain of social order or strives to upset the morals of the "elders," then that being will find their "soul" being cast eternally into a sphere labelled as "damnation," which is said to be torturous and an existence of constant pain. Such half-weaved tales have planted themselves into the framework of many present civilisations and the human psyche is now a torn and damaged instrument, affected by bad programming and mental shocks. There will never be a cure for this disintegration until the humanoids begin to become aware of this problem themselves.

Human life has, to a great degree, been pushed into an unsustainable direction. Too many natural laws are being broken, and the human being has not aligned himself into a correct harmonious relationship with the resonance of the planet. Stuck in financially constricted work-labor lifestyles, forced into nutritionless packaged foods, humanity is loosing sight of the goals of harmonious development. Because we as a species are breaking too many natural laws simultaneously, there has to be radical change. We need to adjust actual human societal thinking—to shift from a linear society to a conceptual society: a manifestation of imagination and vision into reality. Conceptual thinking attempts to join the dots within the "bigger picture" rather than being tied down to what we falsely imagine to be causes and effects.

If we do not change the direction of our very thoughts and way of thinking—our expression of consciousness—then what type of world are we preparing? We may remain consigned to living a life of abstractions, of offered theories, lies, and illusions with little or no true lived experience. This can only offer us a future in which we are inadequate to deal with the necessary changes. If we are submissive and do not manifest a suitable strength of will—collectively and individually—to deal with the possibility (and needs) of the next stage of our evolutionary growth, then we may fail ourselves. Human civilization thus opens itself to extreme vulnerability to be controlled completely or to break down. To take back our minds is about breaking out of vague abstractions and reengaging with the strength of positive human intention and willpower.

A NEW VISION OF SOCIETY AND SPIRITUALITY

There is an Eastern proverb that roughly translates as, "You may ride your donkey up to your front door, but would you ride it into your house?" In other words, when we have arrived at a particular destination we are often required to make a transition in order to continue the journey. In this sense we can acknowledge those elements, factors, knowledge, influences—even obstructions—that have helped us to arrive at where we presently stand. Yet it is now imperative that we move forward. Throughout this book I have suggested that how we move forward is connected to our understanding of consciousness. As I described in the previous chapter, new discoveries show that a form of nonlocal connected consciousness has a physical-scientific basis. This goes some way toward demonstrating that certain spiritual or transcendental states of collective consciousness have a valid basis within the new scientific paradigm. If we are willing to step down from the donkey we will find that our new path ahead has a place for reconciling science and spirituality. That is, there is a place for rational analysis (material world) to exist in harmony with subjective understanding (inner world). Collaboration between both worlds of our perceptive capacities proposes a state of cooperation, not conflict and competition. Again, division weakens people (divide and rule) while cooperation strengthens. Deep in our historical past there were periods where these two forms of perception (external and internal) were not in conflict, but were understood to complement each other. That is, an inner understanding helped to illuminate an awareness of the universe that surrounded humankind. Ancient Eastern teachings have described human beings as having five layers of experience: the environment, the physical body, the mind, the intuition, and our self or spirit. Thus our connection with the environment is an important primary level of "first contact" experience. If this physical experience is tainted, polluted, or manipulated, then we are in danger of affecting our other perceptive sensibilities. However, the disconnection that we have unfortunately suffered from for far too long has separated humanity not only from a healthy cosmic relationship, but also from the very terrestrial environment we were entrusted to steward.

An intimate relationship with the environment is an inherent built-in feature of the human psyche. The denial of the primacy of human consciousness in this reality has resulted, both directly and indirectly, in desacralizing Nature into a commodity to be used and exploited by human beings. Each of us needs to reassert the primacy of consciousness and to acknowledge that the deepest elements of our thoughts, emotions, and even spiritual states are ultimately connected to the world in which we live. We need to assert the qualitative value of our individual lives and to strive for meaning beyond transient psychological states and fleeting sensual gratifications. It is therefore important that we have the opportunity to experience our world with an open mind that is free from stress, fear, and petty divisive tendencies. For this to happen, human consciousness must rise above the negative influences and characteristics that have plagued our many modern cultures. The experience of one's own personal nature, to touch one's inner sense of spirit, is vital in nurturing this relationship between the human species and our many, varied levels of external world(s). An act of sincere and focused awareness can have a tremendous effect on the world around us, not only in the ways we think or believe but also in indirect metaphysical ways. In this respect we need to be more careful of the forces interacting with us and influencing us within our everyday environments. We can assist our growth by reconnecting with the spiritual side of our nature, and to recognize that life is not only physical but rests upon very real and tremendous nonphysical forces. By learning to accept these deeper levels of nonmaterial existence we can assist a shift away from constricting paradigms of perception that narrow our vision and dampen our energetic spirit. As Gopi Krishna says, "An individual, a society or even a whole civilization, which makes the perishable body the sole object of its concern, cannot but perish in the long run."[5] Krishna also noted that while our human global civilization has advanced to a high material degree, with new technologies of communication, travel, health, and so on, and even with stellar exploration, we have failed, collectively as a species, to adequately explore our inner worlds. If this deficiency is not rectified, Krishna warns us, our present civilization may meet the same fate as the vanished civilizations of the past.

We are still being cleverly caught in the binary arguments, debating whether science is the answer or if religion holds the truth. And while we squabble in what Gurdjieff would sardonically call our mental masturbation, we become more deeply entrenched within the rabbit hole of illusion. We don't need to exist within an either/or; such verbal and physical confrontations can be replaced with references of collaboration and coexistence. Our old mind programming sees us attempting to solve the problems bubbling around us. New mind thinking will make us ask, How can we create what we really want to see? Yet no one else is going to do this thinking for us; we need to get our own hands wet, so to speak.

Jack and Jill are in a sailboat with their friend Jason, enjoying the sea. One morning they awake to find the boat sinking.

"What are we going to do?" shouts Jill.

"Don't worry" says Jack, "Jason is very ingenious, he'll know what to do."

Jason calls to Jack and Jill to abandon ship. Jill is worried by this but Jack reassures her that Jason wouldn't let them down.

"We're only a hundred metres from shore; come on, let's go!" shouts Jason.

"But how are we going to save ourselves?" both Jack and Jill ask.

"We're going to swim for it, of course!" answers Jason. Seeing the look of disappointment on their faces, Jason asks them what is wrong.

Jack replies, "We were hoping you could find a way of getting us directly to shore, without our having to get wet."[6]

It just doesn't work that way—it never has and it never will.

We need to reignite our sense of mythos and be inspired to pass on our information, ideas, and learning—to cultivate a coherent form of transmission. Neurogenetic evolution is a biopsychic transmission, yet this needs to be paralleled with a transmission of "cultural memory": a merging of inspiration with past information. This cannot be achieved successfully when the majority of people exist in a sleeping state. It has been achieved in the form of oral histories, stories, and myths passed down by the generations. To our detriment many of these forms are now dismissed by modern culture; the art of storytelling is a fringe activity and myths are relegated to the realms of fantasy or scholarly trappings. Rarely are such myths and stories implanted as living codices within our material cultures. Awake and aware minds need to plan; current generations need to act as conscious and responsible transmitters and cultural carriers for the coming generations. It is not only about taking back our minds for ourselves; we need to achieve this for those who follow so that during difficult times there will always be lights that shine. Remember what was said in chapter 6 about how one individual at consciousness level 300 counterbalances 90,000 individuals below level 200, and one individual at level 400 counterbalances 400,000 individuals below level 200? Well, these could be the tipping points: it takes a minority of conscious-minded people to spread the energy of change exponentially.

There is nothing wrong in saying that we should aim to bring spiritual concerns back into our daily lives, to respiritualize human life. However, the spiritual in this context doesn't mean going around wearing colorful clothes and beads (although that's fine if you wish to!), nor does it suggest that we should be humming mantras or blessing everyone we meet with a bow and a *Namaste*. Of course, this is all fine and may be suitable for some people. Yet what I wish to point out is that such clichés are part of the old programming. We think that being spiritual means adhering to these stereotypes that have been rammed down our throats by coarse and lowest-level-denominator media entertainment. Instead we can start with just having appreciation and an awareness of our own thoughts and behavior. It also means stepping away from too much intellectualism, as what we grasp through the pure intellect will be lacking in spirit. As Rudolf Steiner reminds us, "You cannot truly experience the spirit if you get no further than mere intelligence. The reason why intelligence is so seductive is that it yields a picture, a reflected picture of the spirit—but not the spirit itself."[7] Within each person lives something more than the physical, whether we care to acknowledge its presence or not. We have within us something that is not dependent on the physical events, disruptions, and influences that surround us daily. Yet it is a constructive power that does not equate to dense and heavy forms of control and greed. Part of this inherent energy manifests through the quality of our thoughts and mental behavior. Lower thoughts based on greed, acquisition, control, and material gains keep us trapped within social institutions that are very well placed to supply and create these mental demands and desires. However, such thought forms belong to automatic, mechanical thinking and do not benefit us. Gurdjieff would often refer to these forms as useless thinking that only serves to "Feed the Moon." In this respect, by remaining mechanical we are feeding into those forces that seek to keep us psychically restrained and under embargo. It will also serve as a buffer, a blockage, against the energetic impacts and wave interferences of a potentially rising form of quantum consciousness (as discussed in chapter 7). Yet with well-being and appreciative, aware behavior we can likewise resonate our quantum energy fields with other fields in which we are energetically entangled.

As previously discussed there is the possibility that energetic impacts may alter the vibratory rate of biophoton emission within our human DNA. This in turn, I speculate, could increase the coherency of our quantum energy field that affects our sense and our general perceptions. At the moment we are seeing anomalies arise in the new generations being born within our various societies, and people who exhibit these anomalies are being publicly ridiculed; reconditioned to confer with existing paradigms; or taken into "care," observed, and trained for private gains.* Yet we will gradually witness a rise in the number of younger generations exhibiting these genetic evolutionary differences, which will serve to alter the Earth's vibratory field

---

*See *China's Super Psychics* by Paul Dong and Thomas Raffill.

and contribute to a general rising of species consciousness. We can see visionary elements of this in people's testimony from various transcendental states. One person in particular, A. J. Peterson, wrote of a vision he had while pursuing a program of personal development. Some of these extracts include the following:

> There seems to be a framework—a structure . . . a whole new design for life and inner development . . . moving into manifestation immediately ahead of us in time . . . filtering already through an intermediary strata to specially selected points. Every detail preplanned; originating from above to below . . . not in linear time at all . . . thus superseding our planetary laws of cause and effect. And absolutely nothing can stop it . . . it's already there, out of range of our vision, but as real and solid as life itself. How it will manifest I can only surmise . . .
>
> . . . A new force, or influence, is reaching us—coded to produce precise results that will supersede the old modes of development— almost a forced process which will have effects unique in world history as we know it . . . A stepping-up of transformative force must cause resistance . . . and in this respect, the animal kingdom and all natural life will fare much better than humanity—having followed its own instinctive laws without deviation . . .
>
> . . . I was merely one pupil amongst many, all undergoing some manner of quickening and applied stimulus. Mankind is a cradle, or chrysalis, in which such potential exists as a possibility, or in an embryonic latency. In this state I perceived a vast act of direct intervention in the life of mankind, like realignment with the source of all manifestation, which necessitated the prior removal of an obstruction to its correct development. This occurrence coincided with the release of a fresh inflow of magnetic influences, also a stepping-up of vibrational pressure, like entering a more powerful force-field, or submission to a forced process of growth—designed to produce an evolutionary "leap." But it all happened in the dimension

of the higher Self, and has not yet externalised into our world of linear time, though its foreshadowings are already apparent.[8]

The vision ahead of us cannot be taken from our past references—a new model must come into being. Remember the Buckminster Fuller quote at the beginning of this chapter? "You never change things by fighting the existing reality. To change something, build a new model that makes the existing model obsolete." Or, as Rudolf Steiner prefers to phrase it: "A power for building afresh can only be drawn from a source not belonging to Earth's previous evolution."[9]

A reenvisioning of society with spiritual impulses requires of us that we develop an awareness of the ecology of our minds as living intelligences with endless connectivity in which we exist in an ecosystem of people, Nature, and mental paradigms/systems of thought. As such, we need to cooperate in harmony within our overlapping ecology. The laws of Nature that surround us are steady and constant and have remained so for countless known and unknown past civilizations. Those civilizations are just that: *past*. For us to evolve as a species and as a civilization we need to coexist with the Earth system and to understand those laws we are to live in balance with. This may be the only way toward advancing the evolution of the human being, and it is common sense too. Yet common sense has not always been welcome with rational societies that are based upon power and control. This case was recently highlighted by the "Climategate" scandal that erupted between November 2009 and March 2010. In this incident a reputable climatic research unit at a prominent UK university was hacked into and e-mails leaked that appeared to substantiate the claim that climate research was being tampered with—information withheld, dissenting papers prevented from being published, and similar tactics. In other words, there had been extensive pressure for researchers to follow the consensus line on climate research: namely, that climate change is human induced. This is another example of how peer-reviewed, high-level research is being controlled by corporate and financial interests. This, sadly, is how higher education and university research is conducted nowadays— via corporate financing (grants), which then puts the research under corporate control or at least external pressure. The social matrix has woven its web through all avenues of material science and thought. This has placed us within a dangerous illusion: that our science and technology has released us from dependence on Nature. We desperately need to reenvision this position.

The changes we are witnessing over the Earth in these years are catalyzing many people into rethinking this human-Earth relationship. At the same time, the increase in individual worries and insecurities are eclipsing this longer-term vision. We thus need to have vision and optimism while simultaneously being realistic over the uncomfortable realities of resource depletion, social fractures, and Earth changes. There are too many anomalies within the Earth changes for there to be a simple relationship between humans polluting the air and incredible Earth shifts. What is more likely is that we are witnessing the natural environmental shifts between ice ages as ice continually melts and reforms over thousands of years. This is a natural part of the Earth's water cycles, yet since they occur over a long period of human time we have no immediate recognition of these changes. Still it has presented an almost perfect situation for governing powers to hijack the science and declare carbon taxes and extra monitoring of movement and expenditure. And many of us think, *Science good; humans bad* (*Four legs good; two legs bad*). Where is the information?

The famous historian Arnold Toynbee claimed that civilizations emerge and evolve when they are governed by a creative minority that inspires the people. In turn, civilizations enter decline when the dominant minority fails to inspire the rest of its people and prefers to follow a status quo of power rule. Yet treading water is no good for any person or any civilization. And are we being inspired?

It appears that we are in danger of our worldviews collectively stagnating and thus our individual thought processes halting; worldviews must also evolve like our social structures and our relationships. The constant rigid belief sets that claim that our present knowledge is superior to prior sets of knowledge and wisdom is not only erroneous but also misleading and damaging. These belief sets also close the door to more aware and spiritual relationships that can be opened up when a person accepts that she is a part of the living fabric of the cosmos. This includes our connection with Nature (her laws and forces), the solar system, the galaxy, the universe, and all the living intelligences and energies that reside within such interconnected systems. New information needs to be introduced into our thinking patterns so that the new science will have spiritual implications (such as quantum consciousness discussed in chapter 7). For example, increased knowledge about the nature and function of energy fields and how our lives and this planet are influenced to a large degree by electromagnetic waves and fluctuations will start to put matters in a different perspective. We will then understand that the Earth carries and transmits electromagnetic energy through natural flows such as water and air movement, and that some areas of the Earth are positively charged while others are negatively charged. This will then show us how the Earth's weather patterns depend on the attraction and flow of positive/negative electromagnetic currents. From this we will learn that some of our current technologies, and indeed our military weapons, affect this balance.

The knowledge of the Earth's energy grid and lines and the geomagnetic properties by which the grids influence the surface of the planet needs to shift in the near future from the fringes of alternative science (where it has been relegated by the mainstream) to an important science. We may then come to realize that natural events such as hurricanes and earthquakes are not haphazard in their movements but are connected to magnetic flows and/or disturbances. Continued ignorance of such forces of nature will come at a great cost.

Just as species evolution and mental-paradigm mutations begin to emerge before the ending of evolutionary stages/social cycles, so too do the next signs of civilization/culture begin to sprout in pockets. With the ending of our present stage of culture and its attendant consciousness of control and containment, we see examples of new thinking emerging as cultural movements: a return to respecting energy use and natural resources, the benefits of regionalism/localism, growing our own food and/or patronizing local farmers' markets, and moves toward local sustainability. Returning to these more naturally balanced systems does not imply going backward to more primitive lifestyles; rather, it signifies moving forward into more fundamental ways of being. These include the development of mental, emotional, and spiritual awareness for creative and life-sustaining purposes, such as creating goals around how best to utilize each person's individual skills and capacity, and to engage these capacities for the good of the whole. Individual lives should be based around self-development and wisdom learning, developing personal skills into useful contributions, working as part of larger communities, and working/growing in harmony with nature and natural laws. There is no contradiction between being a creative individual and being part of an inspired community. There is no ridicule to be a part of larger, extended families. The pressure to leave home and to "make it" in the world are consumerist patterns that have helped to destroy the family and community unit. New emerging patterns may likely see larger families increasingly being a part of growing communities. This may lead once more to the growth of community/family businesses, community gardens and self-grown food, and a rise in community self-sufficiency.

Is it really so difficult to take back our minds from the repetitious groove of our consumerist control social matrixes, where our beliefs, emotions, and desires are so blatantly manipulated? What if just *being* is enough? We don't have to be the best of the best if we are comfortable with the person we are. There is no social competition if we see the social as collaborative, communicative, and sharing. Perhaps one of the great contributions we can each make is by spreading positivity and *lack of fear* through all our social interactions—in other words, to have our aware conscious minds functioning alongside our intuitive hearts.

MERGING OF THE MIND AND HEART

Throughout this book I have stressed the need to think for oneself and to break from old programs and conditioning. I have emphasized how important it is for a person to be consciously aware of her own thoughts and behavior, as well as the impact and unfolding of external events. This alert awareness—state of conscious activity—has a fundamental effect on the state of one's being. It also has a primary influence on our emotions and emotional well-being. This is of particular importance since it is often through the emotions that the social matrix attempts to influence and coerce. The human heart has thus been transformed, in a careful and deliberate manner, to represent base emotional signifiers. The heart now has saccharine overtones, of Valentine offerings, pursuit of desire, conquered lust, and endless similar connotations. Within our advancing technological world—our rational modernity and positivistic science—our heart qualities have largely been based on lower emotions and desires. Due to this many people often unknowingly manifest unbalanced and underdeveloped emotional energies.

Our social conditionings have erected a sense of fear over unmasking and expressing our emotional hearts. Many men fear being called feminine, and emotion has often been targeted as a female "weakness." Human emotional energies have thus suffered a control-and-containment process similar to that of our conscious minds. And the result of this has been the same: an underdevelopment of our human potential. After all, imagine trying to control (sorry, govern) the mass of people who are in full control and expression of their own emotional selves? The fear would roll off our backs like balls of jelly. Human encounters have been stunted by emotional fears of social expression. Yet we would do well to establish a distinction between the sentimental heart—the heart of indulgence and desire—and the heart of emotional empowerment. This form of empowerment translates our conscious awareness into our practical behavior and actions, as in the famous dictum "You shall know them by their deeds." Let us look at the rational world around us, at our pinnacle of intellectual technocultures. What do we see? How is the human world treating its people, its relationship to Nature?

The human family is a single organism that connects through the heart. We do not need any secret code or password; we are eligible for our inherent emotional and conscious empowerment by being human. Yet as I have discussed throughout the book we have been relentlessly manipulated into turning our attention in the wrong direction. We have been distracted and fed misleading and disempowering information that weakens rather than strengthens our potential and self-resolve. As was shown in chapter 7 each living entity is surrounded by and emits a quantum field of energy. If these energy fields/states are vibrant, then it is possible for each person to transmit—pass on—this energy in their physical encounters as well as in their thoughts/prayers. Such energy could go viral and act to reenergize and rebalance people in need of regaining strength and equilibrium. This could facilitate a behavioral shift as each of us realizes the potential of our actions. It could be a merging of the mind and heart—of consciousness and compassion—where the ideals of the Enlightenment (new science/quantum consciousness) unite with the spirit of the troubadours (compassion of the heart).

Just as the Enlightenment was a revolution in seeding a higher mental-creative impulse into society and an attack against orthodoxy and control, so too was the troubadour "event" a seeding of the higher emotional impulse. The troubadours brought about a revolution in the way "love" was expressed, thought about, and experienced. It was a time where an interior emotional impulse could be expressed externally in a way never articulated before. It thus created the conditions for others to experience and share in these feelings and conscious expressions. The experience of falling in love was deliberately introduced into the cultural stream of human consciousness, and the experience of being in love was given a structure, a vessel, for its growth and evolution. Although the word *troubadour* is often credited with deriving from the Provençal verb *trobar*, meaning "to find" or "to invent," it is more likely to have come from the Arabic root *TRB* (with the *ador* suffix added).[10] The TRB root suggests a range of words that include a meeting place of friends, a master, playing the viol, and the idealization of women. The troubadours appeared to encapsulate these meanings in their mysterious gatherings and dissemination of a new consciousness of longing. Courtly love provided a vessel for bridging interior yearning to an exterior expression. Through this channel other courtly endeavors could arise, notably in the court chivalry that grew rapidly around the same time. Chivalric ideals were absorbed into literary works such as Chretien de Troyes's romantic Arthurian legends and the Holy Grail. Dante's Divine Comedy too owes much to this conscious influence. Chivalric orders such as the Knights Templar can be seen as having a debt to the troubadour influence. The injection of this deliberate developmental impulse spread rapidly through both mental and physical channels.

By injecting into public consciousness expressions of longing and chivalric etiquette, there have arisen codes of conduct, artistic aspirations, architectural monuments, and various other cultural reminders for the human psyche. The troubadours offered a revolution in higher emotions and behavior and allowed a person's love and yearning to be expressed unsentimentally in correct and laudable actions. Yet this creative impulse has also been corrupted by the human realm into three-minute pop songs and commercial love sentiments. It needs to be asked, however, if humanity is prepared for a future in which the spirit, mind, science, emotion, and technology are fused into one.

Again referring to our quantum energy field, we can reevaluate the human race as a generator of immense electromagnetic energy that is produced from our thoughts and our emotions. This is why there will always be those who, knowingly or unknowingly, attempt to use humanity's emotional energies for their own purpose. The energy of the human race should be directed as an evolutionary impulse and not left to leak and dissipate. Regardless of our social conditioning—status, religious beliefs, and personal views—we are all primarily energetic beings. Every part of us is alive: our cells are electric, our DNA emits biophotons, our hearts pump out an electromagnetic field. As such we are constantly creating an energetic signature—a footprint. This is our mark in the world. If we work on this, we move differently through our external world. To focus on our own mindful and energetic states will give us the energy we need to be able to break away from the energetic constraints and impulses of material life. We can break the spell cast upon us by creating sufficient energetic resources within ourselves. This is our rightful inheritance; it should be our acquired education too. Sadly, we have been denied the information crucial to our personal and collective evolutionary development. We have been kept in the dark for too long, shielded from the knowledge of our own inner resources. Many revolutions have been fought in blood for social change; too few have been fought compassionately for inner development.

As we are increasingly enmeshed within levels of environmental static, EM pollution, and external distortions/distractions, it will be critical in these years that we radiate focused intentions. This may force some people to change their life situations. There are many competing currents and energies within Earth's electromagnetic realm that are giving off chaotic emissions now, affecting each person's energetic balances. In these times we will need balanced emotions of positivity, creativity, motivation, enthusiasm, and joy to raise the body's vibratory frequency and break away from the threat of dis-ease and immunity weakness. Along with conscious awareness it will greatly benefit people to maintain higher emotional states and to avoid being sucked down into the negative emotional trappings of fear, helplessness, and insecurity. The danger is that we get caught up in a world of increasing acceleration and we give diminishing time and attention to the "timeless" resources within us. We become too distracted to the time-oriented life outside us; in contrast, our timeless realm inside seems to us to have no power, no attraction, no control (or no place) in our outer existence. We may allow ourselves a brief ten minutes of meditation in our busy lives to connect with our inner "timeless space," and then we shelve it, relegate it to an ephemeral side of us that we speak to only in rare moments or when stressed. We fail to see that it is exactly this part of us that has the capacity to enhance each physical moment, to infuse the external with our energy signatures. Our heart is like a huge galactic center, emitting energetic pulsars with each beat. The latest scientific research has in fact found the human heart to be a biological electromagnetic pump that pounds out an electromagnetic energy signature within each moment of our physical life.[11] This signature pattern of our EM field/pulse is connected to our state of emotions and thoughts. This in turn reacts with other external EM fields and to some degree affects how events/people interact with us. In other words, our energetic imprint is a factor in the attraction/creation/response of external encounters. We literally carry ourselves around with us, imprinting our every step, interacting at various visible and unseen levels at each moment of our lives. This is why our social matrixes have been constructed to distract and detract from practices of the self. Yet at this moment during these transition years it is of utmost importance that we should *practice our lives:* live out the moments of appreciation, gratefulness, compassion, understanding, humility, and overall positivity.

The merging of the conscious mind and heart, especially in these transition times, will ask that we become fluid, aware yet open, and that we reject all components of fear and thus manipulation. All walls eventually crumble: lightness and being just are. In these times ahead, as the energies around us begin to change, as the struggle for control of human consciousness seems chaotic, let us remember to focus our energies through a more intentional form of living. This includes, but is not limited to:

Being aware of our EM environments and our exposure time to such influences.

Eating consciously and carefully—knowing what we are putting inside our energetic bodies. Food affects the quality of our physical, mental, and emotional health. We should also drink lots of purified water. If drinking tap/household water, check its chemical composition first.

Spending some moments with yourself. Choosing to listen to the inner "timeless space." Enjoying meditation in whichever form you are comfortable with.

Taking walks into Nature and connecting with the natural world and showing appreciation for the livings forms, soil, air, water, and so forth.

Exercising the physical body when you can. It doesn't necessarily have to be long exercise—simple walks are fine. And breathing properly!

Reducing negative thoughts and thinking. Thinking consciously, not storing hatred, and always forgiving and letting go.

Exercising self-discipline and impeccability. There is no need for mechanicalness or laziness of thought.

Trusting yourself and not giving in to fear. Fear is nothing—do not give it a home.

Preparing for the flow: being relaxed, fluid, and open to change and the unpredictable. Trusting your instinct and intuition (use and strengthen the muscle!).

Being at ease with your emotions yet not allowing them to become polluted by coercive sentimentality.

Seeking beautiful things around you: if you entered a garden would you sit next to a bed of weeds or a rosebush?

Avoiding people and things that make you feel bad/negative. Avoiding impacts of a lower vibratory nature.

Asserting your right to manifest your higher mental and emotional states and their higher vibrational qualities. Asserting your right to be—intending and willing your future!

A new reality of life will be ushered in, not as a sudden rapturous dimensional shift or an Armageddon-type cataclysm, but as a transition through human participation, awareness, and, above all, effort. The newer generations that are being born will be inheriting the world to come. It will be a world of unprecedented promise, capacity, and potential. We are all a part of this grand cycle of change, learning, and growth. It is indeed a monumental time to be here.

9
NEW PERCEPTIONS
Creating Energetic Change in Ourselves

Improving the energy balance of one person ultimately affects us all.

ADAM (ENERGY HEALER)

As the preceding chapters in this book have discussed, our collective consensus reality is a bewitching spell. It is a hallucinatory shared "reality" that both fascinates and beguiles. Tolstoy wrote that "truth, like gold, is to be obtained not by its growth, but by washing away from it all that is not gold." Thus by cleansing ourselves of the distractions and distortions we may help to clean the lens of our perception. The new currency here is not fiat money but conscious awareness. As the aphorism goes, "'Take what you want,' says God, 'but pay for it.'" Yet nothing in our world is free. Even the act of changing one's thinking patterns comes at a price. We should remember that all genuine transactions are reciprocal. With real effort comes reward. However, real effort is best practiced when absent from the need or desire for reward.

Throughout this book I have discussed thought patterns and the need to break free from mental conditioning. I have spoken little, except briefly in the previous chapter, about our personal energies. Yet since thought itself is an energy force all mental acts are thus energetic projections. As outlined in chapter 7, each biological entity exists within a form of shared informational field(s); this underlies the Hermetic principle that *everything is mind*. The Hermetic dictum states that "The Universe is Mental,"[1] suggesting that the cosmos resonates with energy that is conscious, dynamic, and creative. In this respect human beings can be viewed as organisms that both filter and create energy. Further, it is through this energy that we hold the capacity to alter our sense and perception(s) of our immediate environment. In other words, we exist in a "sense" environment where our energy fields operate as extensions of our physical five senses. We have the capacity to "feel" our reality, which then gets filtered through our physical sense apparatus. At the fundamental root of physical matter, everything is energy. This is not speculation; it is hard physics that now forms the basis for the most sophisticated scientific experiments, such as the Large Hadron Collider (LHC), the world's largest and highest-energy particle accelerator. With this in mind, taking back our minds is also about learning to manage the interactions between interior and exterior energy fields/flows. By learning how to free up energy a person is then able to save some energy from daily use and wastage. This stored energy can then be used for a person's own focused intentions and awareness. Thus it is also about *creating energetic change in ourselves.*

Our "civilized" societies often direct attention away from the need for an individual to act authentically—that is, driven not by externally motivated desires but from genuine internal impulses. This necessitates the formation within a person of disciplined intention. The intention involves the capacity to direct oneself in life without imitation or need for recognition and approval. The cultivation of inner intention can itself lead to knowing "right action." This is when conscience is operating in balance with the creative imagination of a person's interior life. When we act in balance with our inner nature, our outward actions often appear as if directed by a form of conscience and feel *right*. When conscience and genuine intuition are operating together there is an intention that is not thought, wish, or an object. It is an intention that can override the thoughts of conditioning. It creates a form of internal strength and control that can resist the daily barrage of social memes and manipulative impacts. However, power is not the force we have over others but rather the force we have within ourselves. It is through this force that a person is able to manifest sincere intent through their actions and behavior.

It will be necessary during the years ahead of sociocultural change that our intentions also connect with the accompanying shift in human consciousness. What we are currently passing through is another revolution of the human imagination. It is a time to be open to changing the rigidity of our embedded thoughts, beliefs, and "sacred" attachments. What enslaves a person is what holds her attention externally. There is an oral anecdote about the Sufi mystic Rabia (of Basra), who when asked by a friend on a beautiful spring morning to come outside to see the bounteous works of God, replied, "Come you inside that you may behold their Maker. Contemplation of the Maker has turned me aside from what He has made." Like Rabia's friend the majority of us are focused on the secondary in a way that occupies us totally. It is a consuming relationship, and one that requires all our available energies. This manner is what many mystics have referred to when they say that humanity is asleep.

Breaking out of our many and varied social conditionings requires that a whole new system of perception be brought into being. It calls for mental, emotional, and energetic reserves of concentration that can replace a person's old conditioned terms of reference for new terms of reference, which are more positive and useful. It also involves knowing when to include and when to exclude. With lesser energy a person can often feel helpless in the face of external influences and impacts. It is necessary to hold some disciplinary power over those things, people, and events that we wish to either include or exclude from the realm of our daily world. In other words, we need to rearrange our storage of experiences. When an encounter, event, or impact is received we should immediately ask ourselves about its nature and whether it is a benefit to us. The question of conscious-level storage is sometimes more of a question of what to throw away. Failure to activate this filtering only adds to our loss of internal power and discipline. From this a person can become weaker within his or her life, pushed around by the influence of arbitrary forces. By being an independent presence in the world we are being asked to assume responsibility for this gift. The average person far too often acts on his thoughts and desires without taking responsibility for them. Thus we need to assume the responsibility of our presence in the world: in this time, now, and through each moment and encounter.

By taking responsibility in this way we make each moment and encounter our own. By not taking responsibility we let events drift away from us and are powerless to defend against their disruptive influence. In each moment is the opportunity for the reciprocal exchange of energies; such exchanges are the binds that serve to arrange a person's life. Creative inner discipline allows a person to grab onto more things in life. Life is shorter than we may realize; or rather when we eventually realize how short life can be, it's often too late. This is nicely indicated by the following story.

> A miser had accumulated, by effort, trade, and lending, three hundred thousand dinars. He had lands and buildings, and all kinds of wealth. He then decided that he would spend a year in enjoyment, living comfortably, and then decide as to what his future should be. But, almost as soon as he had stopped amassing money the Angel of Death appeared before him, to take his life away.
>
> The miser tried, by every argument which he could muster, to dissuade the Angel, who seemed, however, adamant. Then the man said: "Grant me but three more days and I will give you one-third of my possessions."
>
> The angel refused, and pulled again at the miser's life, tugging to take it away. Then the man said:
>
> "If you only allow me two more days on earth, I will give you two hundred thousand dinars from my store."

But the Angel would not listen to him. And the Angel even refused to give the man a solitary extra day for all his three hundred thousand pieces. The miser then said:

"Please, then, give me just time enough to write one little thing down."

This time the Angel allowed him this single concession, and the man wrote, with his own blood:

Man, make use of your life. I could not buy one hour for three hundred thousand dinars. Make sure that you realize the value of your time.[2]

Time often appears to speed up for an individual as experiences accumulate. Inner awareness can be helpful here by arranging how each moment is consciously stored and re-created. We have the capacity to embellish our lives through how we perceive and interpret our encounters.

The aim of this final chapter is to reinforce the notion that a person's "cultural spell" can be broken. New and creative perceptions, thought patterns, and behavior can be brought into focus. In a way, we need *to learn how to learn.* And we need to refresh our sense of self— our convictions and inner feelings. Revitalizing these energetic and creative capacities is thus about managing one's energy, being vigilant with oneself, and learning to step away, as the rest of this chapter will discuss.

MANAGING ONE'S ENERGY

Energy is a force of informational exchange and transmission, whether we are able to recognize this or not. In all moments our bodies are involved within an informational field of instructions, feedback, control, and maintenance. These interactions are also occurring within a network of fields between people, society, environment/Nature, and a range of unobservable impacts. As such we can say that energy is a force of material quantity and should be considered in terms of its quantitative value. A person has the capacity (or access) to only so much energy in her lifetime. Energy should be thus viewed not as a limitless resource but as an endowment. Too many people too much of the time spend energy needlessly on unnecessary and unpleasant emotions, thoughts, and actions. Energy gets used up on expectations, mood swings, nervousness, irritability, negative imagination, negative thoughts/intentions, self-pity, and so forth. Desires and misplaced attention, for example, are primary ways of losing this quantitative energy. The fanciful desires that come into us from the exterior social carnival distract and sap our energies. If we could but form small specific goals within our everyday life and achieve them, this would create more permanent energy within us. As an exercise, try to begin with small aims that are realizable before moving onto larger goals. Allow these aims to be formed not from want but from need. To know what one needs is a higher form of thinking than by being influenced by wants.

A helpful formulation is *Energy retention; energy intention,* whereby storing and retaining as much personal energy as possible helps to strengthen other faculties. This personal energy can then be made available for physical aims and achievements through focused intention. A lack of a conscious aim within life goes hand in hand with unfocused and undisciplined interior energy. It is a basic fact of our lives that we give away our energy too easily. It is thus necessary to save, store, and manage one's personal energy, even if for the primary reason that a person needs enough personal energy for self-evolution. To manage one's energy then requires that we become more conscious of the reciprocation of energies—mentally, physically, and emotionally. Energy is thus lost through unnecessary physical/muscular exertion, unfocused mental distractions, and emotional nervousness or stress.

The picture may become clearer if we consider that one of the functions of the human being is to assist in the movement of energies. Humans are agents of transmission—for themselves, for people around them, and for their environment. It can be said that humans both individually and collectively operate as transducers of energies. The human body is like a biological battery—it accumulates, develops, and distributes energies. As such it is necessary for a person to be in harmonious relation with her interactions: with people, situations, emotions, and physical posturing. These concepts are not new; in fact they form the basis of our everyday world. People often talk of sensing "bad vibes" between people or even in places. When something just doesn't feel right we need to trust these instinctual signs. It is our responsibility to find and nurture right alignments. For example, when in the presence of some people we may recognize that we always have a feeling of being drained of energy. It is as if these people were sucking the energy away from us. In these circumstances we can refer to such people as psychic vampires, not because they are necessarily evil, dangerous, or denizens of the night. It is because their energy alignments are such that they pull in the energy around them. The reasons for this are various, yet the outcome invariably the same. If it is not your function to "feed" them, then move away—just don't entertain their energy. Ancient teachings have long recognized that the human being also exists as an energetic entity.

> The human form is a conglomerate of energy fields which exists in the universe, and which is related exclusively to human beings. Shamans call it the human form because those energy fields have been bent and contorted by a life-time of habits and misuse.[3]

The interior health of the human can be related to the shape and form of one's energy body. As one young energy healer recently noted: "Every physical object emits its own quantum hologram, which contains all information about it. From this field of quantum information, I can zoom in on specific information or views."[4] This same healer also noted how a person's attitude (mental and emotional state) affected the health of their energy fields. The quality of a person's energy fields/vibrations is thus relative to his mental and emotional condition. Negative mental states will be accompanied by discordant vibrations. Some of these vibrations will remain within the energy of the person's body, affecting him physically, while the remainder will resonate into the exterior environment. Just as in the vibration of musical sounds, a person's vibration affects the people around him by a form of induction. In simpler terms, everything is in resonance with every other thing (quantum information fields). Every thought we have, every act we perform, has its direct and indirect results through the resonance and transference of energies. It is a universal law taught by all the perennial wisdom traditions that *like attracts like*. A person is liable to attract the positive just as he can attract the negative. One's interior mental state is thus a valve to exterior energies and conditions. Being mindful of one's thoughts and state of mind is primary to a disciplined management of personal energy.

The *attention distractor* (AD) that is increasingly a part of our modern social matrixes often draws a person's attention outward to events that are of a superficial, vacuous, and inane nature. In this way ordinary life operates to distract the focused energy of individuals. It is thus necessary for each person to carefully manage her daily mental and emotional energies. For example, material objects/events can drain us of our conscious energy, demanding more and more of our awareness and concentration, until we are leaking our energy like a bucket with holes.

If an external influence impacts your mental state, as in feeling stressed or confused, then create a mental stop. Assess the situation and restart by calling forth and generating *intent*. By putting deliberate mental intention into a situation or event a person is creating an energetic force that both fuels and protects them. Similarly, to alter a disagreeable state of mind we each should seek out those activities that feel harmonious to us. For example, when the mind is confused or frustrated, we can listen to some relaxing music. Or we can go for a favorite walk in the woods or be near to Nature. By engaging in activities that create a favorable resonance we can learn to revitalize and plug our seeping energies. This is a necessary practice when dealing with energy management. After all, if you had a pot of gold you wouldn't go about throwing out handfuls of gold coins. Why do the same with our personal energy? A dictum that expresses this situation is *Energy flows where attention goes*. By being aware of where we place our attention and to what degree, we are better placed to manage our store of energy. In this sense we need to be ever vigilant in how we exercise our attention.

BEING VIGILANT

The general behavior that manifests in various social forms is mechanical. And the more mechanical human behaviour is, the more external forces we are under the influence of. By exercising self-vigilance a person can learn to become more aware of the multiple interactions we each engage in with the exterior environment, its forces, and its influences. For example, how many of us are aware of our breathing? It is significant that the most fundamental physical act of our survival passes largely unnoticed. Yet the simple act of being attentive to our breathing can help us to become more aware of the present moment. This doesn't mean that we should each go about totally fixated upon our breathing, or that we should try to count each breath obsessively. It is about calmly, during the course of the day, bringing the attention to observe the breathing process. Not only can this act bring some measured calm but also it works to discipline and "tighten" personal energy. An individual will find, after practicing this exercise, that it will gradually become easier and will require less attention. Soon it will become natural for the attention to keep an almost constant awareness on the breathing process. After all, breathing has an important function in that it allows for the exhalation of stale gases and cleans the physical system. Deep breathing especially helps to regulate and "tone" the body as it takes in more oxygen. It can also help a person relax. But it should never be overdone or forced, as artificial or coerced breathing can lead to hyperventilation. Rather, it is a matter of allowing the breathing to stabilize itself. The breathing should be in harmony with one's own natural rhythm.

The body benefits from a good, balanced intake of oxygen, which should be neither labored nor in short rasps. Being aware of one's breathing is not the same as being wary. There should be no tension or anxiety involved. This doesn't mean that we should each occupy ourselves with questions such as "Am I breathing correctly?" The most appropriate approach is one of relaxed calm, where gentle awareness of the breathing can lay the groundwork for a greater sense of cohesion and communication with the body and self. With this attentiveness a person is bringing into focus the present moment. Gradually this practice of breathing awareness should catalyze and bring into play a person's faculties of vigilance and watchfulness.

Another step in developing vigilance is through awareness of one's own "steps" that are taken within daily life. What this calls for is observation and attention to those times when either action or inaction is required, and in such situations, to always act positively. There are also situations when positive inaction is important. When a person can observe and feel when correct action or inaction is required, this triggers the right use of energy. In our daily lives it is critical that each person uses his store of energy correctly. This involves correct thinking and/or right action at the right time. It is not about being critical of oneself or observing with the intention of finding fault. Self-vigilance is more about producing a state of watchful harmony. This state can then further attract (and benefit from) the positive. By being more open to positive impacts and situations a person can be more alert to develop and capitalize on such beneficial moments and conditions. These moments can be developed further and the energies extended. Yet we should also be careful not to contrive or manufacture artificial conditions that are not in genuine harmony with our state or inner priorities.

Being vigilant also requires that each of us feel natural and at ease with ourselves. In other words, we should become used to observing ourselves and come to feel quietly confident with the relationship. Within this vigilant state a person can also observe her own thought processes and exert greater control and discipline over them—instead of letting them run around like wild tigers causing internal havoc and distress. So it is about being aware of coincidences and how these serendipitous moments can be opportunities or circumstances for action.

This disciplined attentiveness to one's own actions, thoughts, and general participation in everyday life does not concern critical judgment or chastising oneself. We can each be gently critical, for sure, yet it is all too easy to become hostile toward oneself and then the blame game begins. It is necessary to make sure that we are comfortable observing ourselves—sometimes passively, and other times in a critically constructive manner. In this way we can learn to travel through our own "inner homeland."

A person's inner homeland represents the internal realm with which an individual develops an intimate communication. It should therefore become a place of familiar travel, where a person visits regularly and becomes familiar with the communication. It should also become the place where a person examines herself from an objective viewpoint. This act of self-observation is an inner muscle that strengthens each time it is used. A person's homeland represents a journey of reflection for examining and considering recent motivations, actions and their consequences, and daily recollections. It should be a welcome place where at the end of the day a person can sit down and recollect how the day's events and experiences passed. Such moments form a kind of self-review; yet in these moments of recollection and analysis a person is also retaining energy rather than letting energy dissipate through scatty and disorganized emotional flourishes and remembrances. It is thus important that any review be as objective and as sympathetic to the self as possible. Harshness and/or emotional indulgence is no good for the inland journeys. These trips to internally review events are about getting to know yourself better and better, and to live with yourself in a more harmonious relationship. It is essential in these present times of attention distraction to maximize on moments of quietness and reflection. Even to take just a few minutes each day within a busy schedule can help to calm, balance, and focus personal energies and mental attention. In our industrialized technocultures time is sped up to the maximum rate of revolutions per minute. This needs to be counterbalanced by snatching, creating, and insisting on five or ten minutes per day of visiting one's homeland. In this time period instead of battering yourself with mental worries you can create a relaxed space where you can enter into a state of balanced self-vigilance. While you may not be able to dictate the length of time you have, you most certainly can influence the sense and quality of your time.

To exercise self-vigilance and to travel within is a learning journey, a path to better know our strengths and weaknesses and to understand what each of us knows and does not know. Yet to accomplish this we need also to exercise a certain degree of balanced humility. There is a joke that goes: "There were three monks arguing as to which order was the best—the Jesuit, the Benedictine, and the Dominican. After hearing the Jesuit and the Benedictine, the Dominican said, 'For logic and argument and organization we all know that the Jesuits are best. And the Benedictines are best for their friendliness and for their great wine. But when it comes to humility we Dominicans are really the best!'" It takes a lot to be genuine and sincere with oneself. Yet by exercising such traits we can each work toward strengthening our management of physical, mental, and emotional energies. In a world of increased external manipulations, conditioning, and insecurities such capacities can bring great benefits.

By developing inner focus and perception we can each gain awareness over the multiple layers of conditioning that impact us throughout our lives. A person who is thirty or forty years old has thirty or forty years of conditioning; this cannot easily be dealt with. The question is not about dropping all conditioning like a sack of old clothes—this would be a bombshell and could do more harm than good. Also without some form of social conditioning we would find it very hard to get along in our everyday lives. So conditioning is required to a degree in order for us to live communal lives (such as conditioning of social politeness). The question, rather, revolves around being made aware of what conditioning is operating at a given time, how it is operating within us, and whether we actually need it or not. And if not how can we halt or sidestep these conditioned beliefs.

The intention behind self-vigilance is to stimulate a degree of awareness so that a person may be in a better position to observe his forms of conditioning (physical, mental, and emotional). He can then develop this knowledge to gain a better understanding of himself. Developing awareness involves a level of discipline that in turn helps to focus an individual's personal energies. The qualities (vibrational nature) of such energies are important in that within a universe of interacting energy/information fields, all thoughts, words, and deeds carry their own vibratory quality. These energies affect the quality of a person's life, his environment, and the people around him. Therefore, what each person "puts out," so to speak, is his own responsibility. Within such a conscious universe each of us should learn how to behave! This does not imply being more than human; rather what is required of us is that we become more fully human.

This may involve moments when it is not only possible but desirable to step more lightly, which means not overindulging in situations and/or emotional matters. As is often said, it is not what happens to you that is important but rather how you deal with it. This requires "strengthening the muscle" of one's disciplined vigilance. For example, emotional energy is all too easy to give away through petty encounters and ignoble disputes. Remember that to feel angry at other people means that you consider his acts/words to have importance—but this is often not the case. People can waste an incredible amount of time feeling offended by the words and/or deeds of others. To feel offended is a form of self-indulgence that succeeds in making the inner person lazy. If you feel offended, perhaps it means you are worrying too much about others' words and not enough about your own state.

Physical energy too also requires a healthy and balanced management. We can learn to be attentive to our physical positions, for example, when seated, standing, or in movement. We can watch how we move and note which movements are most comfortable for us. Also we should pay attention to how we sit—which positions are more favorable and conducive to a sense of well-being and comfort. We should aim to become more conscious of our physical movements and more aware of our body positions. We should aim to be conscious when eating, for example, and be aware of the senses: smell, taste, touch, sight, and hearing. The intention is not to become automatic to the senses. This form of self-vigilance involves a sensing of the being and the body. Within this awareness a person takes some time to sense how the body is generally feeling, to see if there is any unconscious stress or imbalance within the system. Thus in this state a person is sensing her inner self and assessing its condition. Further, each individual should be able to distinguish between a normal pain, such as a headache, for instance, and a sort of nagging inside, which is the inner self trying to communicate. This communication bridge to the inner self should be strengthened.

Being vigilant also involves being on the alert for people, places, moments, and experiences that have a positive energy. That is, being open to impacts of a positive nature. One should be open and "scanning" for harmonic encounters—as positive contacts may come in forms that are not expected or predictable. Unpredictable encounters and impacts are available even within the everyday life of most people. This does not mean that one cannot earn a reasonable living and be exposed to the blows and distractions that being in the world delivers, and still be able to open oneself. The balance concerns being both *in the world* while maintaining a healthy and harmonious inner self and integrity *not of the world*. A person can be exposed and subjected to external stresses and still remain master of her internal imaginative self; there does not need to be a conflict. If a person gives in and conforms to all of their social conditioning, they use up valuable energy that could have been used for inner work. For this reason, it is important to be aware when social conditioning is operating and to observe its working. In this manner part of the social spell can be broken. Another important aspect in developing intuitive perception is knowing when negativity is acting within and against a person.

Let it be said that negativity seeks to disturb, disrupt, and distract us away from the positive. Negativity by itself has no capacity for control; it seeks only to exploit vulnerable situations and circumstances. For example, if a person's state is not fully balanced the negative will try to sneak in to give a further push away from the positive. In this case each individual needs to exercise discipline and be on the lookout for negative intrusions. When negativity is sensed to be present a person needs to act quickly as it often takes longer for the positive to "wake up" and counteract the situation. In normal circumstances, however, the average person has only between 10 and 15 percent negativity within them (and often less). Yet the positive, which is much more present, is less alert than the negative and a person can be momentarily taken over by negative impulses if she is not careful. The positive needs more time to kick in and get the situation under control. This is why being vigilant is so important when guarding the self against unwanted impacts, intrusions, and loss of personal energy.

Let's face it, many of our social contexts and circumstances concur to magnify certain negative impulses and traits. If an individual's social environment is more exposed to negative impacts (from work or people), the more imperative it is to be on guard during these situations. The negative is nothing to be feared; otherwise there is the tendency to give it more importance than it deserves. Try to remember that every negative experience contains its own learning factor. In general, negativity seeks confusion, to react against the opposing energy, which is balance and harmony. Negative energy thus acts to disturb harmonious and developmental thinking. Yet it cannot control you or take you over—unless you yourself give power to the negative energy. It is also a matter of how a person perceives the situation at hand. All of us at some point have been faced with a problem; however, most of the time we are faced with daily situations. Every problem is also a situation, yet not every situation is a problem. First we must ask ourselves what we are facing: Is it a problem or a situation? Once a person knows this they are better equipped to deal with the matter, and with an appropriate investment of energies.

If there is a feeling/sense of disharmony with certain events or circumstances, then one should try to define the reason for this lack of harmony. Once identified, a person can then introduce positive thoughts and intentions into the situation. For example, before entering a situation that you know will make you tense, nervous, or angry (such as a relationship or job interview), prepare beforehand by creating a positive charge of energy within yourself. Being vigilant with oneself is also about being prepared—and energetically armed!

Again, the communication bridge to the inner self should be strengthened. Listen to this communication and be vigilant for warning signals. Are you attracting the negative? An individual, a group, and even a nation can receive warning signals of the negative. No one goes to ruin innocently!

When a person is being vigilant of her internal and external worlds a greater amount of energy is made available. This energy is useful in attracting the positive and in dealing with everyday impacts. In this state a person can perform to the best of her ability and capacity. And because of the law of reciprocal influence, all actions create an influence in the world that will manifest in some way. Therefore, it is in our personal interest that we each should think and behave impeccably. How we measure ourselves also mirrors how we measure the world around us: we share the same terms of reference. If we are vigilant with ourselves we will refrain from jumping to conclusions or making assumptions. We will be more aware of our external influences, where they come from, how they impact the self, and how we ultimately respond. This is a genuine bridge of communication between the external world of social conditioning and our internal world of the energetic self. And once this bridge of communication is formed it will always remain. However lightly or mildly the contact is used it can never be lost. Like a muscle it needs to be strengthened and developed through use.

Being vigilant is one technique for dealing with the everyday social matrix of distracting influences and impacts. The other technique is what can be referred to as stepping away.

STEPPING AWAY

The technique of *stepping away* involves a person detaching from situations that she may find distracting, noisy, or confusing. What this suggests is that a person should be able to move inward for a short time when she feels it necessary to have some space away from tensions or events that are antagonistic or disruptive to one's state. It is also about stepping away from using all of one's physical faculties in order to conserve energy. For example, if you are sitting quietly you don't need all your senses on full awareness. Sometimes it can be beneficial to drop oneself into a lower running gear, as if on standby. A person should learn when to step back not only from physical engagements but also from emotional attachments and other involvements of the senses. This can be achieved in various moments throughout the day, five minutes here or there. It can be done on the subway, while traveling to work, or on a bus. You don't need to detach to the point that you are not aware of external circumstances—especially if you are on the street! It is about shifting your priorities of internal and external involvement.

Each of us can successfully insulate ourselves from unnecessary external noises and impacts by a reasonable and calm, organized withdrawal. There is no need to put cotton balls in the ears! This technique can be used whenever appropriate; there is no hard-and-fast rule. As with everything, it depends on each individual's circumstances and their state of being. It also allows for each person to create moments throughout the day for quiet reflection, moments to halt the flow of chatter. These can be small moments to be enjoyed and that refresh us mentally and physically. In a sense it is like taking a break, only the break is often in the middle of everyday life. For example, you are traveling on the subway and the carriage is packed with commuters all squeezed together with an armada of free newspapers. There is the screech of brakes, the hum of the train, the almost inaudible buzz of music seeping through earphones. The situation is both disturbing and stressful. Why should you always begin your day like this? So step back within yourself. Pull your focus inward, turn down some of your senses, recollect some fond memories, or recite some words to yourself. Don't allow the external impacts to affect you or to enter into your inner space.

There is no need to leave the world behind: you still need to be relatively alert in case there is a madman loose in the carriage. You need only step away from the bustle of external impacts and impressions. In effect you are suspending a part of your social involvement; you are conserving your self and your energies. This also involves a measured degree of restraint. Exercising restraint means imposing self-discipline in avoiding conditioned reactions and sudden impulses. As with being vigilant, we can, after observation, decide to refrain from exercising conditioned responses. Such impulses, judgments, and preconceived attitudes are put to one side. This is a halting, or stepping away, from indulging in particular social terms of reference. A person is thus learning to restrain herself at specific moments when conditioned factors and references come into play. This technique also suggests that at times a physical withdrawal is necessary.

Being able to step away requires us to exercise patience. It also means that sometimes inaction is as valuable as action, so patience can be used to assess the situation. Some situations may demand instantaneous action, whereas others may be better served by refraining from involvement. Of course, there needs to be a modicum of common sense. If there is a car hurtling toward you, this is no time for exercising patience with the car driver by letting yourself get hit and squashed. No one will say, "What a shame. Yet she did manifest the most admirable patience with that car driver." They will most likely say, "What an idiot!"

So stepping away infers exercising patience and restraint under the right conditions until a situation is better understood. The alternative may be an impulsive response based on layers of conditioning. So if you are not sure about how to act within a particular situation, pull back a little and show some personal restraint. By doing this you are in fact looking after yourself. You are learning how to detach from unnecessary baggage, whether mental or emotional. This also helps us to refrain from acts of pettiness and unwarranted attachment. Forms of pettiness and attachment are traits that quickly drain personal energies and in the end become something that a person is unable to let go of. There is an old dervish story about this.

There were two dervishes traveling together. One of them was old and the other was the younger student. They had traveled together for many years; all the time the younger student believing he was learning to be righteous in the shadow of his teacher. His own belief in the value of his actions gave him faith along his Path. One day both travelers came to a river crossing. Yet the water had recently risen and was waist high. At the side of the river was a young attractive lady, sensual yet distressed. She was afraid of water and sought help in crossing.

The younger student immediately shunned her as he felt it was not right for him to touch such a lady who was clearly disreputable. Suddenly, without hesitation, the older dervish picked up the young lady, slung her on his back, and carried the young woman across the river. When he got to the other side he put her down and carried on walking. Not a word was spoken.

The young dervish hurried after his teacher, surprised and bewildered. He could not believe that his teacher, whom he had trusted and followed all these years, could act in such an immodest way. The young man was fuming. He wanted to confront the older man yet knew it best to keep quiet until a suitable moment. All day though the younger student trailed behind the older man, shaking his head and cursing himself for wasting so many years. The whole day went on like this. The younger man's faith was in turmoil. Finally, they came to a place where the older dervish wanted to rest for the night. They sat in silence for a while.

Knowingly, the older dervish finally smiled and said to the younger one: "Now you can tell me what is on your mind."

The younger man spilled his day's frustrations and anger; his incredulity at the other's "non-spiritual" behavior. When he had finished ranting the older dervish quietly turned to the young man and said:

"I picked that woman up and carried her across the river. When I got to the other side I put her down. But you are still carrying her."[5]

What we cannot refrain from becomes our extra baggage. We are, as in the ancient edict, our own worst enemies. We often get pulled into situations by our desire for attention and self-esteem. Yet by "inflating" ourselves for others we diminish our own being. We need to be aware when to give attention and when to step away. People rarely understand that each one of us craves attention. It is like food for us, from childhood to adulthood and even to the end of our days. So stepping away is another technique for working with one's attention: when to be active and when to be inactive. This swing between the two poles of activity and inactivity also marks out the strong presence of polarity within human lives.

We should refrain from too easily jumping into the polarity game: step away and view the processes more objectively. In truth, it is not about our likes or dislikes. This is an emotional seesaw that sways a person from one encounter to the next. A person who moves between likes and dislikes will find it more difficult to achieve a harmony in his life. Getting tied into polarities, between beliefs and nonbeliefs, is a subjective entanglement supplied by the physical world. After all, belief in nonbelief is still a belief.

Polarity, then, is a way of fixing one's attention onto externalities: we are generous or mean, we indulge or deny, we do good or bad. However, it is often the case that by following the attachment to a particular polarity we are in fact indulging more. For example, the urge in some people to do good (the "do-gooders") is often a need to feel self-gratification, which is an internal reward. It is a form of greed. Greed to be generous is still greed; to indulge in our denial is still indulgence. Often, the desire to be this or that is in fact a need to indulge our desires. There is no simple and pure act as long as a person exists through polarity. It is an illusion we rarely see and thus it draws each of us into this distraction almost completely.

By stepping away we can each practice a form of patience that allows us to have a more objective understanding of events and influences. We may not be able to escape the effects of polarity completely but we can shift ourselves to a more harmonious position. Physical life will ensure that the pendulum will continue to swing, but with awareness and restraint we may escape being totally carried along with it.

> Perhaps it is only by standing back, emotionally, and testing our assumptions that we can become more the masters of ourselves and correspondingly less the slaves of circumstance.[6]

Responsibility to oneself involves taking the opportunities to act properly, whether this means through action or inaction. A degree of restraint and patience can enable this capacity to function more effectively. To step away thus involves an awareness of physical and emotional participation within circumstances, events, experiences, and beliefs. Stepping away also involves an inward move (or shift) for a short time when a person feels it necessary to detach from noisy or distracting situations. It is about being aware of how to conserve one's personal energies.

In a modern world that increasingly seeks to control and manage human consciousness these are small yet useful and significant techniques. After all, as we walk our individual paths we each need to learn about the innate powers we possess to change the perspective of our lives. All of us are passing through a pivotal transition period.

Choices will be upon us, as will impacts, influences, and events. We should never forget that despite the constraining forces that surround our social lives we have at our disposal a great reservoir of human energy. We each must step forward into the driving seat of our own change, and learn to steer our own futures.

Afterword
A HUMAN STORY

If they can get you asking the wrong questions, they don't have to worry about answers.

THOMAS PYNCHON

So we have to begin asking ourselves the right type of questions—questions about the nature and potential futures of our unfolding human story.

The struggle for our minds is about waking up to the great social and cultural change happening in our midst; pulling our minds away from distraction, ignorance, and old programming; and realizing the transitions that our physical and spiritual worlds are moving through. It is imperative that we each begin to recognize the presence of spiritual impulses in our lives and that we work toward transforming any negativity into positive energy. The struggle for our minds is about taking back our right and ability to *act* in accordance with evolutionary necessities, to provide for the newer generations that are arriving with an increased frustration and bemusement with the world. The struggle for our minds is about changing our present ways of thought, emotion, and behavior in order to prepare for future needs, requirements, and obligations.

In this book I have attempted to highlight the influences that face our individual and collective evolution. While there are nefarious, distracting, and manipulating obstacles at play, the outcome will be—*must be*—a positive one. I say this because I have unwavering faith in the capacity for conscious evolution and the power of positive, creative, and energetic forces. In my understanding, the future is never fixed. The game is never a "done deal." Our future potential timelines are always open to adjustments and realignments. With enough conscious critical mass on our rich, varied, and amazing planet we can—*and do*—have the power for change. With focused, energetic, and positive intentionality I firmly believe that we can, as a conscious species, have a participatory role in co-creating the future. Further I feel that each of us can begin by first creating this change in our lives. It is all about the personal force of *creative intention*.

Each of us must identify the type of future we wish to be a part of, then focus our creative intentional energies toward this goal. The choices we make must be coherent with the direction we wish to move toward. By creating and feeling this intention we accumulate great amounts of supporting energy. In this way we can overcome the array of debilitating social forces that fear this change.

The future is very much a human story. A story where the heart and consciousness together create what is truly needed for the future: a balance of our human relationships; expanded development for our children, not arrested development; harmonious work with the land and resources; and, above all, appreciation and gratitude. Each of us is a great bundle of energy and we vibrate and resonate within a confluence of energy fields, waves, and connections. In other words, the human family shares a collective energetic field from which we can gain strength, support, and well-being. We are on the verge of *coming together*.

We should feel privileged that we are placed right in the middle of something that will change the future of humanity. We are not here for nothing, and so it would be a great shame for such a grand opportunity to go wasted. So let's rise to the challenge. There are great things to come.

NOTES

INTRODUCTION.
A FUTURE WE NEED TO WIN

1. Becker, *The Body Electric*.
2. See the work of Emoto, *Hidden Messages in Water*.
3. Narby, *Cosmic Serpent: DNA and the Origins of Knowledge*.
4. Lilly, *Programming the Human Bio-Computer; Leary, Info-Psychology*.
5. Ho, *The Rainbow and the Worm*.
6. McFadden, *Profiles in Wisdom*, 235.
7. Milgram, *Obedience to Authority*.
8. Cited in Mumford, *The Pentagon of Power*, 426–27.
9. Mumford, *Technics and Civilization*, 215.
10. Krishna, *The Wonder of the Brain*, 26.

CHAPTER 1.
GOVERNING THE SOCIAL MIND:
PROPAGANDA, POWER, AND THE MASSES

1. Toch, *The Social Psychology of Social Movements*.
2. Winn, *The Manipulated Mind*, 37.
3. Ibid.
4. Toch, *The Social Psychology of Social Movements*.
5. Winn, *The Manipulated Mind*, 112.
6. Shah, *Reflections*, 140.
7. Cull, Culbert, and Welch, *Propaganda and Mass Persuasion*.

8. Ibid.

9. Bernays, *Propaganda*.

10. Ellul, *Propaganda: The Formation of Men's Attitudes*.

CHAPTER 2.
THE MODERNITY PROJECT:
THE RISE OF SCIENTIFIC TECHNIQUE

1. Russell, *The Impact of Science on Society*.

2. Ibid.

3. Black, *IBM and the Holocaust*.

4. Russell, *The Impact of Science on Society*.

5. Simpson, *Science of Coercion*.

6. Graham and Marvin, *Splintering Urbanism*.

7. Ellul, *The Technological Society*, 125.

8. Laszlo, *The Chaos Point*.

9. Marcuse, *One-Dimensional Man*, 5.

10. Ellul, *The Technological Society*, 140.

11. Zerzan, *Future Primitive and Other Essays*, 22.

12. Cited in Farnish, *Time's Up*, 151.

13. Ibid., 17.

14. Douglass, *Narrative of the Life of Frederick Douglass, an American Slave*.

15. Lewis-Williams, *The Mind in the Cave*.

16. Baudrillard, *Simulacra and Simulation*.

17. Atwater, *Beyond the Indigo Children*.

18. Ibid.

19. Ibid., 111.

20. Hill, "Healthy food obsession sparks rise in new eating disorder."

21. Ellul, *The Technological Society*.

22. McLuhan, *Understanding Media*, 3.

23. Ellul, *The Technological Society*.

24. Men, *The 8 Calendars of the Maya*, 38.

CHAPTER 3.
LIVING UNDER QUARANTINE:
THE MANUFACTURE OF SOCIAL CONTROL

1. Chomsky, *World Orders, Old and New.*

2. Wells, *The Open Conspiracy,* 20.

3. Russell, *The Impact of Science on Society.*

4. Engdahl, *Seeds of Destruction.*

5. Russell, *The Impact of Science on Society.*

6. Ellul, *The Technological Society,* 427.

7. Marcuse, *One-Dimensional Man,* 10.

8. Billington, *Fire in the Minds of Men.*

9. Russell, *The Impact of Science on Society.*

10. Marcuse, *One-Dimensional Man,* xvii.

11. Brzezinski, *Between Two Ages,* 5.

12. Ibid., 61.

13. Ibid., 44.

14. See Leontief, *Studies in the Structure of the American Economy.*

15. Unknown, *Silent Weapons for Quiet Wars.*

16. Ibid.

17. Ibid.

18. Information Commissioner, UK, *A Report on the Surveillance Society.*

19. U.S. Department of Defense, *Information Operations Roadmap* www.gwu
    .edu/~nsarchiv/NSAEBB/NSAEBB177/info_ops_roadmap.pdf.

20. IWGEO, *Strategic Plan for the U.S. Integrated Earth Observation System,*
    1–166.

CHAPTER 4.
UNDUE INFLUENCE:
PLAYING GAMES WITH THE MIND

1. Bertalanffy, cited in Baines, *The Stellar Man,* 36–37.

2. Becker, *The Body Electric.*

3. Becker, *Cross Currents.*

4. Blank and Goodman, "Do electromagnetic fields interact directly with DNA?" 111–15.

5. See www.iegmp.org.uk/report/summary.htm.

6. See www.i-sis.org.uk/FOI2.php.

7. Recommended reading is Becker, *The Body Electric* and Becker, *Cross Currents*.

8. Brzezinski, *Between Two Ages*, 7.

9. Lynch, "Neurotechnology and Society (2010–2060)," http://lifeboat.com/ex/neurotechnology.and.society.

10. See "Moscow Microwaves," *Time*, February 23, 1976; "The Microwave Furor," *Time*, March 22, 1976.

11. O'Connor, "Psychological Studies in Nonionizing Electromagnetic Energy Research," 33–47.

12. See "The Microwave Furor."

13. DIA, *Controlled Offensive Behavior—USSR*, 1–174.

14. Horgan, "The Forgotten Era of Brain Chips."

15. Delgado, *Physical Control of the Mind*.

16. Pravda, "Mind Control: The Zombie Effect," 2004, www.omegatimes.com/article.php?intid=1333.

17. Thomas, "The Mind Has No Firewall," 84–92.

18. Ibid.

19. AFRL, "Controlled Effects (Air Force Research Laboratory Long-Term Challenges)," www.dtic.mil/cgi-bin/GetTRDoc?Location=U2&doc=GetTRDoc.pdf&AD=ADA504868.

20. USAF, *New World Vistas: Air and Space Power for the 21st Century*.

21. Thomas, "The Mind Has No Firewall," 84–92.

22. Simpson, *Science of Coercion*.

23. See http://emotiv.com.

24. Tae-gyu, "Acoustic Wave Prevents Game Addiction."

25. Hogan and Fox, "Sony patent takes first step towards real-life Matrix," 10.

26. Sample, "The brain scan that can read people's intentions."

27. Schwartz, Taylor, and Koselka, "Quantum leap: Brain prosthetics.

Telepathy. Punctual flights. A futurist's vision of where quantum computers will take us."

28. Miller and Miller, "The Schumann Resonances and Human Psychobiology."

29. Becker, *The Body Electric*.

30. Becker, *Cross Currents*.

31. McTaggart, *The Intention Experiment*; Radin, *Entangled Minds*.

CHAPTER 5.
CONSTRUCTIONS OF FEAR:
THE ARMAGEDDON MEME

1. Russell, *The Impact of Science on Society*.

2. Ibid.

3. Quigley, *The Anglo-American Establishment*.

4. A paraphrased quote from www.kryon.com/k_channel09_seattle.html.

5. Winn, *The Manipulated Mind*.

6. Ring, "Precognitive and prophetic visions in near-death experiences," 47–74.

7. See www.nasa.gov/mission_pages/themis/main.

8. Joseph, *Apocalypse 2012*.

9. Dmitriev, "Planetophysical State of the Earth and Life," See www.tmgnow .com/repository/global/planetophysical.html.

10. Joseph, *Apocalypse 2012*.

11. Shah, *Reflections*, 11.

CHAPTER 6.
WINNING THE WAR OF MINDS:
CHANGING THE MENTAL GAME-PLAY

1. Bennett, *Needs of a New Age Community*.

2. Hawkins, *Power vs. Force*, 12–13.

3. Ibid.

4. See McLuhan, *Understanding Media*; McLuhan, *Counterblast*.

5. Russell, *The Global Brain Awakens.*

6. de Chardin, *The Phenomenon of Man.*

7. Ibid., 278.

8. de Chardin, *Let Me Explain.*

9. Bache, *Dark Night, Early Dawn.*

10. Ibid.

11. Thompson, *Passages about Earth,* 119–20.

12. Needleman, *New Religions.*

13. Dmitriev, "Planetophysical State of the Earth and Life," See www.tmgnow
    .com/repository/global/planetophysical.html.

14. LaViolette, *Earth under Fire.*

15. See www.jsasoc.com/docs/JSE-LST.pdf.

16. Ouspensky, *The Psychology of Man's Possible Evolution.*

17. Steiner, *Secret Brotherhoods and the Mystery of the Human,* xxi.

18. Three Initiates, *The Kybalion,* 26–27.

19. Rifkin, *The Empathic Civilization.*

20. Three Initiates, *The Kybalion.*

21. Cited in Harman, *Global Mind Change,* 7.

22. Krishna, *The Wonder of the Brain,* 92.

CHAPTER 7.
OUR EVOLUTIONARY FUTURES:
AGENTS OF MUTATION

1. Krishna, *The Dawn of a New Science,* 56.

2. Popp, Li, Mei, Galle, and Neurohr, "Physical Aspects of Biophotons,"
   44, 576–85.

3. Ho and Popp, "Gaia and the Evolution of Coherence."

4. Ho, *The Rainbow and the Worm,* 210

5. Ibid., 241.

6. Becker, *The Body Electric.*

7. Krishna, *Kundalini,* 226.

8. Laszlo, *Science and the Akashic Field.*

9. Narby, *Cosmic Serpent.*

10. Narby, *Intelligence in Nature.*

11. Krishna, *Higher Consciousness and Kundalini,* 166.

12. Ibid., 147.

13. Gulbekian, *In the Belly of the Beast,* 251.

CHAPTER 8.
USHERING IN THE NEW LIFE:
A REENVISIONING OF SOCIETY
AND SPIRITUALITY

1. Quinn, *Beyond Civilization,* 10.

2. Shah, *The Sufis.*

3. Ibid., 9.

4. Quinn, *Beyond Civilization,* 20.

5. Krishna, *The Dawn of a New Science,* 113.

6. Quinn, *Beyond Civilization,* 188.

7. Steiner, *The Incarnation of Ahriman,* 81.

8. Peterson, *Approach to Reality,* 139–41.

9. Steiner, *The Incarnation of Ahriman,* 100.

10. Shah, *The Sufis,* 319.

11. Pearce, *The Biology of Transcendence.*

CHAPTER 9.
NEW PERCEPTIONS:
CREATING ENERGETIC CHANGE
IN OURSELVES

1. Three Initiates, *The Kybalion.*

2. Shah, *The Way of the Sufi.*

3. Castaneda, *The Wheel of Time,* 159.

4. Adam, *Complete Dream Healer,* 44.

5. Shah, *Tales of the Dervishes.*

6. Winn, *The Manipulated Mind,* 212.

BIBLIOGRAPHY

Adam. *Complete Dream Healer*. London: Piatkus, 2009.

AFRL. "Controlled Effects (Air Force Research Laboratory Long-Term Challenges)," 2004. www.dtic.mil/cgi-bin/GetTRDoc?Location=U2&doc= GetTRDoc.pdf&AD=ADA504868.

Atwater, P. M. H. *Beyond the Indigo Children: The New Children and the Coming of the Fifth World*. Rochester, Vt.: Bear & Company, 2005.

———. The New Children and Near-Death Experiences. Rochester, Vt.: Bear & Company, 2003.

Bache, Christopher. *Dark Night, Early Dawn*. Albany, New York: SUNY Press, 2000.

Baines, John. *The Stellar Man (Hermetic Philosophy, Bk. 2)*. New York: John Baines Institute, 2002.

Baudrillard, Jean. *Simulacra and Simulation*. Ann Arbor: The University of Michigan Press, 1994.

Becker, Robert O. *The Body Electric*. New York: William Morrow, 1998.

———. *Cross Currents: Perils of Electropollution, the Promise of Electromedicine*. New York: Jeremy P. Tarcher, 1990.

Bennett, John. *Needs of a New Age Community*. Santa Fe: Bennett Books, 1990.

Bernays, Edward L. *Propaganda*. New York: Ig Publishing, 2004.

Billington, James Hadley. *Fire in the Minds of Men*. New Jersey: Transaction Publishers, 1998.

Black, Edwin. *IBM and the Holocaust: The Strategic Alliance Between Nazi*

Germany and America's Most Powerful Corporation. New York: Crown Publishing Group, 2001.

Blank, M., and R. Goodman. "Do electromagnetic fields interact directly with DNA?" *Bioelectromagnetics 18 (1997)*.

Brzezinski, Zbigniew. *Between Two Ages: America's Role in the Technetronic Era*. New York: Viking, 1970.

Castaneda, Carlos. *The Wheel of Time*. London: Allen Lane, 1999.

Chomsky, Noam. *World Orders, Old and New*. London: Pluto Press, 1997.

Cull, Nicholas J., David H. Culbert, and David Welch. *Propaganda and Mass Persuasion: A Historical Encyclopedia, 1500 to the Present*. Santa Barbara, Calif.: ABC-CLIO Ltd, 2003.

de Chardin, Pierre Teilhard. *Let Me Explain*. London: Fontana, 1974.

———. *The Phenomenon of Man*. London: Collins, 1959.

Delgado, José. *Physical Control of the Mind: Toward a Psychocivilized Society*. New York: Harper & Row, 1969.

DIA. *Controlled Offensive Behavior—USSR*. The U.S. Army Office of the Surgeon General Medical Intelligence Office, 1972.

Dmitriev, Alexey N. "Planetophysical State of the Earth and Life." Published in Russian, IICA Transactions, Volume 4, 1997.

Douglass, Frederick. *Narrative of the Life of Frederick Douglass, an American Slave*. London: Penguin, 1982.

Ellul, Jacques. *Propaganda: The Formation of Men's Attitudes*. New York: Vintage Books, 1973.

———. *The Technological Society*. New York: Vintage Books, 1964.

Emoto, Masaru. *Hidden Messages in Water*. New York: Beyond Words Publishing, 2004.

Engdahl, Frederick William. *Seeds of Destruction: The Hidden Agenda of Genetic Manipulation*. Montreal: Global Research, 2007.

Farnish, Keith. *Time's Up: An Uncivilized Solution to a Global Crisis*. Totnes: Green Books, 2009.

Graham, Steve, and Simon Marvin. *Splintering Urbanism: Networked Infrastructures, Technological Mobilites and the Urban Condition*. London: Routledge, 2001.

Gulbekian, Sevak Edward. *In the Belly of the Beast: Holding Your Own in Mass Culture*. Charlottesville, Va.: Hampton Roads, 2004.

Harman, Willis. *Global Mind Change: The Promise of the 21st Century*. San Francisco: Berrett-Koehler, 1998.

Hawkins, David. *Power vs. Force: The Hidden Determinants of Human Behavior*. Arizona: Veritas Publishing, 1995.

Heinberg, Richard. *Peak Everything: Waking Up to the Century of Decline in Earth's Resources*. Forest Row: Clairview Books, 2007.

Hill, Amelia. "Healthy food obsession sparks rise in new eating disorder." *The Observer*, Sunday, August 16, 2009.

Ho, Mae-Wan. *The Rainbow and the Worm: The Physics of Organisms*. Singapore: World Scientific, 1998.

Ho, Mae-Wan, and Fritz-Albert Popp. "Gaia and the Evolution of Coherence." In Third Camelford Conference on *The Implications of The Gaia Thesis: Symbiosis, Cooperativity and Coherence*. The Wadebridge Ecological Centre, Camelford, Cornwall, 1989.

Hogan, Jenny, and Barry Fox. "Sony patent takes first step towards real-life Matrix." *New Scientist* 2494 (2005).

Horgan, John. "The Forgotten Era of Brain Chips." *Scientific American*, October 2005.

Information Commissioner (UK). *A Report on the Surveillance Society*. London: The Surveillance Network, 2006.

IWGEO. *Strategic Plan for the U.S. Integrated Earth Observation System*. National Science & Technology Council: Executive Office of the President, 2005.

Joseph, Lawrence E. *Apocalypse 2012: An Optimist Investigates the End of Civilization*. London: HarperElement, 2007.

Krishna, Gopi. *The Dawn of a New Science*. Markdale, Ont.: Institute for Consciousness Research, 1999.

———. *Higher Consciousness and Kundalini*. Ontario, Calif.: F.I.N.D. Research Trust, 1993.

———. *Kundalini: The Evolutionary Energy in Man*. Boston: Shambhala, 1997.

———. *The Wonder of the Brain*. New Delhi: UBSPD, 1997.

Laszlo, Ervin. *The Chaos Point: The World at the Crossroads*. Charlottesville, Va.: Hampton Roads, 2006.

———. *Quantum Shift in the Global Brain*. Rochester, Vt.: Inner Traditions, 2008.

———. *Science and the Akashic Field: An Integral Theory of Everything*. Rochester, Vt.: Inner Traditions, 2004.

LaViolette, Paul. *Earth under Fire: Humanity's Survival of the Apocalypse*. Alexandria, Va.: Starlane Publications, 2000.

Leary, Timothy. *Info-Psychology*. Las Vegas: New Falcon Publications, 1988.

Leontief, Wassily. *Studies in the Structure of the American Economy*. New York: International Sciences Press Inc., 1953.

Lessing, Doris. *Prisons We Choose to Live Inside*. London: HarperCollins, 1987.

Lewis-Williams, David. *The Mind in the Cave: Consciousness and the Origins of Art*. London: Thames & Hudson, 2004.

Lilly, John Cunningham. *Programming the Human Bio-Computer*. Berkeley, Calif.: Ronin, 2004.

Lynch, Zach. "Neurotechnology and Society (2010–2060)," (2004). http://lifeboat.com/ex/neurotechnology.and.society.

Marcuse, Herbert. *One-Dimensional Man: Studies in the Ideology of Advanced Industrial Society*. Oxford: Routledge, 2007 (reprint).

McFadden, Steve. *Profiles in Wisdom: Native Elders Speak about the Earth*. Santa Fe: Bear & Company, 1991.

McLeod, Adam. *Complete Dream Healer*. London: Piatkus, 2009.

McLuhan, Marshall. *Counterblast*. London: Rapp and Whiting, 1970.

———. *Understanding Media*. London: Routledge, 2002 (reprint).

McTaggart, Lynne. *The Intention Experiment: Use Your Thoughts to Change the World*. London: Harper, 2008.

Men, Humbatz. *The 8 Calendars of the Maya: The Pleiadian Cycle and the Key to Destiny*. Rochester, Vt.: Bear & Company, 2010.

"The Microwave Furor," *Time,* March 22, 1976.

Milgram, Stanley. *Obedience to Authority: An Experimental View*. New York: HarperCollins, 1974.

Miller, Richard Alan, and Iona Miller. "The Schumann Resonances and Human Psychobiology." *Nexus Magazine* 10 (3), April–May 2003.

"Moscow Microwaves," *Time,* February 23, 1976.

Mumford, Lewis. *The Pentagon of Power: The Myth of the Machine.* London: Secker & Warburg, 1971.

——. *Technics and Civilization.* London: Routledge, Kegan Paul, 1934.

Narby, Jeremy. *Cosmic Serpent: DNA and the Origins of Knowledge.* London: Phoenix, 1999.

——. *Intelligence in Nature.* London: Jeremy P. Tarcher, 2006.

Needleman, Joseph. *New Religions.* New York: E. P. Dutton, 1977.

O'Connor, Mary Ellen. "Psychological Studies in Nonionizing Electromagnetic Energy Research." *Journal of General Psychology* 120: 1(1993).

Ouspensky, P. D. *The Psychology of Man's Possible Evolution.* London: Vintage Books, 1999.

Pearce, Joseph Chilton. *The Biology of Transcendence: A Blueprint of the Human Spirit.* Rochester, Vt.: Park Street Press, 2004.

Peterson, A. J. *Approach to Reality.* Cambridge: Rose King Publications, 1983.

Popp, F-A., K. H. Li, W. P. Mei, M. Galle, and R. Neurohr. "Physical Aspects of Biophotons." *Experientia,* 1988 Jul 15, 44 (7): 576–85.

Pravda, "Mind Control: The Zombie Effect," 2004, www.omegatimes.com/article.php?intid=1333.

Quigley, Carol. *The Anglo-American Establishment.* San Pedro, Calif.: G S G & Associates, 1982.

Quinn, Daniel. *Beyond Civilization: Humanity's Next Great Adventure.* New York: Three Rivers Press, 1999.

Radin, Dean. *Entangled Minds.* New York: Pocket Books, 2006.

Rifkin, Jeremy. *The Empathic Civilization: The Race to Global Consciousness in a World in Crisis.* Cambridge: Polity Press, 2010.

Ring, Kenneth. *The Omega Project: Near-Death Experiences, UFO Encounters, and Mind at Large.* New York: William Morrow, 1992.

——. "Precognitive and prophetic visions in near-death experiences." *Anabiosis: The Journal of Near-Death Studies,* 2 (1982).

Russell, Bertrand. *The Impact of Science on Society.* London: Routledge, 1985 (reprint).

Russell, Peter. *The Global Brain Awakens: Our Next Evolutionary Leap*. Palo Alto, Ca.: Global Brain Inc., 1995.

Sample, Ian. "The brain scan that can read people's intentions." *The Guardian,* Friday, February 9, 2007.

Sargant, William. *Battle for the Mind: A Physiology of Conversion and Brainwashing*. Cambridge, Mass.: Malor Books, 1997 (reprint).

Schwartz, Peter, Chris Taylor, and Rita Koselka. "Quantum leap: Brain prosthetics. Telepathy. Punctual flights. A futurist's vision of where quantum computers will take us." *Fortune,* 154 (3), August 7, 2006.

Scott, Ernest. *The People of the Secret*. London: Octagon Press, 1985.

Shah, Idries. *Reflections*. London: Octagon Press, 1969.

———. *The Sufis*. London: Octagon, 1982.

———. *The Way of the Sufi*. London: Octagon Press, 1980.

———. *Tales of the Dervishes*. London: Octagon Press, 1982.

Simpson, Christopher. *Science of Coercion: Communication Research and Psychological Warfare,* 1945–60. Oxford: Oxford University Press, 1996.

Steiner, Rudolf. *The Incarnation of Ahriman: The Embodiment of Evil on Earth*. Forest Row: Rudolf Steiner Press, 2009.

———. *Secret Brotherhoods and the Mystery of the Human Double*. Forest Row: Rudolf Steiner Press, 2006.

Tae-gyu, K. "Acoustic Wave Prevents Game Addiction." *The Korea Times,* 2007. http://times.hankooki.com/lpage/ 200703kt2007031220190210160.htm.

Talbot, Michael. *The Holographic Universe*. London: HarperCollins, 1996.

Thomas, Timothy. "The Mind Has No Firewall." *Parameters,* Spring 1998.

Thompson, William Irvin. *Passages about Earth: An Exploration of the New Planetary Culture*. New York: Harper & Row, 1974.

Three Initiates. *The Kybalion*. London: Tarcher, 2008.

Toch, Hans. *The Social Psychology of Social Movements*. Indianapolis: Bobbs-Merrill Co, 1965.

Unknown. *Silent Weapons for Quiet Wars*. 1979 (reprint).

USAF. *New World Vistas: Air and Space Power for the 21st Century*. USAF Scientific Advisory Board, 1995.

U.S. Department of Defense. *Information Operations Roadmap* (2003). www
.gwu.edu/~nsarchiv/NSAEBB/NSAEBB177/info_ops_roadmap.pdf.

Wells, H. G. *The New World Order.* New York: Filiquarian Publishing, 2007
(reprint).

———. *The Open Conspiracy: What Are We to Do with Our Lives?* San Diego,
Calif.: Book Tree, 2006 (reprint).

White, John. *The Meeting of Science and Spirit.* New York: Paragon House,
1990.

Winn, Denise. *The Manipulated Mind.* London: Octagon Press, 1983.

Zerzan, John. *Future Primitive and Other Essays.* New York: Semiotext, 1996

———. *Twilight of the Machines.* Port Townsend, Wash.: Feral House, 2008.

INDEX

BOOKS OF RELATED INTEREST

New Consciousness for a New World
How to Thrive in Transitional Times and Participate
in the Coming Spiritual Renaissance
by Kingsley L. Dennis

2012: A Clarion Call
Your Soul's Purpose in Conscious Evolution
by Nicolya Christi

Quantum Shift in the Global Brain
How the New Scientific Reality Can Change Us and Our World
by Ervin Laszlo

Morphic Resonance
The Nature of Formative Causation
by Rupert Sheldrake

The Biology of Transcendence
A Blueprint of the Human Spirit
by Joseph Chilton Pearce

Visionary Shamanism
Activating the Imaginal Cells of the Human Energy Field
by Linda Star Wolf and Anne Dillon

Darwin's Unfinished Business
The Self-Organizing Intelligence of Nature
by Simon G. Powell

Chaos, Creativity, and Cosmic Consciousness
by Rupert Sheldrake, Terence McKenna, and Ralph Abraham

INNER TRADITIONS • BEAR & COMPANY
P.O. Box 388
Rochester, VT 05767
1-800-246-8648
www.InnerTraditions.com

Or contact your local bookseller